ECONOMIC ISSUES, PROBLEMS AND PERSPECTIVES

ECONOMIC GROWTH IN THE 21ST CENTURY

PERSPECTIVES, ROLE OF GOVERNMENTAL POLICIES, POTENTIAL AND CONSTRAINTS

ECONOMIC ISSUES, PROBLEMS AND PERSPECTIVES

Additional books in this series can be found on Nova's website under the Series tab.

Additional e-books in this series can be found on Nova's website under the e-book tab.

ECONOMIC ISSUES, PROBLEMS AND PERSPECTIVES

ECONOMIC GROWTH IN THE 21ST CENTURY

PERSPECTIVES, ROLE OF GOVERNMENTAL POLICIES, POTENTIAL AND CONSTRAINTS

CODY ACCOSI
EDITOR

nova publishers
New York

For permission to use material from this book please contact us:
Telephone 631-231-7269; Fax 631-231-8175
Web Site: http://www.novapublishers.com

Library of Congress Cataloging-in-Publication Data

ISBN: 978-1-63321-589-4

Published by Nova Science Publishers, Inc. † New York

CONTENTS

PREFACE

The Global Financial crisis that led to the Great Recession resulted in differing levels of economic turmoil across developed industrialised economies, with particularly acute implications for eurozone countries where it triggered a sovereign debt crisis given their fundamental lack of economic cohesion and appropriate policy tools. This book discusses the foreign direct investment and economic growth in OECD countries. It also discusses the economic growth and self-consumption in oil producing countries; the drivers of economic growth in Latin America; financial education and economic growth; regional development strategy, market segmentation and economic growth; religion, work ethic and economic growth in modern Turkey; and being happy in uncertain economic times.

Chapter 1 - This chapter summarizes and synthesizes the theories, methodologies, and findings from of a series of studies that investigate the predictors of economic growth at the state-level in the United States (US). In contrast to other studies of state economic growth, the authors look to the wealth of findings from the cross-national research for guidance in predicting economic growth at the subnational level in the US. The authors consequently focus on the capacity of education, infrastructure, population growth, savings, and initial economic growth to predict economic growth measured as per capita income and gross state product (GSP) per capita. Of these classic predictors, the authors take a more in depth look at the role of education-related variables in predicting economic growth.

The authors also investigate the capacity of the cross-national predictors and a series of political variables to predict unemployment in the states. From these studies, the authors establish the most common predictors of economic growth, present common observations and insights gleaned from these studies, and conclude by suggesting future directions for economic growth research.

Chapter 2 - The role of inward FDI on economic growth has attracted the attention of researchers for many years as its beneficial impact has been recognised theoretically by scholars and policymakers; however, the empirical evidence remains ambiguous.

Hence, the objective of this chapter is to investigate the causal relationship between FDI inflows/outflows and economic growth in developed OECD countries. Investigation of the causal link between FDI inflows and growth has important implications such that if there is a unidirectional causality it would support the FDI-led growth hypothesis. Alternatively, if the causal link runs in the opposite direction, it would imply that economic growth may be a prerequisite for countries to attract FDI. Finally, if the causal process is bi-directional, FDI inflows and growth would have a reinforcing causal relationship.

In particular, this chapter contributes to the existing literature by focusing on developed countries as inward/outward FDI has become an increasingly significant factor in influencing the economic activity. In contrast, most previous time-series causality studies focus on developing countries with only a few covering developed countries. However, almost all of the world's FDI originates from developed countries and the majority of FDI is also located in developed countries.

Another feature is that this chapter also tests the causal link between outward FDI and economic growth. Outward FDI might promote the home country's economic growth as it might yield higher profits, transfer technology and management skills to the home country, expand production abroad, secure raw materials overseas and avoid trade barriers and so on.

Following an Introduction, the chapter then reviews FDI trend across OECD countries. Next it discusses the alternative theories and literature exploring the relationship between FDI and economic growth (i.e., the impact of inward FDI on host country's economic growth, the impact of outward FDI on home country's economic growth, together with the impact of economic growth on inward/outward FDI). The authors then describe empirical causality testing methodology, together discussing the empirical results.

Chapter 3 - The design of governmental policies is crucial to face the 21st Century economic growth challenges. Energy will be one of the core issues in economic growth policies. Therefore, this chapter focuses on the energy consumption-economic growth nexus. The perspectives on the role of energy use upon economic growth are grounded on empirical evidence from a panel of oil producing countries that have been examined for a long time span (1965-2012). Both the ratio of oil production to oil consumption, as well as the aftermath of the structural break from the second oil shock were controlled for. The presence of cross-section dependence phenomena within the panel strongly supports that these countries share common features as oil producers. Panel data estimators and co-integration/long memory analyses are both pursued and discussed, namely dealing with the heterogeneity of panels and the countries' specific effects. Comprehensive analysis of the energy-growth nexus requires that both short- and long-term effects should be considered, for which the Driscoll-Kraay estimator with fixed effects proved to be appropriate. The growth hypothesis was confirmed. Energy consumption and the ratio of oil production to oil consumption are drivers of economic growth. The structural break, beginning in 1979, seems to have been persistent. Findings support that expansionary governmental energy policies could not generate an equivalent effect upon the output in the 21st Century.

Chapter 4 - During the current century the evolution of economic growth in Latin America is the result of the learning obtained after several decades of instability and significant economic imbalances. The region was able to overcome the uncertainty generated by the crisis at the beginning of the century, to emerge with high rates of economic growth and improvement in the level of development in most countries. This chapter presents how some key factors affect Latin America´s economic growth. First of all, it examines the influence of government policies on the improvement of regional economic growth. Secondly, it analyzes the role played by two factors such as education and information and communication technologies (ICT) on Latin America´s economic growth. Thirdly, it studies the positive contribution of the external sector to economic development in that region. Finally, it outlines a review of the main challenges and limitations of economic growth in this emerging region.

Chapter 5 - In this paper, the authors adopt glacier model to measure the market segmentation index, and use the inter-provincial panel data from 1985 to 2011 to make an empirical analysis of the relationship between market segmentation and regional economic growth in the context of national regional development strategy. The results show that there will be a trend of consolidation in the domestic regional market, but the regional economic division is stronger than the geographic segmentation. At the same time, the relationship between market segmentation and regional economic growth does not follow a certain rule, and polices bring different gains in four areas with regional development strategy. Therefore, it is of great importance to correctly handle the relationship between government and market, break market segmentation, promote regional cooperation, and thoroughly implement national regional development strategy so as to speed up the regional market integration process in China.

Chapter 6 - In this study the author examines the recent economic boom in Turkey and its relationship with the resurge of Islam. The media have reported the proliferation of "Islamic Calvinism" in Turkey, which stresses pro-business values, the importance of work, and the acquisition of scientific knowledge as component of religious duties. Using Max Weber's study The Protestant Ethic and the Spirit of Capitalism as a theoretical background, the author tests for the impact of this religious development on work ethic values and economic attitudes. First, the author takes a closer look at the message of the neo-Sufi movement and its implantation into the economic and political context of modern Turkey. Second, the author empirically studies trends in economic output, religiosity, and economic values between 1990 and 2007. Analyses are conducted based on survey data from the World Value Survey. Results indicate that the neo-Sufi movement has revalued Turkish Islam in a pro-business direction. Empirically, the author finds that both religiosity and work ethic values significantly increased between 1990 and 2007. However, there is no empirical evidence of organic development of work ethic due to the values of Turkish Islam.

Chapter 7 - Given the uncertain economic times over the past few years, the aim of this research was to investigate whether economic instability affected subjective well-being and if so how. The sample was 135 men and women from a stratified sample of adults living in metropolitan Western Australia. Using scores from the Satisfaction with Life Scale and the Short Happiness-Depression Inventory two happiness groups were formed: adults with high subjective well-being; and adults with lower subjective well-being. Group differences on homeownership, financial liquidity and stress, attitudes towards credit, pursuit of extrinsic goals were assessed. The results showed that income level per se did not make people happier, although not being able to make ends meet was associated with more unhappiness. Happier people were more likely to own their home, to pay off credit balances each month, pay rent/mortgage on time and could save even a small amount of money on a regular basis. Attitudes to credit, number of credit cards owned, and extrinsic life aspirations were not associated with levels of happiness. The results and applied implications of the study are discussed with an emphasis on promoting happiness and avoiding financial stress during times of economic uncertainty.

Chapter 8 - Particularly since the financial crisis, it is widely recognized the importance of consumers' financial decisions around the world. At the same time, several studies have shown that consumers worldwide have an insufficient knowledge of financial issues and a limited confidence in financial institutions and how that factors may complicate making informed financial decisions. That is the main reason why financial education is identified as a key driver to improve the stability of the financial system which would be a positive factor for economic growth. During the last years many public and private institutions have launched initiatives in the field of financial education, but now it´d be necessary to ensure the efficiency and usefulness of those programmes. The first objective of this chapter is to present a review of some relevant initiatives on financial literacy and education, developed by public and private organizations around the world. Secondly, it focuses on the effectiveness and efficacy of those initiatives, analyzing how those programmes could have a positive impact on economic growth.

In: Economic Growth in the 21st Century
Editor: Cody Accosi
ISBN: 978-1-63321-589-4

Chapter 1

ECONOMIC GROWTH IN THE STATES OF THE UNITED STATES: FINDINGS AND LESSONS FROM FOUR EMPIRICAL STUDIES

J. Norman Baldwin[1*], William A. McCracken III[2] and Michael J. New[3]

[1]Department of Political Science, The University of Alabama
Tuscaloosa, Alabama, US
[2]Department of Political Science, The Ohio State University
Columbus, Ohio, US
[3]Department of Social Sciences, University of Michigan, Dearborn
Dearborn, Michigan, US

ABSTRACT

This chapter summarizes and synthesizes the theories, methodologies, and findings from of a series of studies that investigate the predictors of economic growth at the state-level in the United States (US). In contrast to other studies of state economic growth, we look to the wealth of findings from the cross-national research for guidance in predicting economic growth at the subnational level in the US. We

---

* Email: nbaldwin@bama.ua.edu. Phone: (205) 345-1694.

consequently focus on the capacity of education, infrastructure, population growth, savings, and initial economic growth to predict economic growth measured as per capita income and gross state product (GSP) per capita. Of these classic predictors, we take a more in depth look at the role of education-related variables in predicting economic growth.

We also investigate the capacity of the cross-national predictors and a series of political variables to predict unemployment in the states. From these studies, we establish the most common predictors of economic growth, present common observations and insights gleaned from these studies, and conclude by suggesting future directions for economic growth research.

INTRODUCTION

In recent years, we conducted a number of studies on the predictors of economic growth at the state level in the United States. Published in 2008 (Baldwin and Borrelli), the primary intent of our first study was to determine whether the most common predictors of economic development at the cross-national level applied to economic development at the subnational level of the United States. Measuring economic development as per capita income, this research was followed by a similar article that investigated the predictors of state economic development measured as gross state product, a modest change in the operationalization of the dependent variable (Baldwin, Borrelli, and New, 2011). To satisfy our curiosities about the effects of education-related variables on state economic growth, we conducted a third study that expanded the number of variables that tested human capital theory as an explanation for economic growth, thus introducing new independent variables to our previous work (Baldwin and McCracken, 2013). Finally, given the recessionary times beginning in 2008, we decided to conduct a fourth study that investigated the effects of state equivalents of cross-national predictors of economic growth on state unemployment rates, another change in the dependent variable (McCracken and Baldwin, 2014). In this most recent study, we incorporated new independent variables that capture political factors. These variables were added in recognition of the accusations and condemnations associated with the Great Recession as politicians sought to assign blame to the other side for the economic crisis.

This chapter explores what we have learned over the last seven years in conducting state economic growth research.[1] It begins by summarizing the theoretical foundation for our research and proceeds to describe the different methods and analyses conducted in four studies. We next present the findings from individual studies, followed by an assessment of the trends in the aggregate findings from the four studies. We conclude with a presentation of the lessons and insights gleaned from our research agenda and with recommendations for future economic development research at the subnational level.

THE THEORIES OF ECONOMIC GROWTH TESTED

Cross-National Predictors and Theory

Because the cross-national economic growth research boasts such a large, cumulative body of research relative to subnational (state-level in the U.S.) economic growth research, we repeatedly investigated the state-level equivalents of the most common predictors of cross-national economic growth, typically measured as growth in gross domestic product, in per capita income, and in employment. Identified through meta-analyses and reviews of the research (Barro and Sala-i-Martin, 2004; Nijkamp and Poot, 2004; Poot, 2000; Temple, 1999), the common predictors of cross-national economic growth investigated were education, infrastructure spending, population growth, savings, and initial economic growth. With the exception of infrastructure spending, all of these variables are elements of human capital theory and neoclassical economic growth theory, the latter which is based on the Solow-Swan growth model (Solow, 1956; Swan, 1956). This model contends that stable economic growth is a function of labor, capital, and technology, with changes in capital being determined by savings and population growth.

Neoclassical growth theory asserts that economic growth is a function of labor and capital, and that capital grows at a rate determined by investment or

[1] As an article that synthesizes finding from three previously published studies and one unpublished study, this chapter's content draws substantially from Baldwin and Borrelli (2008); Baldwin, Borrelli, and New (2011); and Baldwin and McCracken (2013). To focus on the syntheses of findings, this chapter does not review the body of empirical research on economic growth at the state level. However, details of the empirical research on state economic growth can be found in these previously published works.

savings (Poot, 2000: 520). Savings permit investments that increase capital and employment growth over what can be achieved if all the capital is consumed. Neoclassical theory also asserts that, as populations grow, the ratio of capital to labor falls, therefore reducing returns and the capital available for new jobs (Sedgley, 1998). Beyond increasing the competition for jobs, high population growth lowers the steady-state level of capital and output per worker (Barro and Sala-i-Martin, 2004). Population growth due to immigration also raises short-term unemployment as immigrants consume time to acquire language skills and labor market information (Blackley, 1989).

Human capital theory asserts that skills, knowledge, abilities, experience, aptitude, and training are investments in human capital that accumulate a stream of future benefits when cultivated (Jorgensen and Fraumeni, 1992; Mincer, 1994; Walsh, 1935). Education investments increase economic growth and reduce unemployment through increasing the job qualifications of individuals and reducing the mismatch between the demand for and supply of skilled labor (Borooah and Mangan, 2008; Manacorda and Petrongolo, 1999). Highly educated individuals are, not only more likely to be productive, they have more rare skills and are therefore less expendable (Nickell, 1979; Nistor, 2009).

Higher education has additional economic benefits to the individual and society. Individuals with college and graduate degrees are attractive employees because they increase the value of their work output, develop new products, and bring the best technologies of universities into industry (Bradshaw, Kennedy, and Davis, 2003; Crown and Wheat, 1995; Feller, 2004: 140; Senter, 1999). The R &D functions of universities facilitate economic growth through developing environments and cultures that stimulate innovation, entrepreneurialism, and business creation (Jones and Vedlitz, 1993).

Another variable from the cross-national research, initial economic growth, is tested because it allows us to test Solow-Swan predictions that economic growth experiences convergence—that economic growth is negatively related to initial levels of per capita income, gross state product (GSP), and employment. More specifically, rich states experience decreasing returns to capital, while poor states experience higher rates of return from investment that increase economic growth and employment rates (Barro and Sala-i-Martin, 2004; Cass, 1965; Solow, 1956; Temple, 1999). Economic growth is more likely to occur in poorer states because poor states learn what works from advanced states and avoid sunk costs that advanced states have incurred in developing new technology and means of production (Crihfield, Giertz, and Metha, 1995; Evans and Oneal, 1995; Temple, 1999).

Convergence is especially germane in a study of state economic growth because the mobility of resources, including unemployed citizens, and technology transfer, are less regulated between states than across nations (Crihfield et al., 1995: 553)

The impact of infrastructure spending on economic growth can be traced to regional economic theory, which is grounded in development economics (Rephann, 1993). Infrastructure capital and the flow of spending on infrastructure increases economic growth through increasing spatial accessibility and reducing transportation costs. They also raise the social return to ongoing investments that allows organizations to retain and expand their labor forces (Gramlich, 1994; Nijkamp, 2009; Temple, 1999: 146). Infrastructure investments also facilitate economic growth through making business locations more accessible to new markets and larger labor forces (Crown and Wheat, 1995; Garcia-Mila and McGuire, 1992; Rephann and Isserman, 1994).

Theory and Political Predictors of Unemployment

Explanations for the relationship between political variables and economic growth and unemployment can be derived from theories of political rationality in decision making. Scholars such as Landau (1969), Wildavsky (1964), and Stone (2002) would argue that political outcomes are a function of political reasoning rather than the rationality of economic selfinterest found in public choice theory. Political rationality pertains more to the community, not the market, and commonly explains policy as the outcome of conflicts involving political actors who define problems, values, and objectives differently (Stone, 2002). Closely related to political rationality theory, theories of the policy-making process also help explain the relationship between political variables and economic growth and unemployment (see Sabatier, 2007). Originating in the biological sciences (Von Bertanlanffy, 1950), pioneered by Pfiffner and Sherwood's (1960) research, and popularized in the study of politics and organizations by Easton (1965) and Katz and Kahn (1966), systems theory, in turn, would view economic growth and unemployment as outcomes of the complex interactions of an array of variables in the external and internal environments of a dynamic system. Depending on the unit of analysis representing the internal environment, or throughput, political variables would be critical factors in either the internal or external environment of the system.

A more specific case for the relationship between political variables and unemployment is made by Kalecki (1993) who contends that, even in ardently capitalistic societies, public opinion widely supports government intervention in the market in order to stimulate employment. Given that elected leaders are often held responsible for the performance of the economy, Kalecki (1993) and Jacoby (2000) also emphasize the importance of incumbents being able to hang their hat on achieving lower unemployment rates.

Cross-national research on industrial democracies (Alt, 1985) reveals that unemployment falls under left-wing governments and rises under right-wing governments. Building on Hibbs's (1977) quantitative and qualitative work, Alt found that Democratic (US) and Labour (UK) governments pursue policies that decrease unemployment, while Republican and Conservative governments pursue policies that increase unemployment. Alt also found the governments with single-party working parliamentary majorities are more likely to exhibit the expected effects on unemployment based on right- and left-wing positions.

Examining monetary policy, Chappell and Keech (1986, 1986a, 1988) found right-wing parties to be more tolerant of unemployment and left-wing parties to be more tolerant of inflation. Clark, Fordham, and Nordstrom (2011) present evidence that Democratic politicians prefer to take action to stimulate the economy and reduce unemployment, while Republican politicians prefer to take military action abroad to distract from high unemployment. Wright's (2012) investigations of gubernatorial and Presidential elections reveal that higher unemployment tends to benefit Democratic candidates at the ballot box and consequently leaves Democrats more room to demonstrate reductions in unemployment, which also means that high unemployment is often associated with Democrats holding office.

METHODS OF ANALYSIS

In all of our studies, we investigated economic growth in the 48 contiguous states in the continental United States. We also investigated the effects of the most common predictors of economic growth found in the cross-national research—specifically infrastructure spending, savings deposits, population growth, initial economic growth, and several education-related variables. The education-related variables were all lagged because of their delayed effects on economic growth.

In all of the studies, the variables measured in dollars were divided by the annual state population to derive per capita measures. Barro and Sala-i-Martin (2004) emphasize that per capita measures of capital, consumption, and GSP give one a better sense of the nature of a state because they capture how people are affected. Historically, studies on education and economic growth also investigate the effects of per capita spending (see Fisher, 1997 for review).

Study One: Predicting Per Capita Income Growth

In our first study (Baldwin and Borrelli, 2008), we conducted cross-sectional regression analyses on the 48 states. Although pooled cross-sectional analysis would have increased our sample size substantially, we believed multi-year averaging yielded more robust results through reducing measurement error and avoiding the need to correct for violations of traditional regression assumptions associated with pooled analysis (Baldwin and Borrelli, 2008: 191).

To determine both direct and indirect effects on income growth, we also conducted path analyses using ordinary least squares multiple regression. Teacher-pupil ratios and high school and college graduation rates were conceptualized as intervening variables mediating the effects of K-12 expenditures, higher education expenditures, highway expenditures, state savings in FDIC banks, and population growth.

> We ran initial regressions with per capita income growth as the dependent variable and the five independent variables and three intervening variables as predictors. When initial regressions revealed different intervening variables to be related to income growth, we then tested for indirect effects on income growth through regressions involving the intervening variables as criterion (dependent) variables and the hypothesized independent variables as predictors (Baldwin and Borrelli; 2008: 192-193).

In turn, the predictors that were not significantly related to income growth were eliminated from the path analysis and the regressions were rerun to determine the direct path coefficients to income growth.

> The total effect of an independent variable on income growth was the sum of its direct and indirect effects with indirect effects measured as the product of the effect of the independent variables on the intervening variables times the effect of the intervening variables on income growth (Baldwin and Borrelli, 2008: 193).

Study Two: Predicting Gross State Product (GSP) Growth

Our second study tested the same path model as the first study, but changed the dependent variable to economic growth measured as growth in gross state product per capita. However, in contrast to our first study, we calculated four-year moving averages for each of the variables investigated. This allowed us to reduce short-term data volatility caused by business cycles and "fluctuations induced by shifts" in corresponding public expenditures (Bleaney, Gemmell, Kneller, 2001; Devarajan, Swaroop, and Zou, 1996: 322; Federal Reserve Bank of Dallas, 2010).

> A cyclical recession, for example, that lowered K12 spending in 1991 would not necessarily result in lower economic growth in only 2004; nor would a cyclical recession in 2001 be the result of a reduction in education spending only in 1988. Averaging also allowed us to investigate the effects of *broad* state spending trends on economic growth. A common adjustment, averaging captures changes in the direction of the economy better than unsmoothed data and allows for more valid comparisons of results across studies (Federal Reserve Board, 2010). Moving averages (versus ordinary averages) also allowed more time series observations in our panel data (Devarajan et al., 1996), explained more variation in GSP growth than annual data, and revealed more significant relationships (Baldwin, Borrelli, and New, 2011: 230).

Four-year moving averages in annual growth in GSP per capita were calculated for the growth occurring from 1988 to 1996 and from 1997 to 2005. This was necessary because the Bureau of Economic Analysis (BEA) changed from Standard Industrial Classification (SIC) industry definitions of GSP to North American Industrial Classification System (NAICS) industry definitions in 1997. This created discontinuities in the GSP data resulting from differences in data sources and estimation methodologies (U.S. BEA, 2007). For all independent and intervening variables, we consequently calculated four-year moving averages for the 1988-1996 period and four-year moving averages for the 1997-2005 period.

> With time series cross-sectional data, some panels may have greater error variance and the errors of one panel may be contemporaneously correlated with the errors of another. A Generalized Least Squares (GLS) model with panel corrected standard errors (PCSE) is a common solution (Beck and Katz, 1995). Since DurbinWatson tests found evidence of AR1 autocorrelation, a Prais-Winsten transformation was utilized. We also tested the model by running Ordinary Least Squares (OLS), OLS with robust standard errors, GLS with no correction for autocorrelation, and GLS with panel corrected standard errors and different autocorrelation corrections. Since these analyses produced similar outcomes, we conclude that the regressions results are insensitive to type of corrections performed.
>
> Depending on the state and time period, national economic phenomena and national growth can have positive, negative, or insignificant effects on state economic performance (Brace, 1993). We controlled for national trends through indicator variables for the four-year moving average periods. This allowed us to discern how lagged levels of our predictors affect economic growth rates relative to the national trend, and shows which state activities brought about above and below average rates of future economic growth relative to other states (Baldwin, Borrelli, and New, 2011: 233).

Study Three: Predicting Economic Growth with Expanded Education-Related Variables

Still investigating the effects of cross-national predictors of economic growth, in our third study, we investigated an expanded set of education-related variables and directed our research toward an education-related academic audience. This study looked at economic growth measured as both per capital income growth and GSP growth. While the previous studies measured per capita income growth and GSP per capita growth in 2000 constant dollars, in this study, all of the variables measured in dollar amounts were recalculated from current dollars to 2000 constant dollars. To compress high frequency data, expand low frequency data, correct for skew and kurtosis, and allow for more interpretable beta coefficients, we also determine the natural logs of nine independent variables. Because of the change in the way GSP growth was measured in 1997, annual growth in GSP per capita was calculated for the growth occurring from 1988 to 1996 and from 1997 to 2008. More independent variables also appear in the data analysis from 1997 to 2008 because measures of college enrollments per capita, two-year colleges per million population, and four-year colleges per million population were not available for the 1988-1996 period investigated. Because this research attempts to hold constant cyclical trends in income growth and GSP/GDP growth, as well as the effects of monetary and fiscal policy, the data analysis included dummy variables for each year investigated (Baldwin and McCracken, 2013: 193; Carroll and Wasylenko, 1994)

> Given that our research involved longitudinal panel data, we utilized Hausman, Lagrange Multiplier, and F tests to confirm that random effects rather than fixed effects were present. To reduce that likelihood of committing a type I error as a result of serial correlation (Bertrand, Duflo, and Mullainathan, 2004), we then conducted a block bootstrapping of the variables in the regressions that we executed. Consistent with study two, we again tested our models by running GLS regressions with panel corrected standard errors. We also executed a standard AR1 correction for autocorrelation[2] and each model was also tested for multicolinearity (Baldwin and McCracken, 2013: 196).

Study Four: Predicting Unemployment

This study replicated much of the data analysis presented in study 3. However, instead of controlling for nationwide trends through yearly dummy variables, we controlled more specifically for the effects of national unemployment rates and national gross domestic product per capita.

Labels and definitions for the variables in all of the studies are found in Appendix 1. The definitions, however, do not reflect the averaging of variables that was conducted in the first two studies. The data sources for the variables

[2]We also tested our models without an AR1 correction for autocorrelation. Only two of the 32 uncorrected significant findings were dissimilar to those generated with the correction.

can be found in the original studies (Baldwin and Borrelli, 2008; Baldwin, Borrelli, and New, 2011; Baldwin and McCracken, 2013; and McCracken and Baldwin, 2014).

FINDINGS

Table 1 reveals the findings from our first study that averaged all of the variables for the 18 years investigated. It more specifically presents the direct effects of the cross-national predictors on per capita income. Between 1988 and 2005, higher educational spending and highway spending reveal significant positive relationships with growth in per capita income, while K12 expenditures and K12 pupil-teacher ratios have significant negative relationships with income growth. Table 1 further reveals that the model explains a moderate amount of variance in income growth (R^2 = .44). Savings and population growth fail to demonstrate a relationship with income growth, as do two intervening variables—high school attainment, and college attainment.

To explore the applicability of the path model for sub-periods, we tested for direct effects on per capita income growth from 1988-89 to 1996-97 and from 1997-98 to 2004-2005 (see Table 1).

From 1988-89 to 1996-97, high school attainment demonstrates a significant positive relationship with income growth, while college attainment demonstrates a significant negative relationship with income growth. The model explains almost 30 percent of the variation in income growth.

For the 1997-98 to 2004-05 period, two of the independent variables—highway spending and higher educational spending—reveal significant positive associations with income growth (see Table 1). In turn, of the intervening variables, pupil-teacher ratio demonstrates a significant negative association with income growth, while college attainment demonstrates a significant positive association with income growth. Overall, the model explains a moderate amount (R^2 = .44) of variance in per capita income growth. Figure 1 presents the path model that summarizes the findings for the 1988 to 2005 period investigated. The coefficients for the relationships between the independent variables and GSP growth are the results of two re-specified regressions excluding the insignificant variables in Table 1 (contact authors for details).

Table 1. Multiple Regressions Predicting Per Capita Income Growth over Three Periods (Study 1)

	Income 1988-05		Income 1988-96		Income 1997-05	
Predictors	Beta	SE	Beta	SE	Beta	SE
K12 Expends	-.363*	.000	-.207	.000	-.192	.000
HEd Expends	.466***	.000	.199	.000	.350**	.000
Hway Expends	.309*	.000	-.020	.000	.445**	.000
Savings	-.106	.000	-.084	.000	-.069	.000
Pop Growth	-.156	.065	-.133	.117	-.050	.111
Pup-teacher ratio	-.272*	.001	-.096	.001	-.343*	.001
% HS Graduates	.224	.000	.341*	.000	-.001	.000
% College Grads	-.077	.000	-.549***	.000	.312*	.001
R^2	.436		.296		.444	

*p<.10. **p< .05. ***p< .01.
n=48.
Table 1 is reprinted with kind permission from Springer Science and Business Media and *Policy Sciences* 41, 2008, page 194, Table 2, Education and Economic Growth in the United States: Crosse-national Applications for an Intra-national Path Analysis by Norman Baldwin and Stephen A. Borrelli.

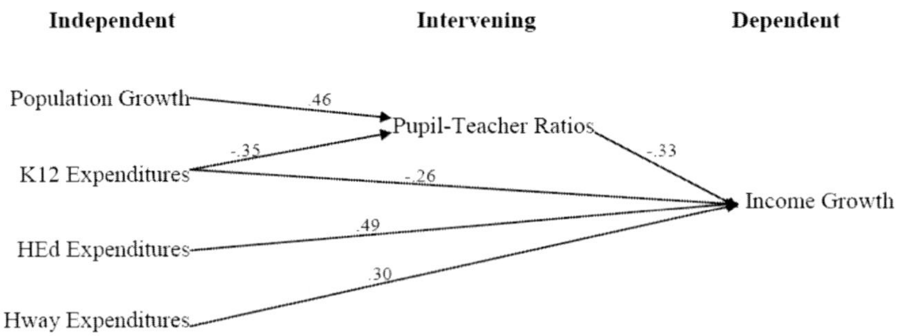

Figure 1 is reprinted with kind permission from Springer Science and Business Media and *Policy Sciences* 41, 2008, page 194, Figure 2, Education and Economic Growth in the United States: Crosse-national Applications for an Intra-national Path Analysis by Norman Baldwin and Stephen A. Borrelli.

Figure 1. Revised Growth Model for 1998-2005.

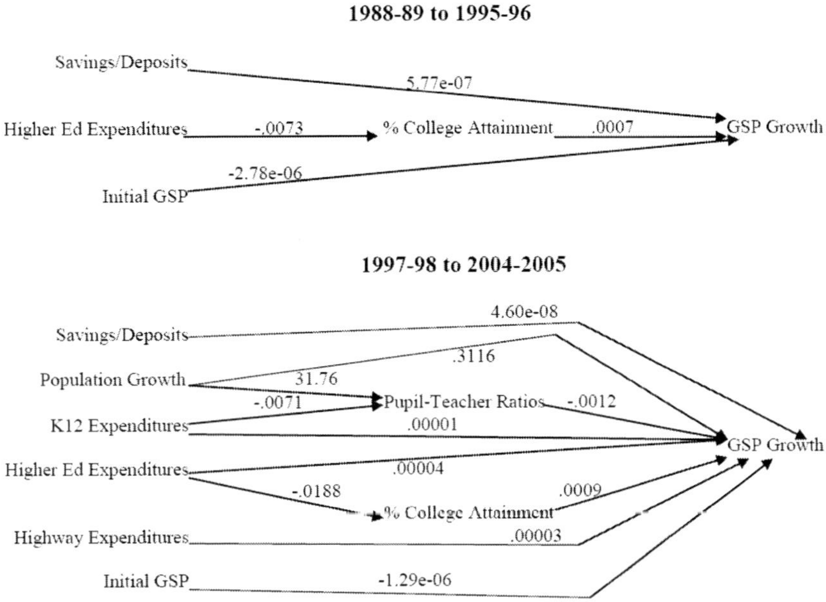

Figure 2 is from Baldwin, J. N., Borrelli, S. A., and New, M. J. (2001). State Education Investments and Economic Growth in America: A Path Analysis. Social Science Quarterly 9(1): 237. Reprinted with permission from Wily Publishing and Social Science Quarterly.

Figure 2. Revised Economic Growth Model.

Table 2 presents the findings from our second study that investigates the predictors of economic growth measured as growth in per capita GSP. It reveals that college attainment rates demonstrate an unpredicted significant negative relationship with GSP growth, and FDIC deposits demonstrate their predicted significant positive relationships with GSP growth between 1988 and 1996. It also reveals conditional convergence—the hypothesized significant negative relationship between initial GSP and GSP growth. However, between 1997 and 2005, all of the independent variables, except high school attainment, demonstrate their predicted significant associations with GSP growth. Moreover, the models for both periods investigated explain a fairly substantial amount of variance (R^2=.63 and .59) in GSP growth.

Figure 2 present the path models statistics based on regressions excluding the insignificant variables in Table 2.

Table 2. Regressions Predicting Per Capita GSP Growth (Study 2)

	GSP Growth 1988-1996		GSP Growth 1997-2005	
Predictors	*b*	SE	*b*	SE
K12 Expenditures	.000017	.000029	.000013**	7.30e-06
Higher Ed Expends	-4.69e-06	.000031	.000035***	.000011
Highway Expends	8.85e-06	8.98e-06	.000026***	7.40e-06
Savings/Deposits	5.68e-07***	1.40e-07	4.57e-08*	3.35e-08
Population Growth	.047195	.127981	.312643**	.179300
Pupil-teacher Ratios	.000635	.000600	-.001192**	.000542
% HS Attainment	.000145	.000266	-.000029	.000262
% College Attain	-.000652**	.000385	.000878***	.000288
Initial GSP	-2.96e-07***	7.78e-07	-1.29e-06***	3.26e-07
1989-90 to 1992-93	-.001754***	.000628		
1990-91 to 1993-94	.003669***	.001211		
1991-92 to 1994-95	.004879***	.001607		
1992-93 to 1995-96	.007024***	.002139		
1998-99 to 2001-02			-.001972***	.000407
1999-00 to 2002-03			-.001504**	.000893
2000-01 to 2003-04			.002767**	.001510
2001-02 to 2004-05			.010100**	.001911
R^2	.63		.59	

*$p < .10$, **$p < .05$, ***$p < .01$.

Table 2 is from Baldwin, J. N., Borrelli, S. A., and New, M. J. (2001). State Education Investments and Economic Growth in America: A Path Analysis. *Social Science Quarterly* 9(1): 234. Reprinted with permission from Wily Publishing and *Social Science Quarterly*.

Table 3. Multiple Regressions Predicting Economic Growth (Study 3)

	Income Growth						GSP/GDP Growth			
	1988-2008		1988-1996		1997-2008		1988-1996		1997-2008	
Predictors	B	SE	B	SE	B	SE	B	SE	B	SE
Log HEd Expends	.00295*	.00210	-.00011	.00344	.00125	.00287	-.00037	.00580	.00052	.00560
% College Grads	.00028*	.00021	.00006	.00025	.00013	.00030	-.00003	.00031	.00025	.00035
Log S & Loc R&D	.00010	.00084	.00251***	.00104	-.00133*	.00098	.00370***	.00137	-.00113	.00132
Log Hway Expends	.00567***	.00237	.00191	.00295	.00649**	.00287	.00505*	.00348	.00786*	.00492
Log Savings	-.00010*	.00076	.00080	.00264	-.00140*	.00088	.00425	.00385	-.00025	.00101
Pop Growth	-.09637	.09546	-.00869	.08953	-.16323	.15261	-.02869	.10596	-.34636**	.18555
Log Init Income/GDP	-.01649**	.00782	-.02375***	.00923	.00080	.01060	-.02228**	.01214	-.00750	.00607
Enrollments					.11271	.13721			.19266	.15795
Log Jr. Colleges					.00474***	.00145			.00300*	.00200
Log 4-yr Colleges						.00258	.00242		.00035	.00290
R^2	.25		.25		.56		.56		.56	

*p< .10, **p< .05, ***p< .01.

[a]Predictors include 19 dummy variables for the 1988 to 2008 growth period,seven for the 1988-1996 period, and nine for the 1997-2008 period.

Table 3 is from Baldwin, J. N. and McCracken, W. A. (2013). Justifying the Ivory Tower: Higher Education and State Economic Growth. *Journal of Education Finance* 38(3): 200.

Table 3 presents the findings from our third study that investigated the predictors of economic growth with a longer time frame and a focus on an extended set of higher education-related independent variables. However, we excluded K12 spending and Other R&D spending from this final set of regressions because they demonstrated only one significant relationship with economic growth in five other models tested (see Baldwin and McCracken, 2013).

Table 3 reveals that highways expenditures and junior colleges per million demonstrate significant relationships with economic growth in a majority of the models. It also demonstrates that conditional convergence occurred in three of the five regressions and was close to being achieved (p < .10) in the prediction of GDP growth from 1997-2008. The findings further reveal that the models explain a somewhat substantial amount of variance (R^2= .56) in income growth form 1997-2008 and in GSP/GDP growth over both periods investigated.

Table 4. Multiple Regressions Predicting Unemployment and Unemployment

	Unemployment		Unemployment Growth	
Predictors	B	SE	B	SE
Log Junior Colleges	-.1821***	.0570	-.0442	.0417
Log 4-year Colleges	-.5898***	.1051	-.1386**	.0683
Population Growth	-22.9581***	5.7917	-4.2083	4.0154
Log Hway Expends	-1.0868***	.2399	-.2310**	.1057
Log Savings	1.30e-06***	4.47e-07	7.59e-07**	3.45e-07
Initial Unemploy	.1927***	.0163	.0061	.0176
Democrat Governor	-.0417	.0943	-.0096	.0554
Democrat Legislature	.0185	.0711	-.0339	.0515
Divided Legislature	.2027*	.1202	.0504	.0639
Democratic Congress	.2986*	.1805	.0301	.8103
Nat'l Political Unity	.3750*	.2135	-3.7141***	.9939
% Nat'l Unemployed	.8816***	.0320	.2322*	.1430
Log National GDP	-.7350*	.4235	6.3002***	1.9822
R^2	.7260		.7674	

*p< .10, **p< .05, ***p< .01.

Table 4 presents the findings from our final study—a study of the predictors of state unemployment and unemployment growth that adds seven political variables to the classic cross-national predictors of economic growth. Junior colleges, four-year colleges, population growth, highway expenditures, and the national GDP have negative relationships with unemployment rates, while FDIC savings, initial unemployment rates, divided legislatures, Democratic Congresses, national political unity, and national unemployment have positive relationships with unemployment. Table 4 further indicates that four-year colleges, highway spending, and national political unity have negative relationships with unemployment growth, while FDIC savings, national unemployment rates, and the national GDP have positive relationships with unemployment *growth*. The findings also reveal that the models explain a substantial amount of variance in unemployment and unemployment growth (R^2=.73 and .77).

SUMMARY OF THE AGGREGATE FINDINGS

Of the predictors of economic growth borrowed from the cross-national research, highway spending as a measure of infrastructure and junior colleges as a measure of education are the most robust predictors of economic growth at the state-level in the United States (see Table 5). Except for the study of unemployment, a majority of the significant relationships also support conditional convergence, or the common cross-national finding of an inverse relationship between initial economic development and economic growth rates. The most consistent significant findings from the four studies reviewed, however, are the control variables that account for national trends. This is captured in the dummy variables for each four-year period in the second study, the dummy variables for each growth period in the third study (contact the authors for the details), and the national unemployment rates investigated in the fourth study.

The summary data in Table 5 further shows that 50% of the significant findings remained the same when the data analysis and model specifications changed. That is, the significant relationships between specific independent variables and per capita income growth and per capita GSP growth found in studies one and two replicated themselves in 16 of 32 relationships in study three.

Table 5. Summary of Significant Findings

	Measures of Economic Growth: Dependent Variables												
	Study One			Study Two		Study Three					Study Four		
Predictors	Income 1988-2005	Income 1988-1996	Income 1997-2005	GSP 1988-1996	GSP 1997-2005	Income 1988-2008	Income 1988-1996	Income 1997-2008	GSP 1988-1996	GDP 1997-2008	Unemp 1988-2010	Uemp Growth 1988-10	% Signif.
Log Hway Expends	Yes	No	Yes	No	Yes	Yes	No	Yes	Yes	Yes	Yes	Yes	75%
Log Savings	No	No	No	Yes	Yes	Yes	No	Yes	No	No	Yes	Yes	50%
Pop Growth	No	No	No	No	Yes	No	No	No	No	Yes	Yes	No	25%
Log K12 Expends	Yes	No	No	No	Yes	No	No	No	No	No	na	na	20%
Log Higher Ed Expends	Yes	No	Yes	No	Yes	Yes	No	No	No	No	na	na	40%
% HS Graduates	No	Yes	No	No	No	na	na	na	na	na	na	na	20%
% College Graduates	No	Yes	Yes	Yes	Yes	Yes	No	No	No	No	na	na	50%
Pupil-Teacher Ratio	Yes	No	Yes	No	Yes	na	na	na	na	na	na	na	60%
Log Initial PC Income	na	na	na	na	na	Yes	Yes	No	na	na	na	na	67%
Log Initial GSP Per Cap	na	na	na	Yes	Yes	na	na	na	Yes	No	na	na	75%

	Study One			Study Two		Study Three					Study Four		
Initial Unemploy	na	na	na	na	na	na	na	na	na	na	Yes	na	100%
Four-year Periods	na	na	na	Yes	Yes	na	na	na	na	na	na	na	100%
Year	na	na	na	na	na	Yes	Yes	Yes	Yes	Yes	na	na	100%
Log State & Local R&D	na	na	na	na	na	No	Yes	Yes	Yes	No	na	na	50%
Log Jr. Colleges	na	na	na	na	na	na	na	Yes	na	Yes	Yes	Yes	100%
Log 4-year Colleges	na	na	na	na	na	na	na	No	na	No	Yes	Yes	50%
Enrollments	na	na	na	na	na	na	na	No	na	No	na	na	0%
Democratic Governor	na	na	na	na	na	na	na	na	na	na	No	No	0%
Democratic Legislature	na	na	na	na	na	na	na	na	na	na	No	No	0%
Divided Legislature	na	na	na	na	na	na	na	na	na	na	Yes	No	50%
Democratic Congress	na	na	na	na	na	na	na	na	na	na	Yes	No	50%
Nat'l Political Unity	na	na	na	na	na	na	na	na	na	na	Yes	Yes	100%[1]
% Nat'l Unemploy	na	na	na	na	na	na	na	na	na	na	Yes	Yes	100%
Log of National GDP	na	na	na	na	na	na	na	na	na	na	Yes	Yes	100%[1]

Note: The variables were measured as 18 year averages in the first study and four-year moving averages in the second study.

[1]Although the two associations are significant, the directions of the significant findings (the signs) are opposite.

Most notably, the more refined and thorough analysis of study three reversed the finding from studies one and two that would have led one to believe that college graduation rates affect both per capita income growth and per capita GSP growth. It also reversed findings from study two that would have led one to believe that FDIC deposit had an impact on per capita GSP growth. Table 5 further demonstrates that 41.7% of the findings from the 1986 to 1996 period are different from those of the 1997 to 2005/2008 period.

However only 33.3% of the finding changed from the 1986 to 1996 period to the 1997 to 2005/2008 period on the basis of the more refined data analysis in our third study. However, on four occasions, the findings in the 1988-1996 period and the 1997-2005/2008 period are the same but different from the full period. The results are actually in keeping with Simpson's Paradox, which states simply that different results can emerge at different levels when splitting data into pieces, and that the levels may not match the aggregate (Agresti, 2007).[3]

CONCLUSION: LESSONS AND FUTURE RESEARCH

One of the more profound observations made in conducting this economic growth research is that different approaches to data analysis yielded different results, yet were found acceptable for publication by different reviewers. Contemporary data analysis in economic development research has become so sophisticated that some reviewers, like researchers, are incapable of catching the shortcoming of the analyses being applied. In turn, those with the expertise to understand the complexities of analyzing longitudinal panel data are often in a suboptimal position for understanding the full context, contributions, and theoretical significance of a lot of economic growth research. We believe the research and review processes sometimes fall short when either the statistically skillful or those with the in depth qualitative understanding of economic growth are overrepresented or underrepresented in economic growth research.

A related general observation is that the economists are much more statistically sophisticated than the social scientists conducting economic growth research. The economists also appear to be more wedded to their models and more focused on refining the calculation of variables and

[3]A classic example of Simpson paradox is "blacks who murder whites are sentenced to death at a greater rate than whites who murder other whites, even though more whites are sentenced to death than blacks overall" Agresti (2007: 51-53).

increasing the validity of their measures through accessing better data sources. In contrast, the social scientists exhibit more freedom in the selection of theories to test and consequently more variation in the component parts of their models tested. Like the quantitative and qualitative scholars, the economists and social scientists have much to learn from one another and, through working together, have the greatest capacity for conducting economic growth research that is innovative, relevant, and both internally and externally valid.

Those with the expertise to identify the appropriate application of statistical tests, however, have led us to a third lesson learned—the data analysis found acceptable for our economic growth research eight years ago is no longer acceptable. Running OLS regressions with data that do not meet the assumptions of linear regression, such as time series or panel data, is problematic, as is averaging variables that reduced one of our studies to as few as 48 observations. Running GLS with longitudinal panel data gave us the ability to consider a cross-section of data resulting in 960 observations. Longitudinal panel data, which is time-dependent, also allowed us to utilize lags in our more recent studies. Moreover, to meet the needs of contemporary reviewers, we became progressively aware of the importance of running PCSE, logging variables, correcting for AR1 autocorrelation, converting all expenditure measures to constant dollars, and testing for fixed effects.

Two other lessons learned that are likely common to any research in which models are tested over time are that no model is ever appropriately specified, and no one agrees on the length of the time (the lags) necessary for education-related variables to have an effect. Indeed, as Box (1987) remarked, "All models are wrong, but some are useful." Reviewers have suggested that we expand our models to include measures of tax burden, health care expenditures, regional variations, specific state characteristics, and an endless number of education-related variables—student population sizes, class sizes, test scores, funding of private sector education, percentage of minorities in schools, students with English as a first language, parents' education level, and where education dollars are spent. Other than insisting on controls for what is going on in the national economy, no two reviewers have suggested similar additions to our models or similar lags for our education-related variables. Commonly accepted standards for the lagged impact of education-related variables on economic growth are needed.

Among the myriad of possibilities in pursuit of a more perfectly specified model, we further believe that the relationship among economic growth, unemployment, and policy and politics begs for further study. For example, while neoclassicism attributes change in the relationship between economic growth and unemployment in the 1990s to technology, the case can also be made that the change was driven by the convergence of unique domestic and international political factors that were absent in preceding decades (Gruber, 2000).[4] We also believe that variations in regional culture reflected in vacation benefits and sick leave are interesting potential predictors of economic growth worthy of further investigation. With respect to data analysis, future economic growth research that investigates national economic and political variables might lend themselves to structural equation modeling. At the very least, future efforts might investigate the covariance structures of the data in order to determine whether structural equations are in fact present. Future research that increases the number of observations is also appealing and becoming increasingly possible as more monthly and quarterly data is being kept and made available to the public. Finally, to compare the effects of the size of the population and the size of the economy, future economic growth research might include spending and income variables measured as per capita variables, as percentages of GSP, and as percentages of total state personal income (Jones, 1990).

In conclusion, our four studies lead us to believe that economic growth at the state level in the Unities States is best served by investing in highways and junior colleges—state-level equivalents of two of the four leading predictors from the cross-national research. However, junior colleges per million population is only one of nine operationalizations of education that predicts all of our measures of economic growth. Of the other two state-level equivalents of the cross-national predictors, FDIC savings was an inconsistent predictor of economic growth and population growth was a poor predictor of economic growth. In contrast, our research demonstrates that what is going on nationally has the most consistent relationship with state economic growth. While state officials are wise to advocate for more junior colleges and more miles of highway, they are equally astute to look beyond the borders of their state to capture what is happening nationwide in order to accurately predict the economic growth of their states.

---

[4] Republicans took control of Congress for the first time since the 1950s and pursued the most radical agenda since the 1930s. On the domestic front, the resulting Contract with America, welfare to work legislation, and an enormously successful deficit reduction act likely impacted employment in the 1990s. On the international front, the politics leading to the end of the Cold War, to the emergence of the U.S. as the lone superpower, to the General Agreement on Tariffs and Trade giving way to the World Trade Organization, and to the liberalization of international trade (e.g., No th American Free Trade Agreement) also likely affected employment.

APPENDIX 1. VARIABLE LABELS AND DEFINITIONS

Label	Definitions[1]
PC Income	growth in personal per capita income
GSP/GDP Growth	growth in gross state (or domestic) product per capita
% Unemployed	percentage of the working-eligible population that is unemployed
Unemploy Growth	year to year growth in unemployment from 1987-2010
Log Hway Expends	logged per capita state disbursement for highways per capita in thousands of dollars
Log Savings	logged per capita state deposits in FDIC insured Commercial Banks in thousands of dollars
Pop Growth	growth in state population
Log Init PC Income	logged per capita income for the initial year in the growth periods investigated
Log Init GSP/GDP	logged gross state/domestic product per capita for the initial years in the growth periods investigated
Init Unemploy	percent of the initial unemployment rate
Log HEd Expends	logged per capita higher education state expenditures for operations in thousands of dollars lagged seven years
% College Attain	percentage of the population 25 years or older with a bachelor's degree or higher
% HS Attain	percentage of the population 25 years or older who have graduated from high school
Pupil-Teach Ratios	the number of students for each teacher in a state
Log State&Loc R&D	logged per capita state and local government R&D expenditures at colleges and universities lagged five years
Enrollments	per capita fall enrollments in public higher education lagged seven years
Log 4-year Colleges	logged per million population four-year public Institutions of higher education lagged seven years
Log Junior Colleges	logged per million population two-year public institutions of higher education lagged four years
Log K12 Expends	logged per capita K12 expenditures in thousands of dollars for operating local public schools lagged 13 years
Dem Governor	dummy variable for sitting Governors who are Democrats
Dem Legislature	dummy variable for legislatures that have Democratic majorities in their House and Senate
Divided Legislature majority	dummy variable for legislatures with a Republican in one chamber and a Democratic majority in the other
Dem Congress	dummy variable for Congresses that have Democratic majorities in their House and Senate

Appendix 1. (Continued)

Label	Definitions[1]
Nat'l Political Unity	the extent that the President & Congressional majority are of the same political party (experience divided government)
Initial Unemploy	the unemployment rate at the beginning of the time period investigated (1988).
% Nat'l Unemploy	percentage of the national population that is unemployed
Log of Nat'l GDP	logged national gross domestic product
Four –Year Periods	dummy variables for 13 four-year periods

[1]The variables were measured as 18 year averages in the first study and four-year moving averages in the second study.

REFERENCES

Agresti, A. (2007). *An Introduction to Categorical Data Analysis* (2nd ed.). Wiley: Hoboken, NJ.

Alt, J. E. (1985). Political Parties, World Demand, and Unemployment: Domestic and International Sources of Economic Activity. *The American Political Science Review* 79(4): 1016-1040.

Baldwin, J. N. & McCracken, W. A. (2013). Justifying the Ivory Tower: Higher Education and State Economic Growth. *Journal of Education Finance* 38(3): 181-209.

Baldwin, J. N., Borrelli, S. A. & New, M. J. (2011)."State Education Investments and Economic Growth in America: A Path Analysis." *Social Science Quarterly* 9(1): 226-245.

Baldwin, J. N. & Borrelli, S. A. (2008). Education and Economic Growth in the United States: Cross-national Applications for an Intra-national Path Analysis. *Policy Sciences* 41: 183-204.

Barro, R. & Martin, X. S. (2004). *Economic Growth*. Cambridge, MA: MIT Press.

Beck, N. & Katz, J. (1995). What to Do (and Not to Do) with Time-Series Cross-Section Data. *American Political Science Review* 89(3): 634-47.

Bertrand, M., Duflo, E. & Mullainathan, S. (2004). How Much Should We Trust Differences-in-Differences Estimates? *The Quarterly Journal of Economics*, MIT Press, 119(1): 249-275.

Blackley, P. R. (1989). The Measurement and Determination of State Equilibrium. *Southern Economic Journal* 56(2), 440-456.

Bleaney, M., Gemmell, N., & Kneller, R. (2001). Testing the Endogenous Growth Model: Public Expenditure, Taxation, and Growth over the Long Run. *Canadian Journal of Economics* 34: 36-57.

Borooah, V. K. & Mangan, J. (2008). Education, Occupational Class, and Unemployment in the Regions of the United Kingdom. *Education Economics,* 16(4): 351-370.

Box, G.E. & Draper, N.R. (1987). *Empirical Model-Building and Response Surfaces*. New York: Wiley.

Brace, P. (1993). *State Government and Economic Performance*. Baltimore: Johns Hopkins.

Bradshaw, T. K., Kennedy, K.M., & Davis, P. R. (2003). Science First: Contributions of a University-Industry Toxic Substances Research and Teaching Program to Economic Development. *The Journal of Higher Education* 74(3): 292-320.

Carroll, R., & Wasylenko, M. (1994). Does State Business Climate Still Matter?—Evidence of Structural Change. *National Tax Journal* 47(1): 19-37.

Cass, D. (1965). Optimum Growth in an Aggregative Model of Capital Accumulation. *Review of Economic Studies* 32(3): 233-240.

Chappell Jr., H. W., & Keech, W. R. (1986). Party Differences in Macroeconomic Policies and Outcomes. *The American Economic Review* 76 (2): 71-74.

(1986a). Policy Motivation and Party Differences in a Dynamic Spatial Model of Party Competition. *The American Political Science Review* 80(3): 881-899.

(1988). The Unemployment Rate Consequences of Partisan Monetary Policies. *Southern Economic Journal* 55(1): 107-122.

Clark, D. H., Fordham, B. O. & Nordstrom, T. (2011). Preying on the Misfortune of Others: When Do States Exploit Their Opponents' Domestic Troubles? *Journal of Politics* 73(1): 248-64.

Crihfield, J., Giertz, J., & Mehta. (1995). Economic Growth in the American States: The End of Convergence? *Quarterly Review of Economics and Finance*, 35(Special issue): 551-577.

Crown, W., & Wheat, L. (1995). State Per Capita Income Convergence Since 1950: Sharecropping's Demise and Other Influences. *Journal of Regional Science* 35(4): 527-552.

Devarajan, S. Swaroop, V., & Zou, H. (1996). The Composition of Public Expenditures and Economic Growth. *Journal of Monetary Economics* 37(2): 313-344.

Easton, D. (1965). *A Systems Analysis of Political Life*. New York: Wiley.

Evans, S. F., & Oneal, J. R. (1995). The Social Returns to Education: The Effects of Income of the Fifty United States Investment in Human Capital, 1963-89. University of Alabama, unpublished manuscript.

Fisher, R. (1997). The Effects of State and Local Public Services on Economic Development. *New England Economic Review* (March/April): 53-82.

Federal Reserve Bank of Dallas. 2010. *Smoothing Data with Moving Averages.* Available at (www.dallasfed.org/data/basics/moving.html).

Feller, I. (2004). Virtuous and Vicious Cycles in the Contribution of Public Research Universities to State Economic Development Objectives. *Economic Development Quarterly* 18(2): 138-150.

Garcia-Mila, T. & McGuire, T. J. (1992). The Contribution of Publicly Provided Inputs to States' Economies. *Regional Science and Urban Economics* 22(2): 229-241.

Gramlich, E. M. (1994). Infrastructure, Investment: A Review Essay. *Journal of Economic Literature* 32(September): 1176-1196.

Gruber, L., (2000) *Ruling the World: Power Politics and the Rise of Supranational Institutions.* Princeton NJ: Princeton University Press.

Hibbs, D. A. (1977). Political Parties and Macroeconomic Policy. *American Political Science Review* 71(04): 1467-1487.

(1982).Public Concern about Inflation and Unemployment in the United States: Trends, Correlates and Political Implications, In R.E. Hall (ed.) *Inflation: Causes and Effects* (pp.211-231). Chicago: National Bureau of Economic Research, University of Chicago Press.

Hooker, M. A. & Knetter, M. M. (1994). *Unemployment Effects of Military Spending: Evidence from a Panel of States. NBER Working Papers: 4889.* Cambridge, MA: National Bureau of Economic Research.

Jacoby, W. G. (2000). Issue Framing and Public Opinion on Government Spending. *American Journal of Political Science* 44(4): 750-767.

Jones, B. D. (1990). Public Policies and Economic Growth in the American States. *Journal of Politics* 52 (1): 219-233.

Jones, B. D. & Vedlitz, A. (1993). Higher Education, Business Creation, and Economic Growth in the American States. In W. Becker, and D. Lewis (eds.) *Higher Education and Economic Growth.* Norwell, MA: Kluwer Academic Publishers.

Jorgensen, D. W. & Fraumeni, B. M. (1992).Investment in Education and US Economic Growth. *Scandinavian Journal of Economics* 94(Supplement): 51-70.

Kalecki, M. (1993). *Socialism: Economic Growth and Efficiency of Investment*. Vol. 4. Oxford, UK: Oxford University Press.

Katz, D. & Kahn, R. L. (1966). *The Psychology of Organizations*. New York: Wiley.

Landau, M. (1969). Redundancy, Rationality, the Problem of Duplication. *Public Administration Review* 29(4): 346-358.

Manacorda, M. & Petrongolo, B. (1999). Skill Mismatch and Unemployment in OECD Countries. *Economica* 66: 181-207.

McCracken, W. A. III. & Baldwin, J. N. (2014). Economic and Political Predictors of Unemployment in the States. Paper presented at the Southern Political Science Association convention January 3, New Orleans, LA.

Mincer, J. (1994). The Production of Human Capital and the Lifecycle of Earnings: Variations on a Theme. Cambridge, MA: National Bureau of Economic Research, NBER Working Paper #4838.

Nickell, S. (1979). Education and Lifetime Patterns of Unemployment. *Journal of Political Economy* 87(5), S117-S131.

Nijkamp, P. (2009). Regional Development as Self-organized Converging Growth. In G. Kochendorfer-Lucius and B. Pleskovic (eds.) *Spatial Disparities and Development Policy*. Washington, DC: The World Bank.

Nijkamp, P. & Poot, N. (2004). Meta-Analysis of the Impact of Fiscal Policies on Long-Run Growth. Tinbergen Institute Discussion Paper. 23 April 2003. http://www.tinbergen.nl/scripts/papers.pl?paper=02028.rdf. (accessed March 2007).

Nistor, A. (2009). Assessing the Effectiveness of Human Capital Investments on the Regional Unemployment Rate in the United States: 1990 and 2000. *International Regional Science Review* 32: 65-91.

Pfiffner, J. M. & Sherwood, F. P. 1960. *Administrative Organization*. Englewood Cliffs, NJ: Prentice-Hall.

Poot, J. (2000). A Synthesis of Empirical Research on the Impact of Government on Long-Run Growth. *Growth and Change* 31(4): 516-546.

Rephann, T. J. (1993). Highway Investment and Regional Economic Development: Decision Methods and Empirical Foundations. *Urban Studies* 30 (2): 437-450.

Rephann, T. J. & Isserman, A. (1994). New Highways as Economic Development Tools: An Evaluation Using Quasi-experimental Matching Methods. *Regional Science and Urban Economics* 24: 723-751.

Sabatier, Paul A. (2007). *Theories of the Public Policy Process* (2nd ed). Boulder, CO: Westview.

Sedgley, N. (1998). *The Role of Industrial Innovation in Growth and Convergence across US States.* Doctoral Dissertation, University of New Hampshire.

Senter, R. Jr. (1999). The Impact of Government Research and Development Spending and Other Factors on State Economic Development. *Public Administration Quarterly* 23(3): 368-384.

Solow, R. (1956). A Contribution to the Theory of Economic Growth. *Quarterly Journal of Economics* 70(1): 65-94.

Stone, D. (2002). *Policy Paradox: The Art of Political Decision Making*. New York: Norton.

Swan, T. W. (1956). Economic Growth and Capital Accumulation. *Economic Record* 32(63): 334-361.

Temple, J. (1999). The New Growth Evidence. *Journal of Economic Literature* 37(1): 112-156.

U.S. Bureau of Economic Analysis. 2007. Gross Domestic Product by State. Available at (http://www.bea.gov/bea/regional/gsp).

Von Bertanlanffy, L. (1950). The Theory of Open Systems in Physics and Biology. *Science* 111: 279-300.

Walsh, J. R. (1935). Capital Concept Applied to Man. *The Quarterly Journal of Economics* 49 (2): 255-285.

Wildavsky, A. (1964). *The Politics of the Budgetary Process*. Boston: Little, Brown.

Wright, J. R. (2012). Unemployment and the Democratic Electoral Advantage. *American Political Science Review* 106(4): 685-702.

In: Economic Growth in the 21st Century
Editor: Cody Accosi
ISBN: 978-1-63321-589-4

Chapter 2

Foreign Direct Investment and Economic Growth in OECD Countries

***Dr. Wenyu Zang**[*1] **and Dr. Mark Baimbridge**[2]*
[1]Division of Economics, Nottingham Business School
Nottingham Trent University, UK
[2]Division of Economics,
School of Social and International Studies
University of Bradford, UK

Abstract

The role of inward FDI on economic growth has attracted the attention of researchers for many years as its beneficial impact has been recognised theoretically by scholars and policymakers; however, the empirical evidence remains ambiguous.

Hence, the objective of this chapter is to investigate the causal relationship between FDI inflows/outflows and economic growth in developed OECD countries. Investigation of the causal link between FDI inflows and growth has important implications such that if there is a unidirectional causality it would support the FDI-led growth hypothesis. Alternatively, if the causal link runs in the opposite direction, it would imply that economic growth may be a prerequisite for countries to attract

[*] Email: wenyu.zang@ntu.ac.uk.

FDI. Finally, if the causal process is bi-directional, FDI inflows and growth would have a reinforcing causal relationship.

In particular, this chapter contributes to the existing literature by focusing on developed countries as inward/outward FDI has become an increasingly significant factor in influencing the economic activity. In contrast, most previous time-series causality studies focus on developing countries with only a few covering developed countries. However, almost all of the world's FDI originates from developed countries and the majority of FDI is also located in developed countries.

Another feature is that this chapter also tests the causal link between outward FDI and economic growth. Outward FDI might promote the home country's economic growth as it might yield higher profits, transfer technology and management skills to the home country, expand production abroad, secure raw materials overseas and avoid trade barriers and so on.

Following an Introduction, the chapter then reviews FDI trend across OECD countries. Next it discusses the alternative theories and literature exploring the relationship between FDI and economic growth (i.e., the impact of inward FDI on host country's economic growth, the impact of outward FDI on home country's economic growth, together with the impact of economic growth on inward/outward FDI). We then describe empirical causality testing methodology, together discussing the empirical results.

1. Introduction

The Global Financial crisis that led to the Great Recession resulted in differing levels of economic turmoil across developed industrialised economies, with particularly acute implications for eurozone countries where it triggered a sovereign debt crisis given their fundamental lack of economic cohesion and appropriate policy tools. For example, the absence of adjustable exchange rates, centralised monetary policy and constrained fiscal policy severely limited scope for economies to both ameliorate shocks and to find a sustainable path to recovery. Indeed, a greater emphasis had previously been placed on long-term supply-side economic policy as discussed in the EU's Lisbon Agenda and its successor, Europe 2020 that seeks to develop a growth model to create conditions for "a different type of growth that is smarter, more sustainable and more inclusive". Hence, this chapter to examines the importance for economic growth of nations shifting the emphasis of their economies towards long-term supply-side economic policy through evaluating the foreign direct investment (FDI) – growth nexus.

FDI plays an important role in influencing the level of economic activity in the world with multinational companies accounting for above one-fifth of world employment in the non-agricultural sectors (Whyman and Baimbridge, 2008). The remarkable growth in FDI has attracted the attention of many researchers on developing countries, as they believe that developing countries have less advanced technology and benefit more from inward FDI through technology spillover (Bengoa and Sanchez-Robles, 2003; Roy and Van den Berg, 2006). However, developed countries might also benefit from inward FDI; yet, there is a risk that inward FDI may transfer the host country's advanced technology to the home country, resulting in a reduction in the comparative advantage of the host country (Dunning, 1994). Another potential drawback is that foreign firms might out compete local firms and drive them out of business (Blomstrom and Kokko, 1997; Hill, 2009).

Outward FDI may also bring significant benefits to the home country, with outward investing firms benefiting from increasing returns to scale and yielding higher profits by investing abroad than by investing in the home market (HM Treasury, 1996). It may also provide routes to transfer advanced technology, management skills and working training to the home country, therefore improving the productivity of domestic firms (HM Treasury, 1996). However, concerns arise over the adverse impact of outward FDI on employment, domestic investment and exports in the home country.

Therefore, this study contributes to the existing literature in the following ways. First, it considers a 'nation' as the unit for analysis and uses data on aggregate FDI inflows into a country from the rest of the world and aggregate FDI outflows from a country to the rest of the world. Second, this study concentrates on developed OECD countries (Australia, Austria, Canada, Denmark, Finland, France, Germany, Ireland, Italy, Japan, Korea, Netherlands, New Zealand, Norway, Portugal, Spain, Sweden, Switzerland, UK and US) as inward/outward FDI might be an important engine to their economic growth and they are the major sources and recipients of FDI. This contrasts with the vast majority of empirical studies focusing on developing countries. Furthermore, many empirical studies pool both developed countries and developing countries into one sample and do not distinguish them in their analysis. Blonigen and Wang (2005) argue that FDI plays a different role in developed countries compared to developing countries such that pooling developed and developing countries in an empirical analysis leads to incorrect inferences. Moreover, this study takes into consideration the importance of outward FDI on the host country's economy, which has been largely neglected in the literature.

2. FDI Trends and Distribution in Developed OECD Countries

In terms of the stylised facts relating to FDI trends, Figure 1 represents the general trend of FDI inflows and FDI outflows in developed OECD countries, which form the basis of the empirical analysis.

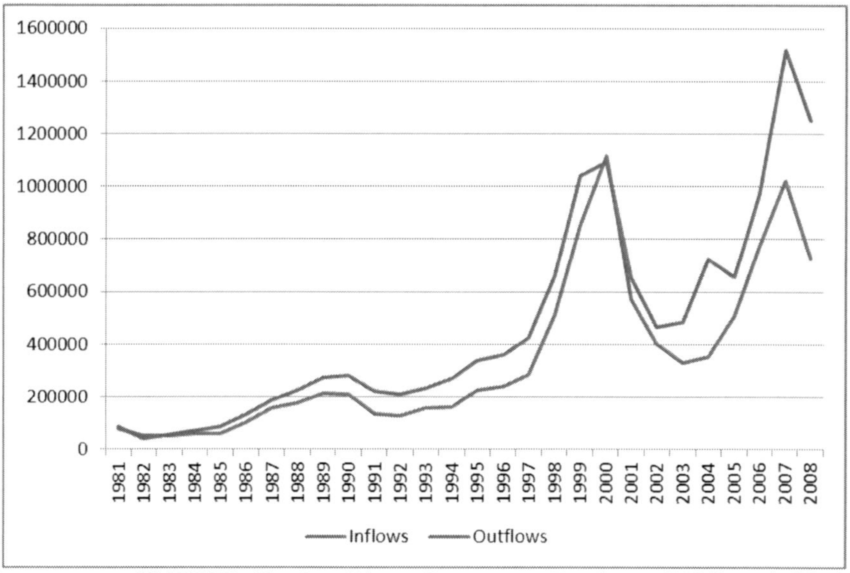

Data source: UNCTAD Foreign Direct Investment Database (2011) and World Development Indicators (2011).

Notes: (1) Data are in millions of 2000 US $. (2) Developed OECD countries include Australia, Austria, Belgium, Canada, Denmark, Finland, France, Germany, Greece, Iceland, Ireland, Italy, Japan, Korea (Republic of), Luxembourg, Netherlands, New Zealand, Norway, Portugal, Spain, Sweden, Switzerland, UK and US. (3) Germany refers to former federal republic of Germany (West Germany) before 1990 and it refers to both former federal republic of Germany (West Germany) and former democratic republic of Germany (East Germany) from 1990.

Figure 1. FDI inflows and outflows in developed OECD countries.

The amount of inflows was relatively small and fluctuated a little between 1981 and 1992. From 1992, it rose steadily to 1997 and increased dramatically to the peak level in 2000. According to UNCTAD (2006), the trends are driven by cross-border mergers and acquisitions (M&As). However, from the highest level in 2000, inflows fell sharply by about 50 percent in 2001, returning to the level in 1998. According to UNCTAD (2002), this decline reflected the slowdown of economic activity in developed countries and a decrease in their stock market activity, which reduced new international investment, particularly the cross-border M&As. The event of 11 September 2001 exacerbated the slowdown, which may also have contributed to the further decline in 2002 and 2003 (UNCTAD, 2002). In 2004, inflows started to pick up following three years of decline, which reflects the recovery and higher growth rates in some countries (UNCTAD, 2006). After four years of consecutive growth, inflows rose in 2007 by more than 30% and reached another high level, which was close to the record high level in 2000. The increase in inflows reflected high economic growth and strong corporate performance in many countries (UNCTAD, 2008). After the global financial and economic crisis in 2007, the decline of corporate profits and stock prices greatly reduced the value of cross-border M&As, which resulted in 29% fall in inflows in 2008 (UNCTAD, 2009).

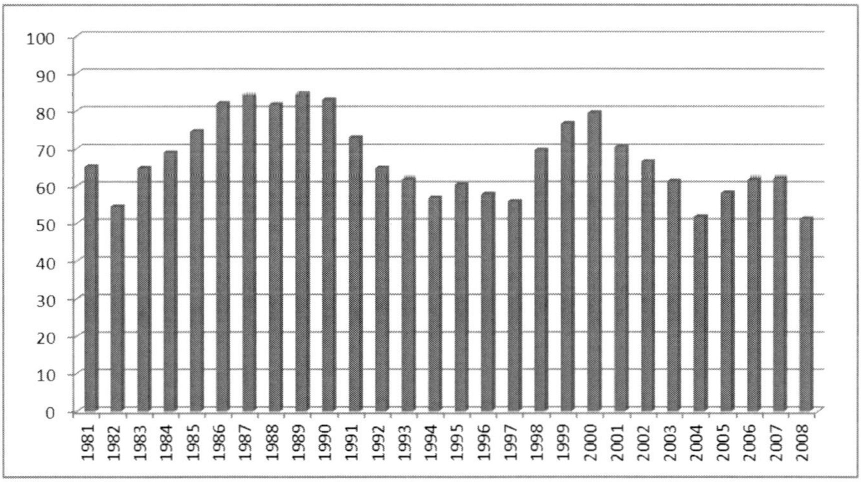

Data source: UNCTAD Foreign Direct Investment Database (2011).

Notes: (1) Developed OECD countries include Australia, Austria, Belgium, Canada, Denmark, Finland, France, Germany, Greece, Iceland, Ireland, Italy, Japan, Korea (Republic of), Luxembourg, Netherlands, New Zealand, Norway, Portugal, Spain, Sweden, Switzerland, UK and US. (2) Germany refers to former federal republic of Germany (West Germany) before 1990 and it refers to both former federal republic of Germany (West Germany) and former democratic republic of Germany (East Germany) from 1990.

Figure 2. Share of world inflows to developed OECD countries (%).

FDI outflows followed a similar pattern to that for inflows from 1981 to 2002. Although in 2003 outflows started to recover, the recovery was short-lived as there was a further decline in 2005, whilst 2006 and 2007 experienced huge increases in outflows. Outflows reached the all-time peak level in 2007, which was 39% higher than the outflows in 2000. However, outflows fell again by 18% in 2008 due to global financial crisis. Another difference between inflows and outflows is that the outflow line is above the inflow line for most years, indicating that outflows are more than inflows in developed OECD countries. According to UNCTAD (2006), outflow trends are also driven by cross-border M&As.

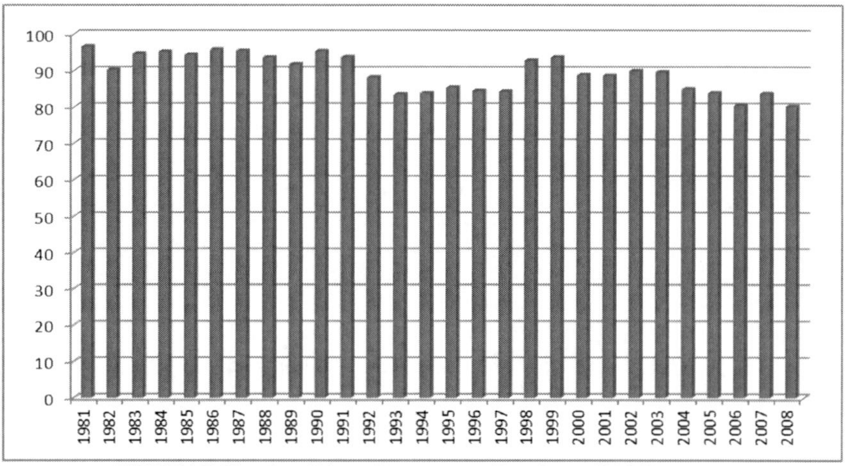

Data source: UNCTAD Foreign Direct Investment Database (2011).

Notes: (1) Developed OECD countries include Australia, Austria, Belgium, Canada, Denmark, Finland, France, Germany, Greece, Iceland, Ireland, Italy, Japan, Korea (Republic of), Luxembourg, Netherlands, New Zealand, Norway, Portugal, Spain, Sweden, Switzerland, UK and US. (2) Germany refers to former federal republic of Germany (West Germany) before 1990 and it refers to both former federal republic of Germany (West Germany) and former democratic republic of Germany (East Germany) from 1990.

Figure 3. Share of World outflows from developed OECD countries (%).

Turning to the share of world FDI inflows shown in Figure 2, we can see that the share of developed OECD countries fluctuates from 51% to 85% between 1981 and 2008, with an average of approximately 67%. Therefore, developed OECD countries account for a significant proportion of world inflows. With respect to the share of world FDI outflows illustrated in Figure

3, developed OECD countries account for most of global outflows ranging from 80% to 97% between 1981 and 2008.

Table 1. Annual average FDI data from 1981 to 2008

FDI as a percentage of total world (%)		FDI as a percentage of GDP (%)	
Inflows	Outflows	Inflows	Outflows
US 23.51	US 19.38	Netherlands 4.22	Netherlands 6.65
UK 8.55	UK 12.99	Ireland 3.89	Switzerland 6.25
France 5.48	Japan 8.85	Iceland 3.73	Iceland 6.17
Spain 3.76	France 8.75	Sweden 3.72	Sweden 4.61
Netherlands 3.24	Germany 8.01	UK 2.86	UK 4.31
Canada 3.12	Netherlands 5.92	Spain 2.46	France 3.08
Germany 2.92	Canada 4.29	Denmark 2.41	Finland 3.04
Australia 2.67	Switzerland 3.29	New Zealand 2.38	Ireland 2.98
Italy 1.70	Sweden 2.81	Switzerland 2.38	Spain 2.71
Sweden 1.65	Spain 2.71	Canada 2.17	Denmark 2.70
Switzerland 1.20	Italy 2.68	Australia 2.14	Canada 2.45
Denmark 0.62	Australia 1.42	Portugal 2.05	Norway 2.35
Japan 0.60	Norway 0.90	Finland 1.88	Austria 1.79
Ireland 0.59	Denmark 0.78	France 1.72	Germany 1.71
Portugal 0.56	Finland 0.74	Austria 1.48	Portugal 1.41
Austria 0.55	Austria 0.62	Norway 1.37	Australia 1.15
Korea 0.48	Korea 0.61	US 1.12	US 1.03
Norway 0.47	Ireland 0.50	Germany 1.03	Italy 1.01
New Zealand 0.42	Portugal 0.27	Greece 0.88	Japan 0.82
Finland 0.41	New Zealand 0.18	Italy 0.61	New Zealand 0.74
Greece 0.40	Iceland 0.09	Korea 0.56	Korea 0.65
Iceland 0.05	Greece 0.07	Japan 0.09	Greece 0.37
Belgium na	Belgium na	Belgium na	Belgium na
Luxembourg na	Luxembourg na	Luxembourg na	Luxembourg na

Data source: UNCTAD Foreign Direct Investment Database (2009).

Notes: (1) na: not available. (2) Germany refers to former federal republic of Germany (West Germany) before 1990 and it refers to both former federal republic of Germany (West Germany) and former democratic republic of Germany (East Germany) from 1990.

The average share is as high as 89%, so developed OECD countries are the dominant FDI exporters. Hence, we conclude that OECD countries are the major sources and recipients of world FDI. FDI inflows/outflows in OECD countries drive the world FDI inflows/outflows pattern. Compared with developed countries, developing countries only contribute a small fraction of world FDI inflows/outflows. However, the majority of current literature focuses on FDI in developing countries, studies on developed countries are relatively scarce. Therefore, it is important to investigate FDI inflows and outflows in developed OECD countries and that is why this study concentrates on this group of economies.

The distribution of FDI inflows/outflows to/from the developed OECD countries has been relatively uneven. Looking at FDI as a percentage of total world. Table 1 shows that the most attractive host developed countries are US, UK, France, Spain, Netherlands, Canada, Germany and Australia in the last three decades, accounting for more than 50% of world inflows. Regarding the outflows of FDI, the largest foreign investors are US, UK, Japan, France, Germany, Netherlands, Canada and Switzerland, accounting about 70% of world outflows. If we take the market size of the host countries and home countries into consideration, the rankings change significantly. The third and fourth column in Table 1 present FDI inflows as a percentage of host country's GDP and FDI outflows as a percentage of home country's GDP. Netherlands, Ireland, Iceland, Sweden, UK are successful in attracting FDI inflows. In terms of FDI outflows, the largest home countries are Netherlands, Switzerland, Iceland, Sweden and UK. However, compared with the first two columns, US is not the largest country in terms of inflows and outflows of FDI.

In summary, Figures 2 and 3 indicate that around 70% of world FDI inflows go to developed OECD countries and about 90% of world FDI outflows originate from developed OECD countries. Therefore, developed OECD countries as a whole contribute the majority of world inflows/outflows. However, there are significant differences in inflows/outflows among individual developed OECD countries shown in Table 1. Hence, it is interesting to examine why different OECD countries have different amounts of FDI inflows/outflows. Current country level studies on the relationship between inward FDI and growth have focused on developing countries (Zhang, 2001; Campos and Kinoshita, 2002; Basu and Chakraborty,2003; Lyroudi and Papanastasiou, 2004; Makki and Somwaru, 2004; Lumbila, 2005; Sylwester, 2005; Hansen and Rand, 2006; Hsiao and Hsiao, 2006; Greenaway and Sapsford, 2007; Qi, 2007; Duttaray and Dutt, 2008; Liu and Shu, 2009), as they take the view that developing countries have less advanced technology and are technological laggards compared to developed countries (Roy and Van den Berg, 2006). Therefore, the role of inward FDI in transferring technology to developing countries is more important. In addition, many studies pool both developed and developing countries into one sample and do not distinguish them (Olofsdotter, 1998; de Mello, 1999; Ram and Zhang, 2002; Choe, 2003; Alfaro and Chanda, 2004; Durham, 2004; Le and Suruga, 2005; Busse and Groizard, 2006; Batten and Vo, 2009). Blonigen and Wang (2005) argue that significant differences exist in developed and developing countries and pooling data together leads to false inferences. However, the empirical studies on only developed countries are limited (Ericsson and Irandoust, 2001; Ekanayake and Vogel, 2003; Kottaridi, 2005; Roy and Van den Berg, 2006; Ghosh and Wang, 2009; Iyer and Rambaldi, 2009). In addition, studies on the impact of outward FDI on the home country's economic growth are relatively scarce (Herzer, 2008; Ghosh and Wang, 2009). Therefore, it is important to analyse FDI in developed countries and that is why this study focuses on developed OECD countries.

3. The Relationship between FDI and Economic Growth

According to the neoclassical growth model, output is a function of labour and capital, technology is considered as an exogenous factor (Barro and Sala-i-Martin, 1995). Inward FDI is a driving force of growth as it increases capital accumulation in the host country. However, it only has short-run effect on economic growth (Ericsson and Irandoust, 2001; Asheghian, 2004). Consequently, the research on the long-run impact of inward FDI on growth has led to the endogenous growth theory, which emphasizes the importance of knowledge and technology in the economic growth process and postulates that technological change is an endogenous determinant of economic growth (Barro and Sala-i-Martin, 1995). Inward FDI increases long-run economic growth not only through capital accumulation, but also through technological progress. Inward FDI can make a positive contribution to the host country by supplying advanced technology, product and process innovations (Dunning, 1994; Whyman and Baimbridge, 2008). The entry of foreign firms might stimulate domestic firms to protect their market shares and profits, which leads to severe competition, low price, wide consumer choice and high quality standards in the host country (Dunning, 1994; Blomstrom and Kokko, 1997; OECD, 2002; Hill, 2009). Increased competition may force local firms to use resources more efficiently, to develop product and process innovation and to promote technological upgrading, etc (Zhang, 2001; OECD, 2002; Ozturk, 2007; Hill, 2009). Therefore, the productivity of local firms can be improved by imitating the more advanced technology brought by inward FDI, by exploiting existing technology and resources more efficiently or by seeking for more advanced technology (Blomstrom and Kokko, 1997, Saggi, 2000; Ozturk, 2007). Furthermore, inward FDI may create forward and backward linkages as foreign firms transfer technology to local suppliers of intermediate goods and customers (Blomstrom and Kokko, 1997; Saggi, 2000; Zhang, 2001; OECD, 2002).

Inward FDI may enhance human capital in the host country by introducing the host country management practices, organizational and marketing techniques (de Mello, 1999; Ericsson and Irandoust, 2001).The foreign firms might provide managerial and working training to their employees. The important information can be transferred to the host country as domestic employees move from foreign to local firms or set up their own businesses (Blomstrom and Kokko, 1997; Saggi, 2000; OECD, 2002; Meier and Rauch, 2005; Hill, 2009). Additionally, the superior skills of foreign firms may stimulate local firms to improve or develop their own skills (Hill, 2009). Furthermore, inward FDI can increase the level of employment in the host country (Baker, 1999; Hill, 2009; Salvatore, 2012). Another benefit is that it improves the efficiency of resource allocation in the host country by engaging in the economic activities where the host country has a comparative advantage (Dunning, 1994; Whyman and Baimbridge, 2008). In addition, the increased competition and demonstration effects encourage domestic firms to use resources more efficiently (Blomstrom and Kokko, 1997; OECD, 2002). Moreover, Inward FDI improves the balance of payments in the host country if inward FDI and imports are substitutes (Hill, 2009). Another benefit to the balance of payments arises when foreign firms undertake production in the host country and export products to other countries (Dunning, 1994; Hill, 2009). Furthermore, the host country can gain through tax revenue from foreign profits (Dunning, 1994; Blomstrom and Kokko, 1997). Finally, inward FDI has the potential to bring environmental benefits to the host country by introducing good practices and clean technologies (OECD, 2002).

Alternatively, there is a risk that foreign technology and working practices cannot accommodate local capacities and needs (Dunning, 1994). Additionally, inward FDI may transfer the host country's advanced technology to the home country, resulting in a reduction in the comparative advantages of the host country (Dunning, 1994). Another potential drawback is that foreign firms might out-compete local firms and drive local firms out of business, which might lead to foreign firms establish monopolies and raise prices in the host country's market (Blomstrom and Kokko, 1997; Hill, 2009). Moreover, the balance of payments in the host country may be deteriorated if the repatriated profits to the home country are more than the initial capital investment in the host country (Hill, 2009) or if inward FDI promotes imports and limits exports in the host country (Dunning, 1994; Hill, 2009). In addition, foreign firms may try to lower tax paid to the host country through transfer pricing manipulation (Dunning, 1994; Blomstrom and Kokko, 1997). Finally, inward FDI might bring harmful impact on the host country's environment, especially in the extractive and heavy industries (OECD, 2002).

In terms of the impact of outward FDI on home country's economic growth, then technology sourcing might be an important motivation behind outward FDI (Neven and Siotis, 1996; Love, 2003). Home countries can benefit from potential spillovers if the firms that invest abroad access the superior technology, organizational and management techniques in the foreign countries and transfer them back to the home country (Dunning, 1994; Hill, 2009). Additionally, it may facilitate the formation of inter-firm networking and cross-border cooperative alliances, which will benefit the home country (Dunning, 1994). Additionally, outward FDI can also exert a positive influence on home country's economic growth in the following channels. First, outward FDI facilitates firms in the home countries to get access to the global market and to expand production/sales in the foreign markets (Dunning, 1994; O'Connor and Walsh, 1998; Wang and Wong, 2007). Second, it can help firms in the home country avoid domestic competition and compete with foreign firms (O'Connor and Walsh, 1998). Third, the profits earned by the firms abroad can be repatriated to the home country, benefiting its economic development (O'Connor and Walsh, 1998). Moreover, outward FDI may secure raw materials and resources supplies in the foreign country and avoid trade barriers to the foreign market (Dunning, 1994; Baker, 1999; Salvatore, 2012). In addition, outward FDI may help the home country reduce the production costs and increase production efficiency. Finally, the home country's balance of payments can be improved if the inward flow of foreign profits is more than the initial outward investment (Hill, 2009). Furthermore, if outward FDI requires the home country to export inputs, intermediate goods, capital equipment etc to the foreign countries, it will benefit the balance of payments in the home country (Hill, 2009). The increased exports will have a positive impact on the employment level in the home country (O'Connor and Walsh, 1998; Hill, 2009; Williams, 2009).

In contrast, one harmful effect of outward FDI on the home country is the loss of domestic jobs (Salvatore, 2012). Furthermore, the unemployment level increases if outward FDI is a substitute for exports (O'Connor and Walsh,

1998; Hill, 2009). In addition, outward FDI might have a detrimental effect on the balance of payments in the home country. The balance of payments suffers if the initial outward capital investment is more than the subsequent inward foreign profits. The situation will get worse if outward FDI and exports are substitutes (Hill, 2009). Moreover, multinational firms can avoid domestic monetary policies due to their access to international capital markets, which might create difficulties on government control over the home country's economy (Salvatore, 2012). Finally, there are costs of adjusting to local language and culture, adapting to local business practices and customer needs, learning about the quality of local infrastructure etc (Dunning, 1994).

However, there might be a reverse relationship from economic growth to inward/outward FDI, whereby ignoring the feedback relationship might lead to biased empirical results and restrict the dynamics (Kim and Seo, 2003). Additionally, Dunning (1981) puts forward the investment development path, which suggests that inward and outward direct investment positions of a country are related to its economic development. The basic hypothesis is that as country develops, the OLI (Ownership, Location, Internalization) advantages facing its indigenous firms that might invest abroad and foreign firms that might invest in the country change; consequently, the amounts of inward and outward FDI also change. The investment development path identifies that countries tend to go through several stages of development (Dunning, 1993, 2001; Dunning and Narula, 1996). Moreover, other impacts of economic growth on inward/outward FDI are where economic growth can be seen as an indicator of future market potential in the host country, whereby higher rate of economic growth ensures long-term commitment by foreign investors as it leads to an increase in income and consumer demand for goods and services (Noorbakhsh and Paloni, 2001). It also implies better infrastructure, provides greater incentive for inward FDI (Tsai, 1994) and influences positively the business climate for inward FDI (Morisset, 2000); indeed, rapid growth may also give rise to the presence of economic rents that will encourage inward FDI (Globerman and Shapiro, 1999).Furthermore, economic growth in the home country is positively related with outward FDI. With higher economic performance and development, the banks in the home country are able to provide more loans for firms to invest abroad (Wang and Wong, 2007). Moreover, firms are more likely to develop their ownership advantages in terms of economies of scale in the production, improvement of marketing expertise, invention and adoption of new technology etc. These are competitive advantages for firms to undertake foreign production (Globerman and Shapiro, 1999; Kyrkilis and Pantelidis, 2003; Kueh and Puah, 2009).

In terms of the empirical studies that investigate the relationship between inward/outward FDI and host/home country's overall economic growth, they examine the impact of inward FDI on growth, the impact of growth on inward FDI and the two-way relationship whereby most studies relate to developing or a mix of developing and developed countries experiences and find a positive impact of FDI on growth. However, the positive impact of FDI is conditional on the host country's threshold absorptive capacity, such as human capital, trade openness, income level, financial development, institutional development etc. Thus, only countries that are above threshold level of development benefit from inward FDI. Alternatively, countries that are above threshold level of development benefit more from inward FDI than countries that are below threshold level of development. There are only three studies (Blonigen and Wang, 2005; Kottaridi, 2005; Ghosh and Wang, 2009) focusing explicitly on developed countries. Blonigen and Wang (2005) do not find a significant impact of inward FDI on economic growth in the developed countries. According to Kottaridi (2005), inward FDI plays a positive role in booting economic growth in the core countries (Belgium-Luxembourg, France, Germany, Netherlands and UK) and the beneficial effect of FDI is enhanced for countries with good human capital. However, inward FDI is incapable of increasing economic growth in the peripheral countries (Greece, Ireland, Italy, Portugal and Spain). In addition, Ghosh and Wang (2009) find the evidence of a positive effect of inward FDI on economic growth in 24 developed countries and the positive effect does not depend on the R&D expenditure in the host country.

Additionally, many studies examine the two-way relationship between inward FDI and economic growth; however, most causality test studies concentrate on developing countries, only five studies (Ericsson and Irandoust, 2001; Ekanayake and Vogel, 2003; Asheghian, 2004; Qi, 2007; Iyer and Rambaldi, 2009) focus explicitly or partly on developed countries. Studies on developed countries find different results based on country sample, time period and methodology. However, these studies do not look for a pattern in the results. Hence, this study tries to fill in the literature gap by examining the causal relationship between inward FDI and economic growth in developed OECD countries. In addition, it tries to look for a pattern in the results to explain why different developed countries experience different FDI-growth relationships. In relation to the relationship between outward FDI and economic growth, empirical studies on the relationship between outward FDI and home country's economic growth are limited. Looking at the studies on developed countries, Ghosh and Wang (2009) find that outward FDI plays a positive role in the home country's economic growth in 24 developed countries. In addition, Lipsey (2000) examines the determinants of outward FDI and finds that economic growth is a factor positively affecting outward FDI in 22 developed home countries. Finally, Herzer (2008) tests the two-way relationship and finds bi-directional causality between outward FDI and economic growth for 14 developed home countries.

4. RESEARCH METHODOLOGY AND FINDINGS

The idea of causality testing was developed by Granger (1969) between two variables X_t and Y_t based on the model of one variable X_t (Y_t) on the lagged values of both variables. Although the Granger (1969) conventional causality test is valid for a VAR model with stationary or trend stationary variables as the Wald tests for causality follow standard chi-squared distribution asymptotically (Toda and Yamamoto, 1995). However, if the variables in the VAR model are integrated or cointegrated, the Wald tests have nonstandard asymptotic properties and the conventional causality test is not applicable (Dolado and Lutkepohl, 1996). For instance, if variables are known to be integrated of order one with no cointegration, VAR in first-order differences of the variables should be estimated (Dolado and Lutkepohl, 1996). Moreover, if the variables are known to be integrated of order one and to be cointegrated of order one, then error correction model (ECM) should be specified (Toda and Yamamoto, 1995). Therefore, tests for unit roots and cointegration rank are usually required before estimating the VAR model. However, this can prove problematic because the unit root tests to test the null hypothesis of stationarity have low power against the alternative hypothesis of (trend) stationarity (Toda and Yamamoto, 1995). Moreover, simulation experiments show that Johansen's tests for cointegrating ranks are not very reliable for sample sizes that are typical for economic time series (Toda and Yamamoto, 1995). Hence, size distortion and pre-test bias may cause serious problems (Yamada and Toda, 1998). In order to overcome the above problems, Toda and Yamamoto (1995) propose a method that is applicable whether the VAR variables are stationary, integrated or cointegrated and ensures that the Wald tests have standard asymptotic distributions.

The advantage of this methodology is that tests for unit roots and cointegration rank are not required, as they have proved to be problematic. Hence, this methodology is applicable whether the variables are stationary, integrated or cointegrated.

There are some limitations on this approach. The Monte Carlo simulations suggest that this approach has advantages in terms of size stability, but might be inefficient in terms of low estimation power (Yamada and Toda, 1998). Toda and Yamamoto (1995) argue that the inefficiency depends on the specific model such that this might be big if a VAR system has many variables and the lag length is one (Toda and Yamamoto, 1995). On the other hand, the inefficiency might be relatively small if a VAR system has a small number of variables and long lag length (Toda and Yamamoto, 1995). In our model, we have a VAR system with three variables and long lag length. Therefore, the methodology is appropriate for our model as the inefficiency is relatively small.

Hence, for our model specification we incorporate inward FDI, outward FDI and economic growth into the VAR model, the equations to be estimated for each country are as follows:

$$X_t = \mu_1 + \sum_{i=1}^{k+d} \alpha_{1i} X_{t-i} + \sum_{i=1}^{k+d} \beta_{1i} Y_{t-i} + \sum_{i=1}^{k+d} \theta_{1i} Z_{t-i} + \varepsilon_{1t} \tag{1}$$

$$Y_t = \mu_2 + \sum_{i=1}^{k+d} \alpha_{2i} X_{t-i} + \sum_{i=1}^{k+d} \beta_{2i} Y_{t-i} + \sum_{i=1}^{k+d} \theta_{2i} Z_{t-i} + \varepsilon_{2t} \tag{2}$$

$$Z_t = \mu_3 + \sum_{i=1}^{k+d} \alpha_{3i} X_{t-i} + \sum_{i=1}^{k+d} \beta_{3i} Y_{t-i} + \sum_{i=1}^{k+d} \theta_{3i} Z_{t-i} + \varepsilon_{3t} \tag{3}$$

t is the number of years
k is the optimal lag order
d is the maximal order of integration of the three variables
ε is white noise error terms.
X is inward FDI
Y is growth rate of real GDP
Z is outward FDI

Annual FDI flow data are used as most previous time-series causality studies use flow data. The variables are FDI inflows as a percentage of GDP, FDI outflows as a percentage of GDP and the growth rate of GDP in constant 2000 US dollars.

Table 2. Unit root test results

		Australia	Austria	Canada	Denmark	Finland	France	Germany	Ireland	Italy	Japan
FDI inflows	DF-GLS test	I(0)	Unknown	I(0)	I(1)	Unknown	I(1)	I(1)	I(1)	I(2)	I(1)
	ADF test	I(0)	I(1)	I(1)	I(1)	I(2)	I(1)	I(1)	Unknown	I(1)	I(1)
FDI outflows	DF-GLS test	I(0)	I(1)	Unknown	I(0)	I(1)	I(0)	I(0)	I(1)	Unknown	I(1)
	ADF test	I(0)	I(1)	Unknown	I(0)	I(1)	I(0)	I(0)	I(2)	I(1)	Unknown
GDP growth rate	DF-GLS test	I(0)	I(0)	I(0)	I(0)	I(0)	I(0)	I(0)	I(2)	I(0)	I(1)
	ADF test	I(1)	I(0)	I(0)	I(0)	I(0)	I(0)	I(0)	I(2)	I(1)	I(1)
		Korea	Netherlands	New Zealand	Norway	Portugal	Spain	Sweden	Switzerland	UK	US
FDI inflows	DF-GLS test	I(1)	I(1)	I(1)	I(1)	I(1)	I(1)	I(1)	I(2)	I(0)	I(0)
	ADF test	I(1)	I(1)	I(0)	I(1)	I(1)	I(2)	I(1)	I(2)	I(0)	I(0)
FDI outflows	DF-GLS test	I(1)	I(1)	I(1)	I(1)	I(1)	I(1)	I(0)	I(0)	I(0)	I(2)
	ADF test	Unknown	I(1)	I(1)	I(1)	I(1)	I(1)	I(1)	I(0)	I(0)	I(2)
GDP growth rate	DF-GLS test	I(1)	I(1)	I(0)	I(0)	I(0)	I(0)	I(0)	I(0)	Unknown	I(0)
	ADF test	I(1)	I(1)	I(1)	I(0)	I(0)	I(0)	I(0)	I(0)	I(0)	I(2)

Note: Data in Germany refer to former federal republic of Germany (West Germany) before 1990, data refer to former federal republic of Germany (West Germany) and former democratic republic of Germany (East Germany) from 1990.

Real FDI values are not used since the investment deflator is not available, instead we use FDI inflows/outflows as a percentage of GDP and GDP in constant 2000 US dollars from World Development Indicators (2011).

Table 3. The number of integration order

Country	DF-GLS test	ADF test
Australia	0	1
Austria	1	1
Canada	0	1
Denmark	1	1
Finland	1	2
France	1	1
Germany	1	1
Ireland	2	2
Italy	2	1
Japan	1	1
Korea	1	1
Netherlands	1	1
New Zealand	1	1
Norway	1	1
Portugal	1	1
Spain	1	2
Sweden	1	1
Switzerland	2	2
UK	0	0
US	2	2

Note: Data in Germany refer to former federal republic of Germany (West Germany) before 1990, data refer to former federal republic of Germany (West Germany) and former democratic republic of Germany (East Germany) from 1990.

The time period is between 1981 and 2008. The country sample includes 20 developed OECD countries – Australia, Austria, Canada, Denmark, Finland, France, Germany, Ireland, Italy, Japan, Korea, Netherlands, New Zealand, Norway, Portugal, Spain, Sweden, Switzerland, UK and US, although we include Switzerland where data are only available between 1983 and 2008. Other countries are not included as there are not enough observations: Belgium (2002-2008), Greece (1999-2008), Iceland (1986-2008), Luxembourg (2002-2008).

The most commonly used test of the unit root in time-series is the augmented Dickey-Fuller (ADF) test. However, Hsiao and Hsiao (2006) argue that the DF-GLS test (Elliot and Rothenberg, 1996) for unit root has higher power in the sense that it is more likely to reject the null hypothesis of a unit root and accept the alternative hypothesis of no unit root. Therefore Hsiao and Hsiao (2006) use both ADF test and DF-GLS test for unit root. So we follow their method and apply both tests for comparison.

Table 2 presents the results from the ADF and DF-GLS unit root tests for each country, which we summarize the order of integration, which is presented in Table 3.

Table 4. Optimum lags

Country	LR	FPE	AIC	HQIC	SBIC
Australia	4	1	4	1	1
Austria	4	4	4	4	4
Canada	4	4	4	4	1
Denmark	4	0	0	0	0
Finland	4	4	4	4	0
France	4	4	4	4	4
Germany	4	2	4	2	1
Ireland	4	4	4	4	1
Italy	4	1	4	1	1
Japan	4	1	4	1	1
Korea	2	2	2	2	1
Netherlands	4	2	2	2	2
New Zealand	4	4	4	4	0
Norway	3	3	3	3	0
Portugal	3	3	3	3	3
Spain	4	4	4	4	1
Sweden	4	1	1	1	1
Switzerland	4	4	4	4	4
UK	3	1	3	1	1
US	4	1	4	1	1

Notes: (1) Data in Germany refer to former federal republic of Germany (West Germany) before 1990, data refer to former federal republic of Germany (West Germany) and former democratic republic of Germany (East Germany) from 1990. (2) Duttaray and Dutt, (2008) set the maximum lag length as 4 using 27 observations and Qi (2007) sets the maximum lag length as 5 using 34 observations. The maximum lag is set as 4 for all countries as the number of observation is 28.

Table 5. Summary of diagnostic tests

Country	Optimum lag *k*	Maximum order of integration *d*	Normality tests	LM test	Stability test
Australia	1	1	X	√	√
Austria	4	1	X	X	X
Canada	1	1	X	X	√
Denmark	4	1	√	X	X
Finland	4	1	√	√	X
France	4	1	√	√	X
Germany	4	1	√	√	X
Ireland	4	2	X	X[a]	X
Italy	1	1	X	√	√
Japan	1	1	X	√[a]	√
Korea	2	1	√[a]	√	√
Netherlands	4	1	X	√	X
New Zealand	4	1	√	X	√
Norway	3	1	√	√	X
Portugal	3	1	√	√	√
Spain	1	1	X	X	√
Sweden	4	1	√	X	√
Switzerland	4	2	X	X[a]	X
UK	1	1	X	√	√
US	4	2	√[a]	X[a]	X

Notes: (1) Data in Germany refer to former federal republic of Germany (West Germany) before 1990, data refer to former federal republic of Germany (West Germany) and former democratic republic of Germany (East Germany) from 1990. (2) Normality tests include skewness statistic, kurtosis statistic and the Jarque-Bera statistic tests for normally distributed disturbances after VAR. The null hypothesis is that the errors are normally distributed after VAR at 10% level. √ means that the null hypothesis is accepted at 10% level. √[a] means the null hypothesis is accepted at 5% level, but rejected at 10% level. X means the null hypothesis is rejected at both 5% level and 10% level. (3) In Lagrange-multiplier (LM) test for residual autocorrelation after VAR, the null hypothesis is that the residual is not auto-correlated after VAR at 10% level. √ means that the null hypothesis is accepted at 10% level until lag 4, √[a] means the null hypothesis is accepted at 5% level, but rejected at 10% level until lag 4. X means the null hypothesis is rejected at both 5% and 10% level until lag 4. X[a]: the exogenous variables may not be collinear with the dependent variables or their lags. (4) In stability test, √ means that the VAR model satisfies stability condition and X means that the VAR model does not satisfy stability condition.

Furthermore, there are different criteria for choosing optimum lag length including Akaike's information criterion (AIC), the final prediction error (FPE), the Hannan-Quinn information criterion (HQIC), likelihood ratio (LR) test, and Schwarz's Bayesian information criterion (SBIC). Most time-series causality studies use only one criterion to select optimum lag order (Ericsson and Irandoust, 2001; Zhang, 2001; Ekanayake and Vogel, 2003; Chowdhury and Mavrotas, 2006; Hsiao and Hsiao, 2006; Chang, 2007; Qi, 2007; Duttaray and Dutt, 2008; Ang, 2009; Lee, 2009; Liu and Shu, 2009). However, we employ all five criteria to select the optimum lag in order to show a broad picture. Table 4 presents the number of optimum lags for each country according to the above five criteria.

Finally, in relation to diagnostic tests, in the time-series causality literature, most studies do not mention, or do not report diagnostic tests results. However, three diagnostic tests are conducted to test the model, namely skewness statistic, kurtosis statistic and the Jarque-Bera statistic tests for normally distributed disturbances after VAR, Lagrange Multiplier (LM) test for residual autocorrelation after VAR, stability test to check stability condition of VAR. These diagnostic tests are carried out using different combinations of integration order (Table 3) and optimal lags (Table 4). According to Toda and Yamamoto (1995), (k+1)-th order VAR model should be estimated when the optimal lag length is k and the order of integration is zero. Therefore the maximum order of integration d is one when the order of integration is zero. Table 5 presents the diagnostic tests results using the best combinations of optimum lags and maximum order of integration for each country. However, most of these countries do not satisfy all three diagnostic tests, which means that the econometric model could be mis-specified and the analysis results could be biased for some countries.

FINDINGS AND CONCLUSION

Table 6 summarizes the causal relationship between FDI inflows/outflows and the growth rate of GDP. The analysis results indicate a one-way relationship from FDI inflows to growth in two countries (Australia and Sweden), a one-way relationship from growth to FDI inflows in two countries (Japan and Korea), a two-way relationship in eleven countries (Austria, Denmark, Finland, France, Ireland, Netherlands, New Zealand, Norway, Portugal, Switzerland and US) and no causal relationship in five countries (Canada, Germany, Italy, Spain and UK). In terms of the link between FDI outflows and growth, the causal link runs from FDI outflows to growth for four countries (Australia, France, New Zealand and Norway), the reverse causality is found in four countries (Germany, Korea, Portugal and UK), the bi-directional causality exists for eight countries (Austria, Denmark, Finland, Ireland, Netherlands, Sweden, Switzerland and US) and no causality is found in four countries (Canada, Italy, Japan and Spain).

Table 6. Summary of causality tests

		Countries
Relationship between FDI inflows and growth	FDI → growth	Australia, Sweden
	FDI ← growth	Japan, Korea
	FDI ↔ growth	Austria, Denmark, Finland, France, Ireland, Netherlands, New Zealand, Norway, Portugal, Switzerland, US
	No causality	Canada, Germany, Italy, Spain, UK
Relationship between FDI outflows and growth	FDI → growth	Australia, France, New Zealand, Norway
	FDI ← growth	Germany, Korea, Portugal, UK
	FDI ↔ growth	Austria, Denmark, Finland, Ireland, Netherlands, Sweden, Switzerland, US
	No causality	Canada, Italy, Japan, Spain

Notes: (1) Data in Germany refer to former federal republic of Germany (West Germany) before 1990, data refer to former federal republic of Germany (West Germany) and former democratic republic of Germany (East Germany) from 1990. (2) It is significant at 10% level.

As shown in Table 6, different countries experience different FDI-growth relationships, hence we analyse whether the reasons depend on country-specific factors (e.g., financial development, GDP per capita, trade openness, domestic investment, R&D expenditure, inflation rate, corporate tax revenue, trade union density, employment protection legislation index and unemployment rate). For example, we try to investigate whether countries with good financial development, higher GDP per capita etc experience FDI-led growth. However, the period average data on country specific factors do not provide evidence why different countries follow different patterns in FDI-growth relationship. The reasons for not being able to find a pattern on FDI-growth relationship might be due to the limitations of Granger causality test proposed by Toda and Yamamoto (1995). First, the causality test suffers from inefficiency because of the artificially augmented lag (Kurozumi and Yamamoto, 2000). In addition, although the empirical size of the test statistic is less distorted when the sample size is small, but the approach is not completely free from size distortion and it still has a large size distortion in some cases (Kurozumi and Yamamoto, 2000). Another limitation is that the causality test only examines the directions of causal links between inflows/outflows and economic growth, but does not check whether the causal links are positive or negative. Finally, most sample countries do not satisfy all the diagnostic tests, so the econometric model could be mis-specified.

In summary, however, this chapter contributes to the existing literature by focusing on developed countries as inward/outward FDI has become an increasingly significant factor in influencing the economic activity in a developed country. Moreover, most previous time-series causality studies focus on developing countries and only a few studies cover developed countries (Ericsson and Irandoust, 2001; Ekanayake and Vogel, 2003; Asheghian, 2004; Qi, 2007; Iyerand Rambaldi, 2009); although almost all of the world's FDI originates from developed countries and the majority of FDI is also located in developed countries.

Another feature is that this chapter also tests the causal link between outward FDI and economic growth. Outward FDI might promote the home country's economic growth as it might yield higher profits, transfer technology and management skills to the home country, expand production abroad, secure raw materials overseas, and avoid trade barriers and so on.

REFERENCES

Alfaro, L. and A. Chanda (2004) FDI and economic growth: the role of local financial markets. *Journal of International Economics* 64: 89-112.

Ang, J. B. (2009) Financial development and the FDI-growth nexus: the Malaysian experience. *Applied Economics* 41: 1595-1601.

Asheghian, P. (2004) Determinants of economic growth in the United States: the role of foreign direct investment. *The International Trade Journal* 18: 63-83.

Baker, J. C. (1999) *Foreign direct investment in less developed countries: the role of ICSID and MIGA*. London, Quorum Books.

Barro, R. J. and X. Sala-i-Martin (1995) *Economic growth*. New York, McGraw-Hill.

Basu, P. and C. Chakraborty (2003) Liberalization, FDI and growth in developing countries: a panel cointegration approach. *Economic Inquiry*41: 510-516.

Batten, J. A. and X. V. Vo (2009) An analysis of the relationship between foreign direct investment and economic growth. *Applied Economics*41: 1621-1641.

Bengoa, M. and B. Sanchez-Robles (2003) Foreign direct investment, economic freedom and growth: new evidence from Latin America. *European Journal of Political Economy19*: 529-545.

Blomstrom, M. and A. Kokko (1997) How foreign investment affects host countries.Policy *Research Working Paper* 1745. Washington D C, The World Bank.

Blonigen, B. A. and M. G. Wang (2005). Inappropriate pooling of wealthy and poor countries in empirical FDI studies. *Does foreign direct investment promote development?* T. H. Moran, E. M. Graham, et al. (eds) Washington D C, Institute for International Economics and Centre for Global Development.

Busse, M. and J. L. Groizard (2006) Foreign direct investment, regulations and growth. *Policy Research Working Paper* 3882. Washington D C, World Bank.

Campos, N. F. and Y. Kinoshita (2002) Foreign direct investment as technology transferred: some panel evidence from the transition economies. *The Manchester School*70: 398-419.

Chang, S. C. (2007) The interactions among foreign direct investment, economic growth, degree of openness and unemployment in Taiwan. *Applied Economics* 39: 1647-1661.

Choe, J. I. (2003) Do foreign direct investment and gross domestic investment promote economic growth? *Review of Development Economics* 7: 44-57.

Chowdhury, A. and G. Mavrotas (2006) FDI and growth: what causes what? *The World Economy*29: 9-19.

de-Mello, L. R. (1999) Foreign direct investment-led growth: evidence from time-series and panel data. *Oxford Economic Papers* 51: 133-151.

Dolado, J. J. and H. Lutkepohl (1996) Making Wald tests work for cointegrated VAR systems. *Econometric Reviews* 15: 369-386.

Dunning, J. H. (1981) Explaining the international direct investment position of countries: towards a dynamic or developmental approach. *Review of World Economics* 117: 30-64.

Dunning, J. H. (1993) Multinational enterprises and the global economy. Wokingham, Addison-Wesley.

Dunning, J. H. (1994) Re-evaluating the benefits of foreign direct investment. *Transnational Corporations* 3: 23-52.

Dunning, J. H. and R. Narula (1996) The investment development path revisited: some emerging issues. *Foreign direct investment and governments - catalysts for economic restructuring*. J. H. Dunning and R. Narula (eds) London, Routledge: 1-41.

Durham, J. B. (2004) Absorptive capacity and the effects of foreign direct investment and equity foreign portfolio investment on economic growth. *European Economic Review*48: 285-306.

Duttaray, M. and A. K. Dutt (2008) Foreign direct investment and economic growth in less developed countries: an empirical study of causality and mechanisms. *Applied Economics*40: 1927-1939.

Ekanayake, E. M. and R. Vogel (2003) Openness and economic growth: empirical evidence on the relationship between output, inward FDI and trade. *Journal of Business Strategies*20: 59-72.

Elliott, G. and T. J. Rothenberg (1996) Efficient tests for an autoregressive unit root. *Econometrica* 64: 813-836.

Ericsson, J. and M. Irandoust (2001) On the causality between foreign direct investment and output: a comparative study. *The International Trade Journal* 15: 1-26.

Ghosh, M. and W. Wang (2009). Does FDI accelerate economic growth? The OECD experience based on panel data estimates for the period 1980-2004. *Global Economy Journal* 9 (4).

Globerman, S. and D. M. Shapiro (1999) The impact of government policies on foreign direct investment: the Canadian experience. *Journal of International Business Studies* 30: 513-532.

Globerman, S. and D. Shapiro (2002) Global foreign direct investment flows: the role of governance infrastructure. *World Development* 30: 1899-1919.

Granger, C. W. J. (1969) Investigating causal relations by econometric models and cross-spectral methods. *Econometrica* 37: 424-438.

Greenaway, D. and D. Sapsford (2007) Foreign direct investment, economic performance and trade liberalisation. *The World Economy* 30: 197-210.

Hansen, H. and J. Rand (2006) On the causal links between FDI and growth in developing countries. *The World Economy* 29: 21-41.

Herzer, D. (2008) The long-run relationship between outward FDI and domestic output: evidence from panel data. *Economics Letters* 100: 146-149.

Hill, C. W. L. (2009) *International business: competing in the global market place*. London, McGraw-Hill.

HM Treasury (1996) Overseas investment and the UK explanations, policy implications, facts and figures. *Treasury Occasional Paper* 8. London, HM Treasury.

Hsiao, F. S. T. and M.-C. W. Hsiao (2006) FDI, exports and GDP in East and Southeast Asia – panel data versus time-series causality analyses. *Journal of Asian Economics17*: 1082-1106.

http://www.cbpp.org/cms/index.cfm?fa=view&id=3441

Iyer, K. G. and A. N. Rambaldi (2009) How trade and foreign direct investment affect the growth of a small but not so open economy: Australia? *Applied Economics* 41: 1525-1532.

Kim, D. D.-K. and J.-S. Seo (2003) Does FDI inflow crowd out domestic investment in Korea? *Journal of Economic Studies* 30: 605-622.

Kottaridi, C. (2005) The 'core-periphery' pattern of FDI-led growth and production structure in the EU. *Applied Economics* 37: 99-113.

Kueh, J. S.-H. and C.-H. Puah(2009) Empirical analysis on emerging issues of Malaysia outward FDI from macroeconomic perspective. *International Review of Business Research Papers* 5: 124-134.

Kurozumi, E. and T. Yamamoto (2000) Modified lag augmented vector autoregressions. *Econometric Reviews* 19: 207-231.

Kyrkilis, D. and P. Pantelidis (2003) Macroeconomic determinants of outward foreign direct investment. *International Journal of Social Economics* 30: 827-836.

Le, M. V. and T. Suruga (2005) Foreign direct investment, public expenditure and economic growth: the empirical evidence for the period 1970-2001. *Applied Economics Letters* 12: 45-49.

Lee, C. G. (2009) Foreign direct investment, pollution and economic growth: evidence from Malaysia. *Applied Economics* 41: 1709-1716.

Lipsey, R. E. (2000) Interpreting developed countries foreign direct investment. *NBER Working Paper 7810*. Cambridge, National Bureau of Economic Research.

Liu, X. and C. Shu (2009) Trade, foreign direct investment and economic growth in Asian economies. *Applied Economics* 41: 1603-1612.

Lumbila, K. N. (2005) What makes FDI work? A panel analysis of the growth effect of FDI in Africa. *Africa Region Working Paper* 80. Washington D C, World Bank.

Lyroudi, K. and J. Papanastasiou (2004) Foreign direct investment and economic growth in transition economies. *South Eastern Europe Journal of Economics*1: 97-110.

Makki, S. S. and A. Somwaru (2004) Impact of foreign direct investment and trade on economic growth: evidence from developing countries. American *Journal of Agricultural Economics*86: 795-801.

Meier, G. M. and J. E. Rauch (2005) *Leading issues in economic development.* Oxford, Oxford University Press.

Morisset, J. (2000) Foreign direct investment in Africa: policies also matter. *Policy Research Working Paper* 2481. Washington D C, The World Bank.

Noorbakhsh, F. and A. Paloni (2001) Human capital and FDI inflows to developing countries: new empirical evidence. *World Development*29: 1593-1610.

O'Connor, C. and E. O. M. Walsh(1998) Irish outward foreign direct investment - The future impetus for economic growth. *Student Economic Review (SER).*Dublin, Ireland, Trinity College Dublin.

OECD (2002) Foreign direct investment for development: maximising benefits, minimising costs. Paris, Organisation for Economic Co-operation and Development. http://www.oecd.org/dataoecd/47/51/1959815.pdf

Olofsdotter, K. (1998) Foreign direct investment, country capabilities and economic growth. *Weltwirtschaftliches Archiv* 134: 534-547.

Ozturk, I. (2007) Foreign direct investment-growth nexus: a review of the recent literature. *International Journal of Applied Econometrics and Quantitative Studies*4: 79-98.

Qi, L. (2007) The relationship between growth, total investment and inward FDI: evidence from time series data. *International Review of Applied Economics*21: 119-133.

Ram, R. and K. H. Zhang (2002) Foreign direct investment and economic growth: evidence from cross-country data for the 1990s. *Economic Development and Cultural Change* 51: 205-215.

Roy, A. G. and H. F. Van-den-Berg (2006) Foreign direct investment and economic growth: a time-series approach. *Global Economy Journal* 6(1).

Saggi, K. (2000) Trade, foreign direct investment, and international technology transfer: a survey. *Policy Research Working Paper* 2349. Washington D C, The World Bank.

Salvatore, D. (2012) *Introduction to international economics.* Hoboken, Wiley.

Sylwester, K. (2005) Foreign direct investment, growth and income inequality in less developed countries. *International Review of Applied Economics*19: 289-300.

Toda, H. Y. and T. Yamamoto (1995) Statistical inference in vector autoregressions with possibly integrated processes. *Journal of Econometrics*66: 225-250.

Tsai, P.-L.(1994) Determinants of foreign direct investment and its impact on economic growth. *Journal of Economic Development*19: 137-163.

UNCTAD (1995) Transnational corporations and competitiveness. *World Investment Report* 1995. New York and Geneva, United Nations Conference on Trade and Development.

UNCTAD (2002) Transnational corporations and export competitiveness. *World Investment Report* 2002. New York and Geneva, United Nations Conference on Trade and Development.

UNCTAD (2006) FDI from developing and transition economies: implications for development. *World Investment Report* 2006. New York and Geneva, United Nations Conference on Trade and Development.

UNCTAD (2008) Transnational corporations and the infrastructure challenge. *World Investment Report* 2008. New York and Geneva, United Nations Conference on Trade and Development.

UNCTAD (2009) Transnational corporations, agricultural production and development. *World Investment Report* 2009. New York and Geneva, United Nations Conference on Trade and Development.

Wang, M. and M. C. S. Wong (2007) Foreign direct investment outflows and business-cycle fluctuations. *Review of International Economics*15: 146-163.

Whyman, P. B. and M. Baimbridge (2008) Labour market flexibility as a key determinant of FDI: evidence from the UK. *Foreign direct investment*. H. G. Blaine (ed) Hauppauge, New York, Nova Science Publishers.

Williams, D. A. (2009) Determinants of outward foreign direct investments from small island developing states. *American Journal of Economics and Business Administration*1: 45-54.

World Bank (2011) World Development Indicators. Washington D C, The World Bank. http://www.esds.ac.uk/international/access/access.asp

Yamada, H. and H. Y. Toda (1998) Inference in possibly integrated vector autoregressive models: some finite sample evidence. *Journal of Econometrics*86: 55-95.

Yang, J. Y. Y. and N. Groenewold (2000) The determinants of foreign direct investment in Australia. *Economic Record* 76: 45-54.

Zhang, K. H. (2001) Does foreign direct investment promote economic growth? Evidence from East Asia and Latin America.Contemporary *Economic Policy* 19: 175-185.

In: Economic Growth in the 21st Century
Editor: Cody Accosi
ISBN: 978-1-63321-589-4

Chapter 3

ECONOMIC GROWTH AND SELF-CONSUMPTION IN OIL PRODUCING COUNTRIES: EMPIRICAL EVIDENCE AND PERSPECTIVES

José Alberto Fuinhas**, António Cardoso Marques and Alcino Pinto Couto
University of Beira Interior, Management and Economics Department and NECE, Estrada do Sineiro, Covilhã, Portugal

ABSTRACT

The design of governmental policies is crucial to face the 21st Century economic growth challenges. Energy will be one of the core issues in economic growth policies. Therefore, this chapter focuses on the energy consumption-economic growth nexus. The perspectives on the role of energy use upon economic growth are grounded on empirical evidence from a panel of oil producing countries that have been examined for a long time span (1965-2012). Both the ratio of oil production to oil consumption, as well as the aftermath of the structural break from the

---

* Corresponding author: E-mail: fuinhas@ubi.pt; and jafuinhas@gmail.com. University of Beira Interior, Management and Economics Department, Estrada do Sineiro, 6200-209 Covilhã, Portugal Tel. +351 275 319 600 Fax. + 351 275 319 601.
Research supported by: NECE, R&D unit funded by the FCT – Portuguese Foundation for the Development of Science and Technology, Ministry of Education and Science.

second oil shock were controlled for. The presence of cross-section dependence phenomena within the panel strongly supports that these countries share common features as oil producers. Panel data estimators and co-integration/long memory analyses are both pursued and discussed, namely dealing with the heterogeneity of panels and the countries' specific effects. Comprehensive analysis of the energy-growth nexus requires that both short- and long-term effects should be considered, for which the Driscoll-Kraay estimator with fixed effects proved to be appropriate. The growth hypothesis was confirmed. Energy consumption and the ratio of oil production to oil consumption are drivers of economic growth. The structural break, beginning in 1979, seems to have been persistent. Findings support that expansionary governmental energy policies could not generate an equivalent effect upon the output in the 21st Century.

Keywords: Oil production; energy; macro panels; governmental policies; economic growth perspectives

1. Introduction

The literature on the energy consumption-economic growth nexus, namely that which focuses on oil production, oil consumption, energy consumption and economic growth, has not been consensual as far as its findings. Several issues contribute to explaining the permanent interest on this subject matter, namely: (i) to shed light on the drivers of economic growth; (ii) to understand the role that the exploration of energy resources could play in the nature of the nexus; and (iii) controlling for the complexities and idiosyncrasies of existing interactions, not only from consumption but also from oil production upon growth.

Most of the literature that analyses oil is focused on exporting countries. However, many countries are oil producers but not oil exporters. Consequently, when focused on exporting countries only, this option excludes from the analysis those countries in which oil production could play a relevant role on their own economic growth path. Accordingly, in order to achieve that goal, an indicator that captures this specificity has been used, namely the ratio of oil production to oil consumption. It is a measure of a country's level of oil self-sufficiency, as it measures oil production units by unit of oil consumption. This option has the great advantage of incorporating oil producing countries into the analysis, either exporting or non-exporting countries.

While resorting to a multivariate approach, the main aim of this chapter is to empirically assess the richness of the energy consumption-economic growth nexus for a set of oil producing countries, for an extended time span, and to infer on the relative magnitude of oil production to oil consumption. But more than that, the chapter also aims at providing support as well as discussing the appropriate design of energy policies for economic growth in the 21st Century.

This chapter brings up new knowledge on the energy-growth nexus by empirical control, for: (i) a set of oil producing countries for which data on primary energy consumption is available over the extended period from 1965 to 2012; (ii) the ratio of oil production to oil consumption; and (iii) the second oil shock of 1979. Our approach resorts to techniques that assess the breakdown of short- and long-run effects, thus providing a deeper understanding on the dynamics of the relationship. The existence of co-integration/long memory was detected. Elasticities seem to be higher in the long-run. The results prove that the oil ratio stimulates economic growth. Moreover, the second oil shock (1979) proved to have a long-lasting effect upon the relationship between primary energy consumption and economic growth.

2. Literature Review

Despite the growing interest observed in the literature over the last few decades, the energy-economic growth nexus remains an open research question: literature outcomes remain quite inconclusive and controversial. Research has focused mainly on trying to explain the role of energy consumption upon economic growth, and predominantly associated to the energy-related concerns of energy importing countries (e.g., Damette and Seghir, 2013; and Mehrara, 2007b). The importance of energy use upon economic growth rests upon the existence, or not, of causality between the variables at stake, their direction, the magnitude of the estimated coefficients, and their impact upon energy policies. Its explanation is crucial in order for public policies to address critical energy-related challenges: the volatility of energy prices, and energy security, as well as to make energy affordable, competitive and environmentally sustainable (e.g., Chu and Chang, 2012; and Al-Iriani, 2006). The actual empirical question behind the causality is to check whether it is growth that leads to energy consumption or the opposite, or both (Pradhan, 2010).

The main types of causalities between energy consumption and economic growth identified and examined by the literature are known as: conservation, growth, feedback and neutrality hypotheses (e.g., Ozturk, 2010; Yuan et al., 2010; Apergis and Payne, 2009; Zhang and Cheng, 2009; and Narayan and Smith, 2008). The first two imply a unidirectional causality. The conservation hypothesis, running from economic growth to energy consumption, argues that economic growth stimulates energy consumption, while assuming that energy conservation policies do not constraint economic growth. The growth hypothesis, running from energy consumption to economic growth, considers energy consumption as a prerequisite for economic growth. In turn, the feedback hypothesis sustains a bi-directional causality between economic growth and energy consumption, whereby the variables are interrelated, working as complements to each other. In this case, energy conservation policies must consider their adverse effects upon economic growth (e.g., Wolde-Rufael, 2009). Finally, the neutrality hypothesis argues that the variables are independent from one another, based on the assumption that the structure of the economy is characterised by low energy intensive activities, in which the cost of the energy is a small share of the GDP.

The findings vary and are conflicting regarding the actual direction of the causality, when it actually exists, (e.g., Payne, 2010; and Chontanawat et al., 2008), as well as to the short- and long term impacts of policies (e.g., Ozturk, 2010; and Padhan, 2010), which should take into account country-specific features (Altinay and Karagol, 2004). In fact, the results depend mainly on: (i) whether the study involves just one single country or a set of countries (Fuinhas and Marques, 2013); (ii) the econometric methodologies used (Alam et al., 2012); (iii) the time span considered (Chen et al., 2012); (iv) the variables studied (Ozturk, 2010); (v) the heterogeneity of the countries' climate conditions; (vi) the different energy consumption standards; and (vii) the countries' structure and development level (Apergis and Payne, 2010, 2009).

More recently, increasing attention has been paid to primary energy producing countries and, in particular, to oil producers. Similar empirical studies have been developed to explain the relationship between energy and growth. These works place oil-producing countries, in particular net oil exporters, in the field of their own oil domestic demand-focused attention. Indeed, they seek to achieve a better understanding of how the nexus energy-growth affects or is affected by the abundance of oil resources, by domestic structural changes, as well as of the arising policy implications. The set of oil producing countries comprises net exporters, net importers and self-sufficient oil economies, as well as developed and developing economies. Could such structural heterogeneities be closely correlated with differences regarding causality hypotheses, oil endowment-domestic oil consumption interactions, and energy policy implications? An answer to this question requires an analysis to the level of oil self-sufficiency.

As pointed out by Kraft and Kraft (1978) in their seminal work, the US - a developed economy, both an oil producer and net oil importer - observed a growth-energy causality relationship. Thus, conservation policies were considered critical in order to face energy-related challenges. On the contrary, net oil exporters were seen for a long time as energy suppliers. Less attention had been paid to the role played by domestic energy demand in the countries' future export prospects and upon domestic energy efficiency. However, research carried out in more recent years (e.g., Gately et al., 2013; Al-Mulali, 2011; Mehrara, 2007a, 2007b; and Al-Iriani, 2006) highlight the need of net oil exporting economies, characterised by higher energy intensity levels, to address efficiency-oriented policies.

These policies are justified in order to secure exports sustainability, to support the increasing domestic energy demand, to sustain economic growth, and to meet environmental goals. Yet, a more detailed approach to the empirical evidence on the energy and oil consumption-economic growth nexus reveals a mixed picture. A summary of the literature could be seen in Yıldırım et al. (2014), Ozturk, (2010) and Payne, (2010). Table 1 discloses recent studies focused on the relationship energy and oil consumption-growth.

Empirical evidence does not point to universal rules. There are differences regarding the direction of causality when testing energy consumption or oil consumption relationships. Nevertheless, the findings suggest three important considerations.

The first one takes into account the causality hypotheses observed. As shown in Table 1, empirical evidence on the relationships between energy and oil consumption–growth is rather inconclusive. The existence of conflicting results and the absence of consensus both on the actual existence and on the direction of causality still remains, just as in similar research anchored in other energy consumption variables. Different reasons could explain the mixed picture in oil producing countries.

Firstly, the different findings could depend on the set of countries under analysis, on the sample period and on the empirical method. Secondly, in the case of oil exporting countries, the energy consumption, in particular oil consumption, benefits from generous subsidies, favouring over-consumption and inefficient resource allocation (e.g., Gately et al., 2013; Damette and

Seghir 2013; Mehrara 2007a; and Al-Iriani, 2006). Thirdly, the oil producing economies show different degrees of vulnerability to external shocks, in particular to price volatility. The economic activity of oil dependent countries is strongly based on oil exports and on foreign exchange earnings. Lastly, a limited body of literature has studied the link between energy and oil consumption, and economic growth in oil producing and exporting countries. Thus, further research is required.

The second one lies in the fact that the studies tend to use a mix of the Granger casualty of more recent generation, namely multivariate co-integration approaches and co-integration, and error correction panel models. As reported by the literature (e.g., Fuinhas and Marques, 2013; and Mehrara, 2007b), differences in methodological approaches affect research outcomes. Applying panel co-integration and panel-based error correction models enables us to tackle three important methodological problems that stem from the use of longer time spans and cross-country analysis. First, the clarification between short-run and long-run effects, by shedding light on the question of whether the findings on energy-growth nexus address different time horizons. Second, the use of nonlinear models, providing some room to examine structural breaks or structural changes in the pattern of energy consumption arising from changes in economic and technological environments, energy policies, and fluctuations in energy prices, among others. Lastly, panel data models seem to be more suitable to reveal a cross-sectional dependence of errors, which may arise from to the presence of common shocks and unobserved components.

Finally, the evidence, both theoretical an empirical, suggest that the approach to energy-challenges of oil producing countries, energy use and policies, must be reconsidered. The increasing demand for domestic energy in the presence of a level of oil endowment creates a tension and it is expected that it could shape the economic performance in the next decades. Could the reduction of the disparity between oil production and domestic oil consumption harm the economic development of oil producers, in particular of net oil exporters, and their capacity to reach higher levels of economic, social and environmental performance? According to the rationale of the resource curse theory, one can sustain that a significant disparity between oil production and oil consumption is a condition that features heavily oil dependent economies. Although, in and of itself, this condition does not explain a better or worse economic performance (e.g., Klein, 2010; Mehrara, 2009; and Rosser, 2006a, 2006b). In turn, a lower disparity appears to favour the efficient use of energy.

Table 1. The literature on the energy and oil consumption-growth nexus

Authors	Countries	Period	Methodology	Main variables	Other variables	Results
Yıldırım et al. (2014)	11 countries	1971-2010	Autoregressive moving average models (ARMA)	*Per capita* energy consumption GDP *per capita*	Gross capital formation	(Bangladesh, Egypt, Indonesia, Iran, Korea, Mexico, Pakistan and Philippines) GDP→EC Turkey GDP→EC
Mohammadi and Parvaresh (2014)	14 oil-exporting countries	1980–2007	Panel co-integration, Pooled Mean Group	Energy consumption GDP		GDP↔ EC (S-R and L-R)
Lim, et al., (2014)	Philippines	1965–2012	Panel co-integration, ECM	Oil consumption; GDP	CO_2 emissions	OC↔GDP (S-R and L-R)
Park and Yoo, (2014).	Malaysia	1965–2011	Panel co-integration, ECM	Oil consumption; GDP		OC↔GDP (S-R and L-R)
Bildirici, and Kayıkçı (2013)	Major oil exporting Eurasian countries	1993-2010	Panel ARDL approach	Oil consumption; GDP		OP↔ GDP (S-R and L-R)
Behmiri and Manso (2013)	Sub-Saharan Africa Oil importing (OI) region Oil exporting (OE) region	1985-2011	Multivariate panel Granger causality	Oil consumption; GDP		OI region OC↔GDP (S-R) OI region OC↔GDP (L-R) OE region OC→GDP (S-R) OE region OC↔GDP (L-R)
Damette and Seghir (2013)	12 oil exporting countries	1990 -2010.	Panel co-integration	Energy consumption GDP		EC→GDP (S-R) GDP→EC (L-R)
Hossein et al. (2012)	OPEC countries	1980-2008	Panel co-integration, ECM	Energy consumption; GDP		OPEC countries GDP≠ EC (L-R) Iran GDP→EC (S-R) Iraq GDP→EC (S-R) Qatar GDP→EC (S-R) U. Arab Emirates GDP→EC (S-R) Saudi Arabia GDP→EC (S-R) rest of OPEC countries EC→GDP (S-R)
Fuinhas and Marques (2012a)	Portugal, Italy, Greece, Spain and Turkey	1965-2009	ARDL	Energy consumption; GDP		GDP↔ EC (S-R and L-R)

Table 1. (Continued)

Authors	Countries	Period	Methodology	Main variables	Other variables	Results
Fuinhas and Marques (2012a)	Portugal	1965-2009	ARDL	Oil consumption; GDP	Crude oil prices	GDP↔ OC (S-R and L-R)
Farhani and Rejeb, (2012)	MENA	1973-2008	Panel co-integration, ECM	Energy consumption; GDP	CO_2 emissions	GDP≠ EC (S-R) GDP→EC (L-R)
Dantama et al. (2012)	Nigeria	1980-2010	ARDL bounds test and ECM	Oil consumption; GDP	Electricity Coal	OC→GDP
Al-Mulali and Sab (2012)	30 Sub-Saharan countries	1980-2008	Panel VECM			GDP↔ Energy
Akkemik et al. (2012)	China provinces	1986-2008	Heterogeneous panel causality	Energy consumption; GDP		GDP→EC (19) EC→GDP (14)
Al-Mulali (2011)	MENA	1980-2009	Panel VECM	Oil consumption; GDP	CO_2 emissions	OC↔GDP (S-R and L-R)
Sadorsky (2011)	Middle East	1980-2007	Panel VECM	Energy consumption; GDP	Exports Imports	EC↔GDP
Lotfalipour et al. (2010)	Iran	1967-2007	Toda-Yamamoto	Energy consumption; GDP		GDP→EC GDP→OC
Pao and Tsai (2011)	Brazil	1980-2007	Engle-Granger	Energy consumption; GDP	CO_2 emissions	GDP↔ EC
Eggoh et al. (2011)	21 African countries	1970-2006	Pooled Mean Group	Energy consumption; GDP		GDP↔ EC
Costantini and Martini (2010)	OECD	1960-2005	Panel VECM	Energy consumption; GDP		GDP→EC
Chang (2010)	China	1981-2006	Engle-Granger	Electricity; GDP	Oil consumption Coal	Electricity→GDP
Ozturk et al. (2010)	Middle income Low income	1971-2005	Panel VECM	Energy consumption; GDP		GDP↔ EC GDP→EC
Belloumi (2009)	Tunisia	1971-2004	Engle-Granger Toda-Yamamoto	Energy consumption; GDP		GDP↔EC
Lee and Chang (2008)	Asia APEC ASEAN	1971-2002	Panel VECM	Energy consumption; GDP		EC→GDP EC→GDP EC→GDP

Authors	Countries	Period	Methodology	Main variables	Other variables	Results
Yuan et al. (2008)	China	1963-2005	Johansen-Juselius Impulse Response Function	Energy consumption; GDP	Oil consumption Coal	EC↔GDP
Chontanawat et al. (2008)	10 Latin American countries	1971-2000	Johansen-Juselius	Energy consumption; GDP		Chile EC→GDP Colombia EC→GDP Uruguay EC→GDP Bolivia GDP→EC Paraguay GDP→EC Peru GDP→EC Venezuela GDP→EC Argentina GDP→EC Brazil GDP→EC Ecuador GDP≠ EC
Lee et al. (2008)	OECD	1960-2001	Panel VECM	Energy consumption; GDP	Capital stock	GDP↔EC
Mehrara (2007a)	Iran Kuwait Saudi Arabia	1971-2001	Johansen-Juselius Toda-Yamamoto ECM	Energy consumption; GDP		GDP→EC GDP→EC EC→GDP
Mehrara (2007b)	Oil exporting countries	1979-2002	Panel VECM	Energy consumption; GDP		GDP→EC
Yoo (2006)	Korea	1968-2002	Johansen-Juselius	Oil consumption		OC→GDP

Notes:→,↔and ≠ represent respectively, unidirectional causality, bidirectional causality and neutrality. Abbreviations are defined as follows: EC=energy consumption, GDP=gross domestic product, OP=oil production, OC= oil consumption, VECM= vector error correction model, ECM= error correction model, VAR=vector autoregressive model, GMM= generalized method of moments.

Understanding the transition from an oil-abundant landscape, to a more oil-scarce one, requires theoretical and methodological improvements. The movements of oil production and of domestic oil consumption appear to be increasingly intertwined, and their relation could express either structural changes or short-run effects (e.g., El-Katiri, 2013; Gately et al, 2013; and Fattouh and El-Katiri, 2012). The evolution of both variables can also be affected by market forces or stimulated by policy measures oriented to either one or the other. Such evolution will be traced both by external and by domestic drivers. Prospects regarding increased global and domestic energy demands, as well as the structural revolution observed in non-oil and oil supplies, will shape the energy landscape in the 21st Century. Thus, it is expected that oil-producing countries will be confronted with a difficult mix of economic, social and political challenges in the years ahead (e.g., El-Katiri, 2013; Gately et al, 2013; and Al-Iriani, 2006). How will they, in particular the net oil exporters, successfully respond to these challenges will depend, to some extent, on energy production and consumption dynamics, both external and domestic, and on how will energy policies address them. Using a measure that integrates oil production and oil consumption to study the causality hypotheses between energy and economic growth can provide room to improve the understanding of such challenges and to explore new avenues on the issue.

3. Data and Methodology

The aim of this study is to analyse the richness of the relationship between energy consumption and economic growth in oil producing countries, while controlling for the ratio of oil production to oil consumption. The selected countries comply simultaneously with the flowing requirements: (i) being oil producers; (ii) data is available for a large time span, namely on primary energy consumption, oil consumption, and exports of goods and services. Consequently, our analysis focuses upon the following eighteen countries: Australia, Algeria, Brazil, Canada, Colombia, Ecuador, Egypt, India, Indonesia, Italy, Mexico, Malaysia, Norway, Peru, Trinidad and Tobago, United Kingdom, United States, and Venezuela. The period under analysis comprises annual data beginning in 1965 and ending in 2012. The econometric analysis was carried out by using both EViews 8 and Stata 13.1 software. The source of the variables was the World Bank Data, for gross domestic product (GDP); exports of goods and services, and population; and the BP Statistical

Review of World Energy, June 2013, for oil consumption, oil production, primary energy consumption, and crude oil prices. The raw data variables used were: (i) GDP (constant local currency unit); (ii) exports of goods and services (% of GDP); (iii) population (total number of persons); (iv) oil consumption (million tonnes); (v) oil production (million tonnes); (vi) primary energy consumption (million tonnes oil equivalent); and (vii) crude oil prices (US dollars per barrel, 2012). The variables used were the following.

- Gross Domestic Product *per capita* (YPC) – this variable is obtained by dividing the GDP by the total population.
- Exports of goods and services *per capita* (XPC) – this variable is computed in three steps. The first one consists of dividing exports of goods and services, as a percentage, by 100. In the second step, the former result is multiplied by the GDP in order to obtain its absolute value. Finally, the absolute value is then divided by the total population to obtain *per capita* values.
- Primary energy consumption *per capita* (EPC) - this variable is obtained by dividing the primary energy consumption by the total population.
- Ratio of oil production to oil consumption (SO) – this variable is obtained by dividing the oil production by the oil consumption.
- Crude oil prices (P) – As it is the "international" price, this variable is unique, and therefore it is the same for all countries.

For the group of oil producing countries under analysis, it is likely that these variables contain dynamic effects. Indeed, two main reasons can be given for expecting such dynamic effects. Firstly, the time span under analysis is quite long. Secondly, for oil exporting countries that can be expected to have quite constant oil income GDP ratios over time, the presence of long-run relationships (e.g., Esfahani et al., 2014, 2013) is anticipated. Thus, the analysis of both short- and long-term adjustments is required. An autoregressive distributed lag (ARDL) model has been used to breakdown the dynamic interactions into short- and long-run. The ARDL model has the advantage of treating functional relationships among variables, making it possible to breakdown the total effect into its short- and long-run components. Besides the advantage of decomposition, the ARDL also has the important property of being robust in the presence of variables that are I(0), I(1), or fractionally integrated. This feature allows them to cope appropriately either with co-integration or with variables with long memory patterns. Furthermore,

ARDL has consistent and efficient parameter estimates, and the inference of parameters based on standard tests, as the vast literature on the topic has shown. As the specification of the ARDL model used here includes variables that are in natural logarithms, first differences of logarithms, and a ratio, their coefficients are elasticities, semi-elasticities, and impacts, respectively. Therefore, the prefixes "L" and "D" denote natural logarithm and first differences of variables, respectively. The specification of the ARDL model is the following:

$$LYPC_{it} = \alpha_i + \beta_{i1} LYPC_{it-1} + \beta_{i2} LEPC_{it} + \beta_{i3} LEPC_{it-1} + \beta_{i4} SO_{it} + \beta_{i5} SO_{it-1} + \\ + \beta_{i6} LXPC_{it} + \beta_{i7} + LXPC_{it-1} + \beta_{i8} LP_{it} + \beta_{i9} LP_{it-1} + \varepsilon_{it}. \quad (1)$$

Eq. (1) can be re-parameterized in order to capture the dynamic relationship among variables, as follows:

$$DLYPC_{it} = \alpha_i + \beta_{i1} DLEPC_{it} + \beta_{i2} DSO_{it} + \beta_{i3} DLX_{it} + \beta_{i4} DLP_{it} + \\ + \gamma_{i1} LYPC_{it-1} + \gamma_{i2} LEPC_{it-1} + \gamma_{i3} SO_{it-1} + \gamma_{i4} LXPC_{it-1} + \gamma_{i5} LP_{it-1} + \varepsilon_{it}. \quad (2)$$

where α denotes the intercept, β_i and γ_i the estimated parameters, and ϵ_i the error term.

Exports of goods and services *per capita*, and crude oil prices are not statistically significant and were excluded from the model (Eq.2). Some of these countries are heavy oil exporters and, as a consequence, their exports incorporate the oil price effect. Accordingly, the model reveals non-statistical significance of oil prices when exporters are considered. This evidence reinforces the redundancy of considering exports and oil prices simultaneously. Thereafter, the model used is that of Eq. (3), as follows.

$$DLY_{it} = \alpha_i + \beta_{i1} DLEPC_{it} + \beta_{i2} DSO_{it} + \gamma_{i1} LYPC_{it-1} + \gamma_{i2} LEPC_{it-1} + \gamma_{i3} SO_{it-1} + \varepsilon_{it}. \quad (3)$$

When working with an empirical approach it is advised to pay special attention to both the nature of the variables and to the idiosyncrasies of the countries under analysis. For example, it is well known that cross section dependence is a common occurrence in macro panels. Given that it is well known, and that several previous studies point towards specificities among oil-producing countries, as the ones under analysis here, the correct selection of estimators is vital for circumvent misspecifications, inefficiencies, and biased results in the estimates. Accordingly, descriptive statistics, the presence of cross section dependence, and the order of integration of the variables, shall be analysed in order to achieve a full understanding of the characteristics of both series and cross sections. Table 2 discloses both the descriptive statistics and the cross section dependence test made to the variables.

Table 2. Descriptive statistics and cross section dependence

	Descriptive statistics					Cross section dependence (CD)		
Variables	Obs	Mean	Std. Dev.	Min.	Max.	CD-test	Corr	Abs (corr)
LYPC	864	10.2463	2.2522	6.9501	16.1769	60.34***	0.705	0.814
LEPC	864	-13.4603	1.2908	-16.5372	-10.9740	53.77***	0.628	0.687
SO	864	2.7776	3.82712	0.0000	25.5077	2.91***	0.034	0.462
DLYPC	846	.0211024	0.03513	-0.1553	0.2153	11.22***	0.132	0.190
DLEPC	846	.023382	0.0526	-0.2325	0.3192	8.79***	0.104	0.176
DSO	846	-.0245023	0.6967	-7.5098	6.8455	1.22	0.014	0.131

Notes: CD test has N(0,1) distribution, under the H0: cross-section independence. *** denotes significance at 1% level. The Stata routine *xtcd* was used to achieve the results for cross section dependence.

The CD-test strongly supports that the countries under analysis share common developments for all variables except for the differences between the ratio of oil production to oil consumption (DSO) that signal cross section dependence. This shows interdependence among the crosses that occur due to the countries sharing common shocks (e.g., Eberhardt, 2011).

Two kinds of dependence between crosses were recognised. The first, is spatial and takes into account the distance between crosses, while the second, the so called long-range or global interdependence (Moscone and Tosetti, 2010), occurs when the crosses respond in the same way to external shocks. If countries react in a very similar manner to events, this generates correlation among countries independently from the extent of the geographic distance between them. The lack of cross section dependence for the first differences of the ratio of oil production to oil consumption, suggests that in the short-run countries do not react in the same way, as far as production and consumption of oil is concerned.

To check the multi-collinearity among variables, both the correlation coefficients and the Variance Inflation Factor (VIF) were computed (see Table 3). The low correlation values and VIF statistics strongly support that multi-collinearity is far from being a concern.

Table 3. Correlation matrices and VIF statistics

	LYPC	LEPC	SO		DLYPC	DLOCPC	DSO
LYPC	1.0000			DLYPC	1.0000		
LEPC	0.0242	1.0000		DLEPC	0.4093	1.0000	
SO	-0.0213	0.0088	1.0000	DSO	0.1481	-0.2288	1.0000
VIF		1.00	1.00			1.06	1.06
Mean VIF		1.01				1.06	

The usual first generation panel unit root tests, namely LLC (Levin, Lin and Chu, 2002), ADF-Fisher (Maddala and Wu, 1999) and ADF-Choi (Choi, 2001), were carried out (see Table 4) to verify the order of integration of the variables. The LLC, as well as the ADF are consensual in pointing to I(1) variables in levels. The second-generation unit root test CIPS (Pesaran, 2007) was also performed. When compared to those of the first generation, this CIPS test has the advantage of being robust to heterogeneity, and tests the null of non-stationarity under nonstandard distribution. Nevertheless, the CIPS test for variable LEPC with two or more lags is clearly non statistically significant (p-values over 13% with no trend, and 60% with trend).

Table 4. Unit root tests

	1st generation			2nd generation	
	LLC	ADF-Fisher	ADF-Choi	CIPS (Zt-bar)	
	Individual intercept and trend			no trend	with trend
LYPC	0.2538	23.8596	0.8030	1.243	1.763
LEPC	-0.5720	18.5752	2.6714	-2.238**	-1.863**
SO	-0.0902	37.0275	0.4761	0.524	1.928
DLYPC	-12.3637***	185.778***	-10.2186***	-8.641***	-8.394***
DLEPC	-10.5718***	209.589***	-11.0647***	-12.376***	-11.828***
DSO	-9.4938***	183.154***	-9.8499***	-8.798***	-8.532***

Notes: ***, **, * denote significance at 1%, 5% and 10% levels, respectively; the null hypotheses are as follows. LLC: unit root (common unit root process); this unit root test controls for individual effects, individual linear trends, has a lag length 1, and Newey-West automatic bandwidth selection and Bartlett kernel; ADF-Fisher and ADF-Choi: unit root (individual unit root process); this unit root test controls for individual effects, individual linear trends, has a lag length 1; first generation tests follow the option "individual intercept and trend", which was decided after a visual inspection of the series; Pesaran (2007) Panel Unit Root test (CIPS): series are I(1); the EViews was used to compute LLC, ADF-Fisher, and ADF-Choi; and the Stata routine multipurt was used to compute CIPS.

A detailed initial analysis to the data suggests that the second oil shock had a permanent effect upon the elasticity oil-growth. This addition was made by generating a shift dummy with "zeros" before 1979, and "ones" thereafter, while including the year of 1979. This shift dummy was multiplied by the natural logarithm of *per capita* oil consumption and used in the estimations as variable SD79LEPC. This shift dummy captures the elasticity change. The former Eq. (3) was extended accordingly to include this shift dummy, resulting in the following Eq. (4). It is therefore the standard specification for models.

$$DLYPC_{it} = \alpha_i + \beta_{i1} DLEPC_{it} + \beta_{i2} DSO_{it} +$$
$$+ \gamma_{i1} LYPC_{it-1} + \gamma_{i2} LEPC_{it-1} + \gamma_{i3} SO_{it-1} + \gamma_{i4} SD79LEPC_{it-1} + \varepsilon_{it}. \quad (4)$$

When working with several countries, good econometric practices advise testing for the adequacy of using panel data techniques. Thus, the presence of individual effects ought to be tested against random effects. If random effects perform better than fixed effects, then one must test for the use of panel random effects against simple OLS regression. Accordingly, fixed effects (FE) were tested against random effects (RE), using a Hausman test, which null hypothesis is that the best model is random effects. In Eq. (4), the error term takes up the following form $\epsilon_{it} = \mu_i + \omega_{it}$, where μ_i denotes the specific effects for country N-1, and ω_{it} is the independent and identically distributed error. Hausman's statistically significant high p-value ($\chi_7^2 = 48.37$) leads to the rejection of H_0, i.e., it supports FE as the adequate model. The evidence of correlation between countries individual effects and the explanatory variables, i.e., FE, supports that the countries individual effects are significant and must be considered in panel estimations. Furthermore, FE is especially adequate to analyse the influence of variables that vary over time, as the FE estimator removes all time-invariant features from the independent variables. This later feature allows the appraisal of the net effect of explanatory variables.

Considering the outcomes from the unit root tests (see Table 4), and although the order of integration of the variable LEPC could be borderline I(0)/I(1), assessment of the co-integration among variables should be pursued. To that end, two approaches were followed. On one hand, the first generation co-integration Kao's test (1999), which is a test based on residuals and is specified based on the assumption of homogeneity of coefficients. On the other hand, the second-generation co-integration test of Westerlund (2007), which is able to deal with dynamic structures instead of residuals and is built on four consistent statistical tests with a normal distribution. Statistics Pt and

Pa test the co-integration of the model as a whole, and Gt and Ga statistics test the hypothesis of at least one cross having all the variables co-integrated. These tests check whether the error correction term, in a conditional model, is zero and is able to incorporate short-run dynamics for each country, as well as serial correlated error terms, non-strictly exogenous regressors, interceptions, tendencies and slop parameters for each country (Ciarlone, 2011). These specificities are therefore flexible and suitable for working upon a heterogeneous specification. Both, first and second generation tests have no-cointegration as the null hypothesis. The extensively used Pedroni's test (1999, 2004), which considers both heterogeneity and independence among crosses (e.g., Pedroni, 1999), is not appropriate given that the presence of cross section dependence was detected in our sample of countries. The Kao's test definitely does not reject the null ($t = 0{,}3603$). Considering that the series shows cross section dependence, bootstrapping has been used to obtain robust critical values. The bootstrapping method provides proper coefficients, standard errors and confidence intervals, and discloses robust critical p-values. As well known, good econometric practices recommend resampling to be done at least 100 times to achieve robust results. For more accuracy, 800 reps were used. The results from the Westerlund (2007) co-integration test are shown in Table 5, and the presence of co-integration is clearly rejected, both considering the panel as a whole, as well as considering each country individually.

Table 5. Westerlund (2007) co-integration tests

Statistics	Value	Z-value	P-value	P-value robust
Gt	-0.366	5.563	1.000	0.999
Ga	-0.726	4.812	1.000	1.000
Pt	0.109	4.347	1.000	0.993
Pa	0.025	2.885	0.998	0.993

Notes: Bootstrapping regression with 800 reps; H0: no co-integration; Gt and Ga test – co-integration for each country individually; Pt and Pa test – co-integration of the panel as whole; the Stata routine *xtwest* was used.

4. RESULTS

The extended time span of the analysis gives us a large number of observations, enabling the use of various methodologies, both of macro panels as well as of means of individual time series estimations. Considering that we are working with oil producing countries, the possibility of sharing the same events suggests that a panel data approach should be pursued, namely by assessing the phenomena of cross section dependence. Furthermore, as pointed out by Klevmarken (1989) and Hsiao (2003), the panel data approach enables the control of heterogeneity of crosses, which are expected to be present when several individuals are analysed. Indeed, it reveals more information, variability, degrees of freedom and efficiency and, thus, less collinearity than is usually present in time series approaches. Of particular interest is the augmented capacity to detect and measure phenomena, and the possibility of building more complex models than with traditional methodologies. Whenever checking co-integration is of particular interest, the macro panel data structure with a larger time span has the advantage of allowing panel unit root tests, which have a standard asymptotic distribution (Baltagi, 2008).

When working with macro panels, the possibility of the panel being heterogeneous must be assessed. Indeed, the option for a panel approach or for techniques that allow diversity to be accommodated is conditional upon the units' degree of heterogeneity. If heterogeneity is found, then Mean Group (MG) or Pooled Mean Group (PMG) estimators should be applied. MG is the most flexible model. It estimates the regressions for each individual, and then calculates an average coefficient for all crosses. Its estimates of the long run average coefficients are consistent, but inefficient when there is a slope of homogeneity (Pesaran et al, 1999). Moreover, this model is not suitable for countries with few time observations, since an outlier can significantly change the coefficient averages (Ciarlone, 2011).

The PMG also allows for greater flexibility than traditional models when studying a panel, but it is not as flexible as MG. It generates restrictions among crosses in long-run parameters, by pooling them, but not in the short-run ones or in the adjustment speed. Thus, short-run dynamics are allowed to be heterogeneous, while the long-run ones must be homogeneous. It can be based on an ARDL approach, enabling the correction of serial correlation among residuals and the problem of endogenous regressors, as long as an optimal number of lags is chosen. It is an intermediate method in which the intersection, the short-run coefficients and the error variances can be different among countries, while implying homogeneity in the long-run. If homogeneity is actually verified, PMG estimators are more consistent and efficient than MG. However, such as noted by Blackburne III and Frank (2007), these estimators require a large number of both crosses (N) and time observations (T). One way to appraise the appropriateness of using MG or PMG estimators is to test them against the FE estimator.

The FE model is the least flexible model. In fact, it is more restrictive than the previous models, imposing homogeneity for all coefficients and allowing only the interception to be different among crosses. Homogeneity is valid if the parameters have a common convergence. The decision on whether to use one of these models instead of another is done by computing a Hausman test, which tests the null hypothesis that the difference in coefficients is not systematic. Given that the model works with dynamic models inspired in the bounds testing approaches (ARDL), it is prudent to start with the more general specification. As set out by Pesaran et al. (2001), one should begin with the most general specification, i.e., including the constant and the trend.

To ascertain the presence of heterogeneity, the MG estimator is applied and their results carefully analysed, both by means and by crosses. In general, the estimations by crosses show few statistically significant parameters and their values are dissimilar. In accordance, the results of the MG estimator ought to be tested against the PMG estimator, as well as the FE estimator. The efforts to estimate the PMG estimator reveal a difficult task. Indeed, the default maximum likelihood optimization technique, used by the Stata routine, the Newton-Raphson (nr) algorithm, does not converge and so the Broyden, Fletcher, Goldfarb and Shanno (BFGS) algorithm was used to estimate de parameters. However, the long-run elasticity coefficients shown by the PMG model do not make either economic or econometric sense, and so the model was not presented. Thus, the MG estimators were tested against fixed effects. Table 6 presents the estimations for both models, as well as the Hausman tests.

Table 6. Heterogeneous estimators and Hausman tests

Models	MG (I)	FE (II)
Constant	3.4177***	0.7055***
Trend	0.0025***	0.0009***
DLEPC	0.3890***	0.3080***
DSO	0.0255	0.0127***
ECM	-0.1974***	-0.0407***
LEPC	0.0049	0.5284***
SO	-0.5631	0.0446***
SD79LEPC	0.0025	0.0366***
Models	MG vs. PMG	MG vs. FE
Hausman tests	Chi2(5) = 18.24***	Chi2(8) = 0.00

Notes: ***, ** denote significance at 1% and 5%, respectively; Hausman results for H0: difference in coefficients not systematic including the constant and with the option sigmamore; ECM denotes error correction mechanism; the long run parameters are computed as elasticities/impacts; the Stata routine *xtpmg* was used.

The results lead to the rejection of the most flexible model, presenting FE as the most suitable estimator. The prevalence of a homogeneous panel indicates that oil producers share common coefficients, and can be suitable for treating them as a group, as these results could be interpreted as evidence that oil producing countries have shared similar deportments, to the extent that these variables are considered.

Given that the Hausman tests point towards panel homogeneity, a battery of specification tests was performed, namely on the heteroskedasticity, the contemporaneous correlation among crosses, the non-correlation of variances across individuals, and autocorrelation. To check any eventual violations of these hypotheses was crucial given the sensibility of traditional panel estimators to their presence. Firstly, groupwise heteroskedasticity of the fixed effects was appraised using the modified Wald test. It has χ^2 distribution and tests the nullity of homoskedasticity, i.e., $\sigma_i^2=\sigma^2$ for i=1, …., N, with σ^2 being the variance of country i. Secondly, the Pesaran test for cross section independence was computed to assess the presence of contemporaneous correlation among crosses. The null hypothesis of this test states that the residuals are not correlated and that it follows a normal distribution. With the purpose of verifying whether the variances across individuals are not correlated, the Breusch-Pagan Langragian multiplier test of independence was performed. This test follows a χ^2 distribution. Finally, to check the existence of serial correlation, the Wooldridge test for autocorrelation was performed. The null hypothesis of this test is no serial correlation and follows an F distribution.

The results shown in Table 7 support the rejection of the null hypothesis of the modified Wald test, pointing towards the presence of heteroskedasticity. The Pesaran's test points towards the existence of contemporaneous correlation. The Breusch-Pagan LM test does not reject the hypothesis that the residuals are correlated. Finally, the Wooldridge test supports that the data have first order autocorrelation.

Table 7. Specification tests

	Statistics		Statistics
Modified Wald test	623.61***	Breusch-Pagan LM test	269.342***
Pesaran's test	4.181***	Wooldridge test	58.748***

Note: *** denote significance at 1%; results for H0 of Modified Wald test: sigma(i)^2 = sigma^2 for all I; results for H0 of Pesaran's and Breusch-Pagan LM test: residuals are not correlated; results for H0 of Wooldridge test: no first-order autocorrelation.

Given that heteroskedasticity, contemporaneous correlation, first order autocorrelation, cross section dependence and a large time span are present, the Driscoll and Kraay (1998) estimator (e.g., Hoechle, 2007) was used (see Table 8). This estimator is a nonparametric covariance matrix estimator that produces a robust standard error to several phenomena, namely temporal dependence. Additionally, as a benchmark, the FE estimator and the FE estimator with robust standard errors, to control the heteroskedasticity that was previously verified. The only changes were found in FE robust, namely in the statistical significance of the variable DSO that dropped slightly, from 1% to 5%. The high statistical significance of the trend points towards a slight tendency for the acceleration of economic growth over the period under analysis.

Table 8. Estimation results

Models	FE (III)	FE Robust (IV)	FE D.-K. (V)
Constant	0.7055***	0.7055***	0.7055***
Trend	0.0009***	0.0009***	0.0009***
DLEPC	0.3080***	0.3080***	0.3080***
DSO	0.0127***	0.0127**	0.0127***
LYPC(-1)	-0.0407***	-0.0407***	-0.0407***
LEPC(-1)	0.0215***	0.0215***	0.0215***
SO(-1)	0.0018***	0.0018***	0.0018***
SD79LEPC(-1)	0.0015***	0.0015***	0.0015***
Diagnostic statistics			
N	846	846	846
R^2	0.2619	0.2619	0.2619
R^2_a	0.2403	0.2557	
F	F(7,821)=41.62***	F(7,17)=14.35***	F(7,46)=14.31***

Notes: ***, **, * denote statistical significance at 1%, 5% and 10% levels, respectively; and the Stata routines *xtreg*, and *xtscc* were used.

Table 9. Elasticities, impacts, and adjustment speed

Models	FE (III)	FE Robust (IV)	FE D.-K. (V)
Short-run elasticities/impacts			
DLEPC	0.3080***	0.3080***	0.3080***
DSO	0.0127***	0.0127**	0.0127***
Computed long-run elasticities/impacts			
LEPC	0.5284***	0.5284***	0.5284***
SO	0.0446***	0.0446***	0.0446***
SD79LEPC	0.0366***	0.0366***	0.0366***
Speed of adjustment			
ECM	-0.0407***	-0.0407***	-0.0407***

Notes: ***, **, * denote significance at 1%, 5% and 10% levels, respectively. ECM denotes the coefficient of the variable LYPC lagged once.

Table 9 displays the short- and long-run elasticities/impacts for each model. It should be noted that the long-run elasticities/impacts are not directly provided by the estimates (Table 8), and are therefore computed. These elasticities/impacts were obtained by dividing the coefficient of the variables by the coefficient of LYPC, both lagged once, and then the ratio was multiplied by -1.

5. DISCUSSION

Overall, the results reveal a strong internal consistency and the use of the ratio of oil production to oil consumption proves to be appropriate. The set of countries under analysis is a mixture of OPEC and non-OPEC, and developing and developed countries, but the diversity is not enough to be econometrically handled as heterogeneous. Indeed, the presence of heterogeneity in the panel of countries was not confirmed, as can be seen in the MG model. The control for the presence of heteroskedasticity, contemporaneous correlation, first order autocorrelation, and cross section dependence was pursued and no changes with statistical significance were observed on the parameters of the model. This makes the analysis quite rich, allowing general rules to be obtained. The delicate problem of the order of integration of the variables is overcome by the use of econometric specifications that are appropriate to work upon variables I(0) and/or I(1). Furthermore, this approach can operate on wider relationships that range from co-integration to long-memory.

The analysis contributes the literature regarding the energy-growth nexus by incorporating the effects of primary energy consumption, controlling for the ratio of oil production to oil consumption, and the shift in the elasticity of energy-growth. On the whole, the models support co-integration/long memory. Nevertheless, this was not noticed previously (Table 5), given that the error correction mechanisms (ECM) are negative and highly statistically significant. This apparent contradiction stresses the appropriateness of using econometric techniques that are: (i) able to breakdown the total effect into short- and long-run components; and (ii) that can handle the phenomena of long memory. The later feature can be evidenced by the low speed of adjustment, which is statistically highly significant.

The estimates reveal that the effect of energy consumption upon growth is positive, although modest in magnitude, especially in the short-run. Indeed, the total elasticity is below one, revelling an inefficient use of energy. Nevertheless, for this set of countries, energy is the driving force of economic growth. When considering the magnitude of elasticities, both in the short- and in the long-run, energy consumption is the main driving force. The phenomenon is both a short- and long-run one, but more relevant in the long-run. As causality running from energy consumption to economic growth was detected, this fact supports the growth hypothesis of the previously mentioned nexus.

The use of the ratio of oil production to oil consumption is a highly relevant new insight of this chapter. Definitely, it has the advantage of controlling for the oil production level comparing to the domestic oil consumption, throughout the entire period of analysis for different levels of the ratio. The literature, only working with oil exporting countries, is unable to capture this noteworthy effect within the energy-growth nexus. Indeed, to some extent, this ratio is an indicator of the country's oil self-sufficiency: the larger the ratio, the larger the energy security of that country will be. A country with a ratio equal to one is not an oil exporting country, and therefore it is not studied in the literature that focuses on oil exporting countries. However, that country could be not only an oil producer, but also be self-sufficient on oil and the relationship between energy consumption and economic growth must also be studied in these cases.

The SO ratio is statistically highly significant and catches some non-linearity throughout the period under analysis. Being a ratio, it could be the consequence of various combinations, both on the numerator and on the denominator. All constant, to slow down oil consumption, for instance trough energy efficiency measures or by increasing the price to restrict access, could generate economic growth. This is compatible with the statement that says that the lower the energy dependence, the higher the economic growth. The same effect is achieved when the oil production increases, at least in an amount equivalent to the oil consumption.

The literature, for instance El-Katiri, (2013), Gately *et al*, (2013) and Fattouh and El-Katiri, (2012), highlight the propensity of oil producing countries to increase oil consumption, considering the high dependence of their economic structure towards that input. Therefore, the results are compatible with an increase in oil consumption even if in smaller magnitude than that of its production. The short-run impact of the ratio of oil production to oil consumption (DSO) loses statistical significance (only at 5%) in the model FE Robust. Both impacts are positive, but its magnitude is larger in the long-run, although quite modest in value. This result supports that deepening self-sufficiency and oil exports are drivers of economic growth. Given that the variables in the ratio are measured in million tonnes, there is no inherent monetary effect. In other words, when prices increase, a larger production level is expected, enhancing the external oil rent. Higher prices induce higher production, at the same time they could generate some cuts in domestic consumption, making resources available for exports.

The idiosyncrasy of the oil shock of 1979 proved to be persistent in time. Before that, the 1973 Yom Kippur War caused a strong reduction in the production by OPEC countries, which was not fully balanced off by the increased production in non-OPEC countries. Overall, the oil price rose exponentially in the following months and the world became aware of the vulnerability of oil dependence. After that, the second crude oil crisis happened in 1979-80, which main causes were the Iranian revolution in 1978-79, and the Iran-Iraq war, which is also known as the First Persian Gulf War (1980-88). In face of abnormally high oil prices, these two facts arouse concerns on energy dependence and inspired new energy policies focused on energy efficiency goals, as well as incentives to replace energy sources. That structural shock revealed to be positive and highly statistically significant for the elasticity energy-growth. This outcome supports that the mentioned measures were even effective upon the context of oil producing countries. As far as the speed of adjustment is considered, it is very low, slightly above 4%, as revealed in Table 9, by the ECM term. This outcome could result from the predominant nature of long memory that prevails for the countries under analysis, contrarily to a much stronger event of co-integration.

CONCLUSION

Traditionally, the literature focuses on the relationship between energy resources and economic growth, some of it by assessing the role of oil consumption. This chapter innovates by appraising the level of oil self-sufficiency upon economic growth. The extended time span under analysis goes from 1965 to 2012, highlighting a set of 18 oil producing countries. Modern panel data techniques were applied. First of all the heterogeneity of the panel was tested. Secondly, the phenomena of heteroskedasticity, contemporaneous correlation, first order autocorrelation, and cross section dependence were assessed. Thirdly, the Driscoll-Kraay estimator was used in order to obtain more confident standard errors. Fourthly, the model was made dynamic in order to breakdown the total effects into their short- and long-run components. Fifthly, the design of governmental policies capable of facing the 21st Century economic growth challenges were discussed.

Overall, the magnitude of elasticities/impacts in the long-run is larger than on the short-run. The elasticity of energy-growth is less than one, signalling a lack of efficiency in what energy consumption is concerned. The aftermath of the 1979 structural shock was proven. For the group of countries under analysis, evidence was found supporting the traditional growth hypothesis of the energy-growth nexus, both in the short- and in the long-run. Additionally, the dynamic specification detected co-integration/long memory as the ECM term is negative and highly statistically significant. This speed of adjustment of the variables to the long-run balance is fundamental for understanding the nexus.

The chapter does not focus on the duality between fossil and renewable energy sources, which ultimately is a political call. Nevertheless, the results corroborate that a larger oil self-sufficiency promotes economic growth. As a consequence, countries trying to ensure high degrees of energy security could expect to achieve higher levels of economic growth. The low energy-growth elasticity of oil producing countries supports the appropriateness of energy policies focused on promoting energy efficiency during the remaining of the 21st century.

Acknowledgments

The financial support from the NECE – Research Unit in Business Science and Economics, sponsored by the Portuguese Foundation for the Development of Science and Technology, Ministry of Education and Science, is hereby acknowledged.

References

Akkemik, K.A., Goksal, K., Li, J., 2012, "Energy consumption and income in Chinese provinces: Heterogeneous panel causality analysis", *Applied Energy* 99, pp. 445-454.

Alam, M. J., Begum, I. A., Buysse, J., Van Huylenbroeck, G., 2012, "Energy consumption, carbon emissions and economic growth nexus in Bangladesh: Cointegration and dynamic causality analysis", *Energy Policy* 45, pp. 217-225.

Al-Iriani, M.A., 2006, "Energy–GDP relationship revisited: An example from GCC countries using panel causality", *Energy Policy* 34(17), pp. 3342-3350.

Al-Mulali, U., 2011, "Oil Consumption, CO2 emissions and economic growth in MENA countries". *Energy* 36(10), pp. 6165-6171.

Al-Mulali, U., Sab, C.N.B.C., 2012, "The impact of energy consumption and CO2 emissions on the economic growth and the financial development in Sub-Saharan African countries". *Energy* 39(1), pp.180-186.

Altinay, G., Karagol, E., 2004, "Structural break, unit root, and the causality between energy and GDP in Turkey", *Energy Economics* 26(6), pp. 985-994.

Apergis N., Payne, J. E., 2009, "Energy consumption and economic growth in Central America: Evidence from a panel cointegration and error correction model", *Energy Economics* 31(2), pp. 211-216.

Apergis, N., Payne, J. E., 2010, "Energy consumption and economic growth in South America: Evidence from a panel error correction model", *Energy Economics* 32(6), pp. 1421-1426.

Baltagi, B.H., 2008, "*Econometric Analysis of Panel Data*", Fourth edition, Chichester, UK: John Wiley & Sons.

Behmiri, N., Manso, P., 2013, "How crude oil consumption impacts on economic growth of Sub-Saharan Africa?", *Energy* 54(1), pp. 74-83.

Belloumi, M., 2009, "Energy consumption and GDP in Tunisia: Co-integration and causality analysis", *Energy Policy* 37(7), pp. 2745-2753.

Bildirici, M., Kayıkçı, F., 2013, "Effects of oil production on economic growth in Eurasian countries: Panel ARDL approach", *Energy* 49(1), pp. 156-161.

Blackburne III, E.F., Frank, M.W., 2007, "Estimation of non-stationary heterogeneous panels", *The Stata Journal* 7 (2), pp. 197-208.

Chang, C., 2010, A multivariate causality test of carbon dioxide emissions, energy consumption and economic growth in China", *Applied Energy* 87(11), pp. 3533-3537.

Chen, P.-Y., Chen, S.-T., Chen, C.-C., 2012, "Energy consumption and economic growth – New evidence from meta analysis", *Energy Policy* 44, pp. 245-255.

Choi, I., 2001, "Unit root tests for panel data", *Journal of International Money and Finance* 20(1), pp. 249-272.

Chontanawat, J., Hunt, L.C., Pierse, R., 2008, "Does energy consumption cause economic growth? Evidence from systematic study of over 100 countries", *Journal of Policy Modelling*, 30 (2), pp. 209–220.

Chu, H.-P., Chang, T., 2012, "Nuclear energy consumption, oil consumption and economic growth in G-6 countries: Bootstrap panel causality test", *Energy Policy* 48, pp. 762-769.

Ciarlone, A., 2011, "Housing wealth effect in emerging economies", Emerging *Markets Review* 12(4), pp. 399-417.

Damette, O., Seghir, M., 2013, "Energy as a driver of growth in oil exporting countries?", *Energy Economics* 37, pp. 193-199.

Dantama, Y.U., Abdullahi, Y.Z., Inuwa, N., 2012, "Energy consumption - economic growth nexus in Nigeria: an empirical assessment based on ARDL bound test approach", *European Scientific Journal* 8(12), pp. 141-157.

Driscoll, J., Kraay, A.C., 1998, "Consistent covariance matrix estimation with spatially dependent data", *Review of Economics and Statistics* 80(4), pp. 549-560.

Eberhardt, M., 2011, "*Panel time-series modelling: New tools for analyzing xt data*", 2011 UK Stata Users Group meeting.

Eggoh, J. C., Bangake, C., Rault, C., 2011, "Energy consumption and economic growth revisited in African countries", *Energy Policy* 39(11), pp. 7408-7421.

El-Katiri, L., 2013, "Energy sustainability in the Gulf States: the why and the how", Oxford Institute for Energy Studies, http://www.oxfordenergy.org /wpcms/wp-content/uploads/2013/03/ MEP_4.pdf, (accessed January 21, 2014).

Esfahani, H.S., Mohaddes, K., Pesaran, M. H., 2014, "An empirical growth model for major oil exporters", *Journal of Applied Econometrics* 29(1), pp. 1-21.

Esfahani, H.S., Mohaddes, K., Pesaran, M.H., 2013, "Oil exports and the Iranian economy", *The Quarterly Review of Economics and Finance* 53(3), pp. 221-237.

Farhani, S., Rejeb, J.B., 2012, "Energy Consumption, Economic Growth and CO2 Emissions: Evidence from Panel Data for MENA Region", *International Journal of Energy Economics and Policy* 2(2), pp. 71-81.

Fattouh, B., El-Katiri, L., 2012, Energy and Arab Economic Development, Arab Human Development Report Research Paper Series, UNDP, http://www.arab-hdr.org/publications/other/ahdrps/ENGFattouhKatiri V2.pdf, (accessed January 27, 2012).

Fuinhas, J. A., Marques, A. C., 2012a, "Energy consumption and economic growth nexus in Portugal, Italy, Greece, Spain and Turkey: An ARDL bounds test approach (1965-2009)", *Energy Economics* 34(2), pp. 511-517.

Fuinhas, J. A., Marques, A. C., 2012b, "An ARDL approach to the oil and growth nexus: Portuguese evidence", *Energy Sources, Part B: Economics, Planning, and Policy* 7(3), pp. 282-291.

Fuinhas, J. A., Marques, A. C., 2013, "Rentierism, energy and economic growth: The case of Algeria and Egypt (1965–2010)", *Energy Policy* 62, pp. 1165-1171.

Gately, D., Al-Yousef, N., Al-Sheikh, H.M.H., 2013, "The rapid growth of OPEC's domestic oil consumption" *Energy Policy* 62, pp. 844-859.

Hoechle, D., 2007, "Robust standard errors for panel regressions with cross-sectional dependence", *Stata Journal* 7(3), pp. 281-312.

Hossein, S.S.M., Yazdan, G.F., Hasan, S., 2012, "Consideration the relationship between energy consumption and economic growth in oil exporting country", *Procedia - Social and Behavioral Sciences* 62, pp. 52-58.

Hsiao, C., 2003, *Analysis of Panel Data*, 2nd ed., Cambridge, Cambridge University Press.

Klein, N., 2010, "The Linkage between the oil and nonoil sectors –A panel VAR approach", IMF Working Paper, WP/10/118, http://www.imf.org/external/pubs/ft/wp/2010/wp10118.pdf, (accessed March 15, 2012).

Klevmarken, N. A., 1989, "Panel studies: What can we learn from them? Introduction", *European Economic Review*, 33(2-3), pp.523-529.

Kraft, J., Kraft, A., 1978, "On the Relationship between Energy and GNP". *Journal of Energy and Development* 3(2), pp. 401-403.

Lee, C., Chang, C., 2008, "Energy consumption and economic growth in Asian economies: a more comprehensive analysis using panel data", *Energy Economics* 30(1), pp. 50-65.

Lee, C.C., Chang, C.P., Chen, P.F., 2008, "Energy-income causality in OECD countries revisited: the key role of capital stock", *Energy Economics* 30(5), pp. 2359-2373.

Levin, A., Lin, C.-F., Chu, C.-S. J., 2002, "Unit root test in panel data: Asymptotic and finite-sample properties", *Journal of Econometrics* 108(1), pp. 1-24.

Lim, K.-M., Lim, S.-Y., Yoo, S.-H., 2014, "Oil Consumption, CO2 Emissions, and Economic Growth: Evidence from the Philippines", *Sustainability* 6(2), pp. 967-979.

Lotfalipour, M., Falahi, M., Ashena, M., 2010, "Economic growth, CO2 emissions, and fossil fuel consumption in Iran", *Energy* 35(12), pp. 5115-5120.

Maddala, G.S., Wu, S., 1999, "A comparative study of unit root tests with panel data a new simple test", *Oxford Bulletin of Economics and Statistics* 61(S1), pp. 631-652.

Mehrara, M., 2007a, "Energy-GDP Relationship for oil exporting countries: Iran Kuwait and Saudi Arabia", *OPEC Review* 31(1), pp. 1-16.

Mehrara, M., 2007b, "Energy consumption and economic growth: the case of oil exporting countries", *Energy Policy* 35(5), pp. 2939–2945.

Mehrara, M., 2008, "The asymmetric relationship between oil revenues and economic activities: The case of oil-exporting countries", *Energy Policy* 36(3), pp. 1164-1168.

Mehrara, M., 2009, "Reconsidering the resource curse in oil-exporting countries", *Energy Policy* 37(3), pp. 1165-1169.

Mohammadi, H. and Parvaresh, S., 2014, "Energy consumption and output: Evidence from a panel of 14 oil-exporting countries", *Energy Economics* 41, pp. 41-46.

Moscone, F., Tosetti, E., 2010, "Health expenditure and income in the United States", *Health Economics* 19(2), pp. 1385-1403.

Narayan, P.K., Smyth, R., 2008, "Energy Consumption and Real GDP in G7 Countries: New Evidence from Panel Cointegration with Structural Breaks", *Energy Economics* 30(5), pp. 2331-2341.

Ozturk, I., 2010, "A literature survey on energy-growth nexus", *Energy Policy* 38(1), pp. 340-349.

Ozturk, I., Aslan, A., Kalyoncu, H., 2010, "Energy consumption and economic growth relationship: Evidence from panel data for low and middle income countries", *Energy Policy* 38(8), pp. 4422-4428.

Pao, H.-T., Tsai, C.-M., 2011, "Modelling and forecasting the CO2 emissions, energy consumption, and economic growth in Brazil", *Energy* 36(5), pp. 2450-2458.

Park, S.-H., Yoo, S.-H., 2014, "The dynamics of oil consumption and economic growth in Malaysia", *Energy Policy* 66, pp. 218-223.

Payne, J.E., 2010, "Survey of the international evidence on the causal relationship between energy consumption and growth", *Journal of Economic Studies* 37(1), pp. 53-95.

Pedroni, P., 1999, "Critical Values for Cointegration Tests in Heterogeneous Panels with Multiple Regressors", *Oxford Bulletin of Economics and Statistics,* 61(Special Issue), pp. 653–70.

Pedroni, P., 2004, "Panel Cointegration; Asymptotic and Finite Sample Properties of Pooled Time Series Tests with an Application to the PPP Hypothesis", *Econometric Theory*, 20(3), pp. 597–625.

Pesaran, M.H., 2007, "A simple panel unit root test in the presence of cross-section dependence", *Journal of Applied Econometrics* 22(2), pp. 265-312.

Pesaran, M.H., Shin, Y., Smith, R.J., 2001, "Bound testing approaches to the analysis of level relationships", *Journal of Applied Econometrics* 16(3), pp. 289-326.

Pesaran, M.H., Shin, Y., Smith, R.P., 1999, "Pooled Mean Group Estimation of Dynamic Heterogeneous Panels", *Journal of American Statistical Association* 94(446), pp.621-634.

Pradhan, R.P., 2010, "Energy Consumption-Growth Nexus in SAARC Countries: Using Cointegration and Error Correction Modell", *Modern Applied Science* 4(4), pp. 74-90.

Rosser, A., 2006a, "The Political Economy of the Resource Curse: A Literature Survey", Working Paper 268, Institute of Development Studies at the University of Sussex, pp. 1-36.

Rosser, A., 2006b, "Escaping the Resource Curse", *New Political Economy* 11(4), pp. 557 570.

Sadorsky, P., 2011, "Trade and energy consumption in the Middle East", *Energy Economics* 33(5), pp. 739-749.

Westerlund, J., 2007, "Testing for error correction in panel data", *Oxford Economics and Statistics* 69(6), pp. 709-748.

Wolde-Rufael, Y., 2009, "Energy Consumption and Economic Growth: The Experience of African Countries Revisited", *Energy Economics*, 31(2), pp. 217-224.

Yıldırım, E., Sukruoglu, D., Aslan, A., 2014, "Energy Consumption and Economic Growth in the Next 11 Countries: The Bootstrapped Autoregressive Metric Causality Approach", *Energy Economics*, http://dx.doi.org/10.1016/j.eneco.2014.03.010.

Yoo, S., 2006, "Oil consumption and economic growth: evidence from Korea", *Energy Sources, Part B: Economics, Planning, and Policy* 1(3), pp. 235-243.

Yuan, C., Liu, S., Xie, N., 2010, "The Impact of Chinese Economic Growth and Energy Consumption of the Global Financial Crisis: An Input-Output Analysis", *Energy* 35(4), pp. 1805–1812.

Yuan, J., Kang, J., Zhao, C., Hu, Z., 2008, "Energy consumption and economic growth: evidence from China at both aggregated and disaggregated levels", *Energy Economics* 30(6), pp. 3077-3094.

Zhang, X., Cheng, X., 2009, Energy Consumption, Carbon Emissions and Economic Growth in China. *Ecological Economics*, 68(10), pp. 2706-2712.

In: Economic Growth in the 21st Century ISBN: 978-1-63321-589-4
Editor: Cody Accosi

Chapter 4

DRIVERS OF ECONOMIC GROWTH IN LATIN AMERICA: EVOLUTION AND CHALLENGES

***Víctor M. González-Sánchez*[1,*]**
***and Susana de los Ríos Sastre*[2]**
[1]UNED – National University of Distance Education,
Department of Applied Economy, Madrid, Spain
[2]Comillas Pontifical University,
Department of Financial Management, Madrid, Spain

ABSTRACT

During the current century the evolution of economic growth in Latin America is the result of the learning obtained after several decades of instability and significant economic imbalances. The region was able to overcome the uncertainty generated by the crisis at the beginning of the century, to emerge with high rates of economic growth and improvement in the level of development in most countries. This chapter presents how some key factors affect Latin America´s economic growth. First of all, it examines the influence of government policies on the improvement of regional economic growth. Secondly, it analyzes the role played by two factors such as education and information and communication technologies (ICT) on Latin America´s economic growth. Thirdly, it studies the positive contribution of the external sector to economic

* E-mail: vgonzalez@cee.uned.es.

development in that region. Finally, it outlines a review of the main challenges and limitations of economic growth in this emerging region.

1. INTRODUCTION

From the point of view of economic growth, Latin America has enjoyed a generally positive decade since the outset of the 21st century. The growing relative importance of some countries, such as, for example Brazil, and the consolidation and implementation of economic integration processes such as Mercosur and the Pacific Alliance[1], have meant that the Latin American region well deserves to be jointly considered as an "emerging economy"[2]. This area's development has often been based on the influence of foreign circumstances and on the arrival of investments from more developed countries. However, Latin America's potential is also based on the improvement of national indicators relating to aspects like education or technological development. Not forgetting the influence that governments' actions can have to encourage economic growth and development.

This chapter analyses, firstly, the possible relationship existing in the context of Latin America between government policies and economic growth, on the basis of the variable relating to public expenditure in terms of investments to improve a country's production capacity. Secondly, it addresses a study into the influence and mutual interdependence of education and economic growth as driving forces of long-term economic development in Latin America.

Thirdly, it analyses both the technological infrastructure available in the region and its relationship with economic growth. Although by themselves they do not guarantee economic prosperity, greater access and use of information and communication technologies (ICT) by the inhabitants of a country can offer a powerful stimulus to foster economic growth and secure economic development. Finally, it addresses the behaviour of the foreign sector as a key element in the economic evolution of each country and of Latin America as a whole. In any event, the challenges and limitations of the region in each of the aspects considered are also part of this chapter's contents.

[1] See González-Sánchez (2014).
[2] See Casilda Béjar (2013).

2. GOVERNMENT POLICIES AND REGIONAL ECONOMIC GROWTH

Government policies may have different effects on a country's economic growth, and they are not necessarily always of the same kind. As described by Nissan, Galindo Martín & Méndez Picazo (2011), there is no uniform opinion regarding the relationship between government action through public expenditure and gross domestic product (GDP). Accordingly, as these authors point out, some studies say that increasing public expenditure through expansive fiscal policies may negatively impact economic growth as a consequence of the crowding-out effect that leads to a drop in investment (Alesina & Rodrik, 1994; Bertola, 1993; Perotti, 1993; Persson & Tabellini, 1994, among others). Conversely, other studies point in the opposite direction, defending the positive effects of public expenditure on economic growth through different aspects (Bourguignon & Verdier, 2000; Piketty, 1997; Saint-Paul & Verdier, 1993, among others).

Public expenditure can be classified in different ways. Probably the most common is to differentiate between the government's current expenditure and capital expenditure. The first associated with payments relating to the provision of services, civil service salaries and the acquisition of goods and services; while the second is associated with investments aimed at improving the country's production capacity. This section compares the correspondence between public sector capital expenditure and economic growth in Latin America[3] during two periods: 1990-2000 and 2001-2012. As may be seen in Figure 1, the relationship between the two variables is very different according to the years considered.

During the decade of the 90s and the year 2000, the slope of the trend line is negative. That is, the effect that public sector capital expenditure had on economic growth in the region as a whole during that time was not, maybe paradoxically, what might be expected. In the years prior to the Argentinean crisis, public capital expenditure was greater in countries than grew least economically, such as, for example, Venezuela: its average annual growth was almost 2.6% and its public sector capital expenditure was on average above 10.4% annually. Conversely, Panama was the third country in Latin America for which information is available whose public sector spent least on

[3] Includes data available in ECLAC-CEPAL (2014) referring to: Argentina, Bolivia, Colombia, Costa Rica, Ecuador, El Salvador, Mexico, Nicaragua, Panama, Paraguay, Uruguay and Venezuela.

investment (on average slightly above 3.7% per annum) and its average growth between 1990 and 2000 was the largest of the group, at around 5.4%. It could be said that public expenditure in this period could not be exploited as might be expected from the point of view of growth. This was also partly due to the fact that, during this time, foreign circumstances were not as favourable as in the first decade of the 21st century.

The Argentinean crisis at the beginning of the century led to a period of adjustment, not only for the country itself but also for the region as a whole. Since then, economic growth was faster in most countries, at least until 2008, and the relationship between public investment and economic growth changed trend. As can be seen in Figure 1, the slope of the trend line between 2001 and 2012 turns positive, though smaller in absolute terms than during the foregoing period. It does not seem that public sector capital expenditure affects the economic growth of Latin American countries as favourably as might be expected. It could be said that this is one of the challenges facing the region: to position the relevance and influence of the public sector in accordance with its proportional weight in the economy as a whole in order to make it a more useful economic policy instrument. Nevertheless, as pointed out by González-Sánchez (2014), in order to have sustainable, useful public accounts as a tool for economic policy, Latin American countries in general should reform their tax systems to try to increase their tax base, while improving the fairness of tax collection systems.

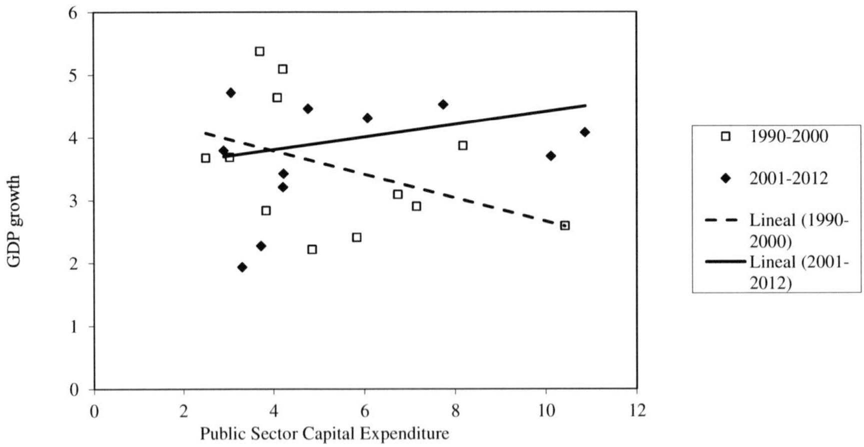

Source: Author's elaboration from information of ECLAC-CEPAL (2014).

Figure 1. GDP growth and Public Sector Capital Expenditure.

3. Education and Economic Growth

The link between education and economy is usually strong and constant. Both variables are interdependent and it is common for one to influence the other and vice versa. As described by González-Sánchez (2009), an increase in the education level of a country's inhabitants usually forms the basis for an improvement in economic growth and, in the long term, a country's development, while this economic development provides greater resources for education. This potential virtuous circle between education and economy means that access to education is not only a fundamental human right, but is also an essential element to achieving equal, sustainable economic and social development (UNESCO, 2006).

The population's literacy is maybe the basic pillar on which to consolidate a country's development. Over the last decade, significant progress has been made as regards literacy and education. Nevertheless, the geographical element is still an essential factor in whether a person has more or less probability of being illiterate. The other element that persists significantly as a discriminating factor in whether or not a person is illiterate is, unfortunately, gender. As can be seen in Table 1, the information provided by UNESCO shows significant differences in the possibility of a person being illiterate or not according to factors such as geographical area, sex or age.

In spite of the progress made over the two preceding decades, the literacy rate[4] observed at present in the world as a whole still cannot be considered acceptable. Despite having improved 4.2% globally per decade since 1993, the persistence of more than one in six illiterate persons of a mature age in the world makes it necessary to increase efforts in this field. By regions[5], Sub-Saharan Africa, South and West Asia and Arab States, in this order, are the areas of the world where efforts to increase literacy should concentrate most.

[4] For measurement purposes, UNESCO has long used the definition of literacy that relates to the ability to read and write, with understanding, a short simple statement related to one's daily life. A parallel definition, however, arose with UNESCO's introduction of the notion of functional literacy in 1978: a person is considered functionally literate if they can engage in activities, or effectively function, in his or her group and community. This definition also refers to the ability to continue to use reading, writing and calculation for personal and community development (UNESCO, 2008).

[5] The most recent statistics in the UNESCO (2014) do not offer information on North America and Western Europe. Nevertheless, as may be seen in González-Sánchez (2009), all references regarding literacy rate relating to this region stood at around around 99% in 2006.

Table 1. Adult and Youth Literacy Rate

	Total Adult / Youth			Male Adult / Youth			Female Adult / Youth		
	1993	2003	2013	1993	2003	2013	1993	2003	2013
WORLD	75.7 / 83.4	81.9 / 87.2	84.1 / 89.5	82.0 / 87.6	87.0 / 90.4	88.6 / 92.2	69.5 / 79.0	77.0 / 83.9	80.0 / 86.9
Arab States	55.2 / 74.2	67.5 / 83.4	76.9 / 89.9	67.9 / 83.1	77.8 / 88.8	84.7 / 93.2	41.9 / 64.8	56.5 / 77.8	68.4 / 86.5
Central and Eastern Europe	96.0 / 98.4	97.4 / 98.8	98.5 / 99.3	98.2 / 99.1	98.9 / 99.2	99.3 / 99.5	94.0 / 97.6	96.1 / 98.4	97.8 / 99.2
Central Asia	97.9 / 99.8	99.0 / 99.8	99.5 / 99.7	99.0 / 99.8	99.4 / 99.7	99.6 / 99.6	97.0 / 99.8	98.6 / 99.8	99.4 / 99.8
East Asia and the Pacific	82.0 / 94.7	91.5 / 98.0	94.7 / 98.9	89.1 / 96.8	95.1 / 98.3	96.9 / 98.9	74.8 / 92.6	88.0 / 97.7	92.5 / 98.8
Latin America and the Caribbean	85.8 / 93.1	89.7 / 96.3	91.5 / 97.1	87.1 / 92.8	90.6 / 95.9	92.2 / 96.8	84.5 / 93.4	89.0 / 96.7	90.9 / 97.3
North America and Western Europe	n.a.	n.a.	n.a.	n.a.	n.a.	n.a.	n.a.	n.a.	n.a.
South and West Asia	46.7 / 59.6	58.9 / 73.8	62.8 / 80.7	58.9 / 69.8	70.4 / 81.3	74.0 / 86.8	33.6 / 48.8	46.8 / 65.6	51.9 / 74.9
Sub-Saharan Africa	53.2 / 65.5	57.2 / 68.2	59.1 / 69.5	63.6 / 72.9	67.3 / 75.1	68.1 / 75.6	43.2 / 58.6	47.9 / 61.8	50.6 / 63.7

Source: Author's elaboration from information of UNESCO (2014).

However, although the differences follow a constant downward trend, what is most striking is the persistence of a higher probability of illiteracy among women. Even though some regions, such as, for example, the Arab States, have reduced the gap in literacy between men and women by almost ten percentage points in twenty years, in South and West Asia the rate of female literacy is still 22.1 percentage points below the male rate for the adult population above the age of 15.

The data on literacy relating to the young population, between the age of 15 and 24 years old, fortunately shows smaller disparities between men and women and with higher rates than in the case of the adult population. In some regions, like Latin America and the Caribbean and Central Asia, the literacy rate of young women is even higher than among men. This fact helps to explain in some way the greater economic strength in both regions over recent years and it contributes to support the idea of interdependence of educational and economic variables with mutual positive effects. The evolution of the literacy rate among the young population is certainly one of the factors that is contributing to change in the international economic scenario; though there remain differences that are hard to accept between men and women in areas where the female population shows the highest illiteracy rates: particularly Sub-Saharan Africa and South and West Asia.

In the specific case of Latin America and the Caribbean, literacy among the young population has traditionally shown high rates, above 90% for both sexes over the last two decades, and with a proportion of literate young women higher than that of men. This characteristic is not exclusive to this region, but it is where it has taken place every year at least since the decade of the 90s. It may therefore be said that, as regards the literacy rate among the youth population, Latin America is the region of the world where gender equality[10] was achieved longer ago and the data even favours women. The foundations for an egalitarian role of women in the economic progress of Latin America have been laid for the present and the future among the younger population. The individual reality of each country is another matter.

The indicator relating to the proportion of people who have fully completed secondary education represents a higher step as regards the use of education. This fact lets us compare the population's educational level, especially the young population, and the possibilities to access jobs of a certain qualification that could potentially generate more economic growth.

[10] For other areas such as the European Union, see González-Sánchez and De los Ríos Sastre (2010).

The data on young adults between 20 and 24 years old that have completed secondary education[11] in Latin America are shown in Figure 2; together with each country's level of economic development. In general, the data refers to the country as a whole[12]; although the differences between rural and urban areas are often considerable: for Latin America as a whole, there are 27.1 percentage points of young men and 29.1 points of young women more in urban areas who have completed secondary education compared with rural areas.

In keeping with the abovementioned higher rate of literate women in the region, it may be seen that in Latin America as a whole, the proportion of women who complete secondary education is 6.1 percentage points above that of men. In fact, only in Bolivia, Guatemala and Peru is the proportion of young men who complete secondary studies higher than that of women. While in Uruguay, the Dominican Republic and Honduras, around a third more young women than young men complete secondary education. This average educational reality, for Latin American society as a whole, in some way shows its recent socio-economic evolution, which maybe the female population has better taken advantage of. What is certain is that women's preponderance as regards the reference in question is not new, but there is no doubt that while in 2005 the proportion of women who completed secondary education was 9.4% higher than that of men, the gap grew to 11.4% in 2012. This relative greater female qualification in secondary education contrasts with the lower rate of women in the Latin American labour market[13]. It may be said that this it is one of the limitations that the region has to take better advantage of the opportunities of future growth economic: to increase the presence of women in the labour market.

Figure 2 also shows significant important differences among countries and in relation to their degree of economic development. On one hand, in only a third of the countries do at least two out of every three young person's complete secondary education. In Chile and Peru, the proportion rises to four out of every five young persons with secondary studies. In another six countries, not even half the population finishes studies at this level.

[11] The data available for Bolivia, Chile and Paraguay is from 2011, the data available for Honduras is from 2010, the data available for Nicaragua is from 2009 and the data available for Guatemala is from 2006 (ECLAC-CEPAL, 2014).

[12] The data available for Argentina only shows the percentage of persons from 20 to 24 years old with completed secondary education in the urban geographic area (ECLAC-CEPAL, 2014).

[13] The proportion of men of working age who were employed in Latin America and the Caribbean as a whole was 75.1% in 2011, while the rate for women was 49.4% (ECLAC-CEPAL, 2014).

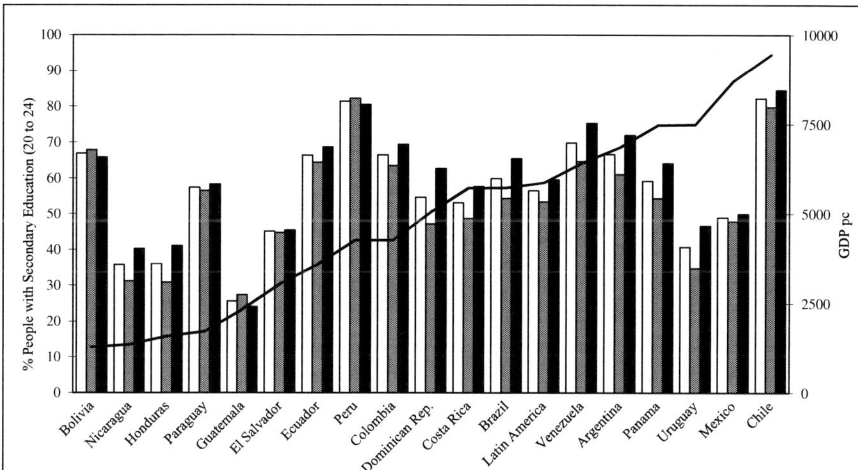

Source: Author's elaboration from information of ECLAC-CEPAL (2014).

Figure 2. Secondary Education vs. GDP pc - 2012.

In those countries, although there exist differences between sexes, not even half the men or women complete mid-level educational. Such low qualification, especially among the young population, becomes a handicap for exploiting the potentials of economic growth in these countries. Additionally, the link between a country's level of economic development, represented by gross domestic product per capita (GDP pc) and the proportion of young persons with completed secondary studies shows some apparent paradoxes such as the presence of Mexico and Uruguay in the top positions in the development index, while their rates of completed secondary education are below average; or such as the contrast that Bolivia is the fourth country in proportion of average completed studies.

4. ICT AND ECONOMIC GROWTH

Growth-generating economic activity is increasingly difficult to explain without the existence of ICT. The use of a country's technological potential to generate knowledge and to increase economic development has become a key factor in the present-day economy. The OECD (2001) noted that ICT had become a key factor in explaining a large part of the economic development achieved by some countries over the preceding decade.

Table 2. ICT in Latin America (per 100 inhabitants)

	Fixed telephone lines		Mobile-cellular telephone subscriptions		Fixed broadband subscriptions		Internet users	
	2001	2012	2001	2012	2001	2012	2001	2012
Argentina	21.8	23.5	18.1	151.9	0.3	10.9	9.8	55.8
Bolivia	6.0	8.4	9.0	90.4	0.0	1.1	2.1	34.2
Brazil	21.2	22.3	16.2	125.0	0.2	9.2	4.5	49.8
Chile	22.2	18.8	32.6	128.2	0.4	12.4	19.1	61.4
Colombia	18.2	13.0	8.1	102.9	0.0	8.2	2.9	49.0
Costa Rica	23.5	20.7	8.1	111.9	0.0	9.3	9.6	47.5
Cuba	5.1	10.8	0.1	14.9	0.0	0.0	1.1	25.6
Dominican Rep.	10.9	10.4	14.4	86.9	0.0	4.3	4.4	45.0
Ecuador	10.5	14.9	6.7	106.2	0.0	5.3	2.7	35.1
El Salvador	10.9	16.8	14.3	137.3	0.0	3.8	1.5	25.5
Guatemala	6.6	11.6	10.0	137.8	0.0	1.8	1.7	16.0
Haiti	0.9	0.5	1.0	59.9	0.0	n.a.	0.3	9.8
Honduras	4.9	7.7	3.7	92.9	0.0	0.8	1.4	18.1
Mexico	13.1	16.7	20.7	83.4	0.0	10.5	7.0	38.4
Nicaragua	3.0	5.0	3.8	86.1	0.0	1.6	1.4	13.5
Panama	12.3	16.8	15.2	178.0	0.2	7.8	7.3	45.2
Paraguay	5.3	6.1	21.1	101.6	0.0	1.2	1.1	27.1
Peru	6.0	11.4	6.8	98.0	0.1	4.7	7.6	38.2
Uruguay	28.6	29.8	15.6	147.1	0.0	16.6	11.1	55.1
Venezuela	10.9	25.5	26.0	101.9	0.0	6.7	4.6	44.0
World	16.9	16.9	15.7	91.2	0.6	9.0	8.0	35.7

Source: Author's elaboration from information of ITU (2013).

Over a decade later, ICT is now an everday tool in economic activity and society. However, despite being a very important component of modern economy, as described by González-Sánchez (2009), whether or not a country has a basic technological infrastructure establishes fundamental differences among economies and conditions a country's potential to develop. Accordingly, although by themselves they do not guarantee economic prosperity, greater access to and use of ICT by a country's inhabitants can create a powerful stimulus for fostering economic growth and strengthening economic development.

By themselves, ICT do not solve the economic problems that the countries of Latin America may have, although they can encourage and stimulate the economy. In any event, the evolution of technological indicators has logically been different in each country. Table 2 shows the information provided by the International Telecommunication Union (ITU, 2013) referring to countries in the region and, for the purposes of comparison, the world average. Basic ICT infrastructure is shown in the first double column with data referring to the indicator for fixed telephone lines per inhabitant. The fact that the world average has remained almost the same over a period of more than ten years reflects the fact that, in many countries of the world, this indicator has dropped as a consequence of the boom in cellular telephony. In any event, this indicator has only dropped in five of the twenty countries considered, as the fixed telephony infrastructure in Latin America is below the world average in almost three quarters of the countries. Bearing in mind the geographical difficulties of establishing this infrastructure, as well as its cost, it is possible that some countries abandon it before strengthening it against the development of cheaper, more competitive cellular technology.

The increase in mobile-cellular subscriptions in Latin America has been, as may be seen in Table 2, greater than in the world as a whole. As pointed out above, this cellular telephony has come to occupy the space that fixed telephony had definitively obtained in the region as a whole. In 60% of the countries analysed, the number of mobile-cellular telephone subscriptions is higher than the number of inhabitants; while only Cuba and Haiti, especially the first, show low figures. Panama, Argentina and Uruguay lead this section; though all the countries have, to a greater or lesser extent, undergone a positive evolution between 2001 and 2012.

As regards the reference showing available technological capacity so that a country's inhabitants can take advantage of an Internet connection, Table 2 shows then data on fixed broadband subscriptions. This indicator represents a greater technical capacity to make connections to Internet[14], so its implementation came later. This explains the low values shown for most of the countries in 2001. In fact, in the world as a whole, no country even reached 10% of fixed broadband subscriptions in relation to its total number of inhabitants, and less than 6% of the countries considered surpassed this reference's percentage unit at the beginning of the first decade of this century. The evolution in Latin America has been positive over the period considered.

[14] The other indicator provided which in the past was given by the ITU to assess Internet connection capacity was fixed Internet subscriptions.

However, only six countries have improved above the world average, though a long way from the most-developed countries in this field, such as the European countries (see González-Sánchez, 2012). Regional leadership in quality Internet access corresponds to Uruguay and Chile, followed by Argentina and Mexico; it is not a coincidence that these four countries are in the top five from the point of view of economic development. The link between ICT and economic growth is clearly positive and this is also backed by the fact that Brazil, despite being the most-populated country in the region, has been multiplying its data in this indicator by four since 2001, while, at the same time, it has become one of the world's emerging economic powers.

Regarding Internet users, Latin America‘s generally positive evolution does not hide the existence of a technological gap between the region's countries. Leadership in Internet access corresponds Chile, Argentina and Uruguay, where more than half their population can do so regularly. This contrasts with other countries, like Guatemala, Nicaragua or Haiti, where less than one in five inhabitants was an Internet user in 2012. It is probably this reference that best shows the degree of practical use of the opportunities offered by ICT whether as a tool for work, commerce or leisure. Therefore, the indicator relating to Internet users probably explains better than others the inequalities among Latin American countries in the global field of ICT. Countries less advanced in the field of ICT should take advantage of the opportunities they offer to boost their development and economic growth. The appeal for investment and government policies in this respect should be a priority in the region.

On the basis of the above, there seems to be a positive link between ICT and economic development. Accordingly, the increase in economic growth as a direct or indirect consequence of a greater availability of ICT in a country fosters economic development in the medium term. Figure 3 shows this positive relationship between an ICT Indicator and GDP pc. The technological indicator summarises the four variables considered in this section[15] referenced to the average for every year. The world-wide average of the indicator in every year has been assigned the unit value, so the fact that a country shows a value higher than one means that it is above the world-wide average regarding the ICT Indicator and it will be below the world-wide average if the value is smaller than one.

[15] Fixed telephone lines, mobile-cellular telephone subscriptions, fixed broadband subscriptions and Internet Users.

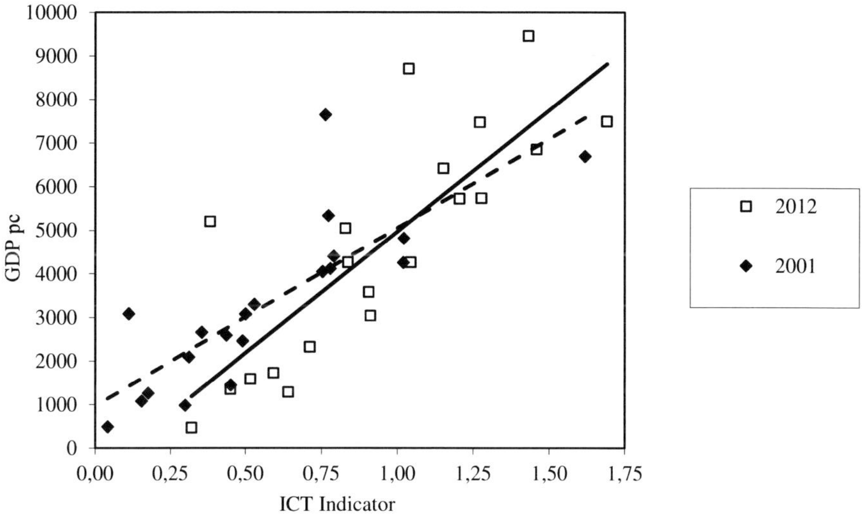

Source: Author's elaboration from information of ITU (2013).

Figure 3. GDP pc and ICT Indicator.

As is the case for other regions and the world as a whole[16], the relationship is positive both in 2001 and more recently. Nevertheless, over the years the slope has increased in gradient, growing more positive. That is, the link between the two references seems to be increasingly more consolidated and more direct. In fact, if we exclude from the analysis any country with an atypical performance from the point of view of ICT development, such as Cuba, the inclination of the slopes would be greater in both periods and they would be also be more representative. The apparent paradox of Cuba is that it increased its GDP pc significantly between 2001 and 2012, but its technological improvement has been much more moderate. While the increase in its average annual development was only lower than the increase seen by Panama and Peru, its ICT Indicator data is only better than the data for Haiti. This decoupled evolution between economy and ICT expansion could represent a major limitation to improving Cuba's economic growth.

Uruguay, Argentina and Chile lead the set of nine Latin American countries whose technological reference was above the world average in 2012. In fact, they were already the only three countries that surpassed the average world-wide reference at the beginning of the 21st century. Chile has lost the leadership it had at the beginning of the period, as the only country that has

[16] See González-Sánchez (2009 and 2012).

moved backwards with respect to the world-wide average during the period considered. This evolution is partly due to the relative saturation of Chile's technological sector as regards its population's needs and, partly, to the negative evolution of some technological indicators over the years, such as the 15.4% drop in fixed telephone lines in eleven years.

Though enjoying high levels of ICT does not sufficiently guarantee that a country's economy achieves full development, it seems that they increasingly represent a necessary factor to obtain and, what sometimes seems more difficult, to maintain an acceptable economic growth that leads to improvement in medium-term economic development. In any event, the absence of appropriate infrastructure and use can limit the economic potential of a country or region. This still seems to be one of Latin America's limitations and, at the same time, it could be an opportunity for future progress.

5. External Sector and Economic Development

A country's foreign sector is the gateway that channels trade: selling national goods and services and acquiring those produced in other economies; but it is also a major element for strengthening growth and development through GDP. The current account of the Balance of Payment registers, among other things, the exchange of goods and services with the foreign sector. Its balance therefore shows whether a country exports a greater value of goods and services than it imports and whether it has a trade surplus or, quite the opposite, a trade deficit. Accordingly, it may be seen whether the foreign trade of goods, services and finance contributes positively or negatively to a country's economic growth and, in the long term, to its development.

Table 3 shows the average current account balance during periods from 1990 to 2013. The data is expressed in relation to each country's GDP as from the original information in US dollars. As may be seen, the norm in the region as a whole and in the countries for there to be a current account deficit; that is, what is most frequent is that the value of imports is greater than the value of exports. Therefore, it may be said that the foreign trade sector's contribution to economic growth is usually negative.

In fact, if we look at the aggregate data for Latin America, we can see that only during the period 2005-2009 was a surplus balance obtained as a consequence of the balance achieved by seven countries, led by Venezuela and Bolivia. The best trade period in the region starts in 2003 following the end of the effects of the Argentinean crisis, with the first current-account surplus, according to data provided by ECLAC-CEPAL (2014), as from 1980, and shows its best period in 2006, with a regional surplus of more than 1.5% of GDP. As from then, Latin America has returned to the path of increasing and even worrying foreign trade deficit, representing a negative effect on economic growth.

Venezuela is the country whose foreign sector performed best over the whole period considered; only in 1992, 1993 and 1998 did it have a foreign trade deficit. The fact that it is a petrol exporter is without doubt thc most significant factor in obtaining a positive current-account result over every period analysed. Paraguay also mostly shows surplus balances and just one period (1995-1999) with an average deficit. Argentina, the end of the crisis at the outset of the century and the corresponding adjustment, gave it constant current-account surplus from 2002 up to 2009. Something similar happened in Bolivia, which has not had a negative current-account balance since 2003. Chile and Ecuador are the other countries that have taken most advantage of the region's best five-year period as regards the foreign sector.

Conversely, proportionally, the largest negative contribution of the foreign trade sector to economic growth comes mainly from countries such as Nicaragua and Honduras; additionally, Panama, the Dominican Rcpublic, Costa Rica and, more recently, Uruguay. These are often countries that, considering their relatively small size, mainly export basic products with lower added value and they need to import products whose price is higher. This imbalance in their terms of trade generates mismatches in their current accounts that lead to deficit. An improvement in terms of trade is another of the challenges that Latin America should address to improve its potential for future economic growth, and to achieve this it should endeavour to produce and export goods with greater added value.

Among the options available to Latin America in order to increase its production capacity and generate greater value added in exports lies in the arrival of Foreign Direct Investment (FDI) (González-Sánchez, 2014). In this respect, the region should endeavour to foster the entry of FDI to consolidate a gradual improvement in the current-account balances that had begun before the recent international financial crisis. In any event, the arrival of FDI can also be useful in financing part of the current-account deficits.

In Latin America as a whole, FDI began to expand at the same time as the end of the periods of hyperinflation and the implementation of stabilisation plans during the last decade of the 20th century. As may be seen in Table 4, the general trend over every period since 1990 is net entry of FDI into the region. Particularly as from the implementation of stabilisation plans such as the Real Plan in Brazil in 1994, which meant, among other things, the disappearance of hyperinflation from the country[17]. Since then, the region has seen net entries of FDI above 1% of GDP.

Latin America's condition as a net receiver of FDI can be verified by noting that only one country shows a period with a net outflow of investments: Venezuela. It could be said that this is a clear example of the negative effects of a certain political situation and legal uncertainty regarding such investments, whose result is the net negative balance of Venezuela in the period 2005-2009. It is not the only country with negative net investments for one year, but it is the one that shows direct foreign disinvestments for half a decade. The other two countries with at least two continuous years of net disinvestments are Haiti (1992-1993) and Peru (1991-1992).

Table 3. Latin America External Sector: Current Account (%GDP)

	1990-1994	1995-1999	2000-2004	2005-2009	2010-2013
Argentina	-2.7	-6.1	1.1	3.4	-0.7
Bolivia	-5.2	-6.3	-1.7	11.5	7.9
Brazil	-0.0	-3.6	-1.0	-0.4	-5.2
Chile	-.1.6	-2.6	-0.2	2.1	-2.7
Colombia	-0.3	-3.1	-0.5	-2.7	-5.5
Costa Rica	-3.7	-3.2	-4.4	-6.1	-7.8
Cuba	-2.9	-1.4	-0.9	0.3	n.a.
Dominican Rep.	-2.2	-1.1	-0.4	-5.2	-7.7
Ecuador	-2.0	-1.6	-1.0	2.7	-1.8
El Salvador	-1.6	-1.2	-2.9	-4.9	-6.0
Guatemala	-2.8	-3.5	-4.6	-3.9	-3.6
Haiti	-0.7	-1.5	-2.1	-3.0	-6.2
Honduras	-3.7	-2.6	-5.9	-8.1	-9.6
Mexico	-3.3	-1.2	-1.7	-1.3	-1.3
Nicaragua	-16.9	-17.1	-13.9	-15.0	-15.2
Panama	-0.8	-5.9	-3.7	-6.1	-15.4
Paraguay	0.7	-1.4	0.9	3.2	2.2
Peru	-4.3	-5.4	-1.4	0.1	-4.8
Uruguay	-0.6	-2.1	-0.9	-2.7	-7.9
Venezuela	1.4	2.0	7.9	13.2	7.4
Latin America	-1.6	-2.6	-0.7	0.2	-2.9

Source: Author's elaboration from information of ECLAC-CEPAL (2014).

[17] See González-Sánchez (2004).

From the outset of the 20th century, apart from Venezuela, only six countries, and for only one year, show net outflows of FDI: Paraguay (2004), Bolivia (2005), Brazil (2006), Colombia and El Salvador (2010) and Mexico[18] (2012).

The increase in FDI registered in Latin America also demonstrates an increase in the region's participation in global capital flows. It may be said that the region's economic growth and the high international prices of natural resources have contributed to sustaining the level reached in recent years by foreign investment in the region. Furthermore, as pointed out by ECLAC-CEPAL (2013), the historical figures regarding FDI received by Latin America took place in a context of international uncertainty, where world-wide flows of FDI showed signs of contraction. Accordingly, although the macroeconomic situation was unfavourable in the United States and the European Union, leading to a drop in global flows of investment, local contexts in Latin America were particularly favourable and attractive for international investors. The explanation for this lies partly in the fact that natural resources saw a prolonged period of high prices, particularly metals; meanwhile, the region's internal markets enjoyed several years of sustained growth and offered business opportunities for developing services (telecommunications, trade and financial services, among others).

In short, despite the recent crisis, though maybe also as a result of being an emerging region that acted as a refuge for FDI during the years of economic uncertainty in developed countries, Latin America received almost 3.5% of their GDP in net FDI between 2010 and 2013. Some countries, such as Panama (especially due to the channel enlargement works), and Uruguay, even managed to reach average and yearly figures in double digits over that time. At the same time, another seven countries obtained an average above 5%. This significantly important influx of investments to the region is undoubtedly an opportunity to consolidate future growth and development that should not be wasted. As mentioned in previous sections of this chapter, Latin America needs to improve its technological capacity and take advantage of its educational progress to face the challenges of economic growth and to combat inequality. In this respect, the arrival of FDI may be the key to changing the pace of the region and driving it towards development.

---

[18] Almost half of the fall of the FDI can be attributed to a specific operation: IPO of 25% stake in the subsidiary of Spain's Banco Santander, by 4.1 billion US dollars which ceased to be classified as FDI and went on to register in the balance of payments of the country as portfolio investment (ECLAC-CEPAL, 2013).

Table 4. Latin America External Sector: Foreign Direct Investment (%GDP)

	1990-1994	1995-1999	2000-2004	2005-2009	2010-2013
Argentina	1.9	5.2	2.3	2.2	3.5
Bolivia	1.3	9.2	5.6	2.4	8.4
Brazil	0.2	2.5	2.2	1.8	5.3
Chile	1.3	4.1	2.4	4.4	3.9
Colombia	0.7	1.9	1.5	3.8	3.7
Costa Rica	2.0	3.3	3.2	6.4	7.4
Cuba	n.a.	n.a.	n.a.	n.a.	n.a.
Dominican Rep.	1.0	2.4	3.0	4.4	5.2
Ecuador	1.0	2.0	1.6	1.0	0.9
El Salvador	0.1	1.9	1.8	3.6	0.8
Guatemala	0.5	1.0	1.1	2.0	3.1
Haiti	0.1	0.3	0.2	1.5	3.8
Honduras	0.8	1.7	4.5	6.8	8.3
Mexico	0.9	1.7	2.6	2.0	1.0
Nicaragua	0.5	4.0	3.8	5.8	9.6
Panama	2.1	6.9	4.5	9.5	12.1
Paraguay	1.5	2.2	0.5	1.3	3.6
Peru	1.6	3.8	2.0	4.8	7.6
Uruguay	0.3	1.0	1.9	7.4	10.5
Venezuela	0.4	2.2	1.4	-0.4	1.0
Latin America	0.7	2.5	2.3	2.3	3.5

Source: Author's elaboration from information of ECLAC-CEPAL (2014).

CONCLUSION

Latin America's positive economic performance over the decade following the Argentinean crisis at the outset of the 21st century is partly due to adjustments made previously, but also to the opportunities arising from the circumstances of the international environment. The region has been positively affected by the growing income of FDI with the two-fold intention of, on the one hand, taking advantage of the economic potential of certain countries and, on the other hand, investing in Latin America as a safe haven from the uncertainties in more developed regions. Likewise, the positive performance of the current account in the Balance of Payment, especially between 2003 and 2007, was a driving force and, at the same time, a reflection of the area's favourable economic evolution. Even despite the need to improve the added value of exportable goods and services. However, the challenges and opportunities that Latin America must address have not disappeared.

The public sectors' presence and capacity of influence in Latin America do not seem to have sufficient impact to positively affect economic progress. It is not so much a question of the public sector's size as its functionality. Thus, as mentioned by González-Sánchez (2014), in order for the countries of the region to have sustainable public accounts and to use them as a tool for economic policy, they should carry out a general reform of tax systems so as to increase their tax base, especially direct taxation, and to simultaneously improve the fairness of collection systems.

The potential of education to generate a virtuous circle along with the economy's evolution makes it a key element in fostering economic growth in Latin America. Although the situation of women in the field of gender equality is more than guaranteed among the region's youth, a challenge remains to extend favourable educational development to rural areas of most of Latin America. And to take advantage of the greater average education among women to foster their incorporation into the Latin American labour market and, as a result, boost regional economic growth.

In the field of ICT, its positive link with economic growth is clear in a Latin American context. However, a major technological gap exists between the regional leaders and the countries that have fallen most behind. Particularly regarding some indicators, such as the rate of Internet users, which best show the degree of practical use of the opportunities that ICT have as a tool for work, leisure and commerce. The region needs to foster investment in this technological sector, while encouraging government policies aimed at improving digital infrastructures and competences among the population as mechanisms for growth and development.

REFERENCES

Alesina, A. & Rodrik, D. (1994). Distribution policies and economic growth? *Quarterly Journal of Economics*. No. 109: 465–490.

Bertola, G. (1993). Factor shares and savings in endogenous growth? *American Economic Review*. No. 83: 1184–1198.

Bourguignon, F. & Verdier, T. (2000). Oligarchy, democracy, inequality, and growth. *Journal of Development Economics*. No. 62: 285–313.

Casilda Béjar, R. (2013). América Latina, una potencia emergente en el siglo XXI. *Boletín económico de ICE, Información Comercial Española*. No. 3039: 25-32.

ECLAC-CEPAL (2014). *Statistics and Indicators*. Chile: CEPALSTAT Databases and Statistical Publications.

ECLAC-CEPAL (2013). *Foreign Direct Investment in Latin America and the Caribbean 2012*. Chile: CEPAL - United Nations Publication.

González-Sánchez, V. M. (2014). Mercosur oder Pazifik-Allianz: konkurrierende Modelle lateinamerikanischer Integration. *GIGA Focus Lateinamerika*. No. 3/2014.

González-Sánchez, V. M. (2012). Information and communication technologies and entrepreneurial activity: drivers of economic growth in Europe. *The Service Industries Journal*. Vol. 33, No. 15, November: 1–11.

González-Sánchez, V. M. (2009). *Education and ICT: Key Factors to Improve the Development in the World*. In: Galindo Martín, M. A. & Nissan, E. (2009). *International Political Economy*. Hauppauge, NY: Nova Science Publishers.

González-Sánchez, V. M. (2004). *Convergencia económica en el Mercosur*. Madrid: UNED Ediciones.

González-Sánchez, V. M. & De los Ríos Sastre, S. (2010). Estrategia Europa 2020: mujer, educación y empleo, *CLM Economía*, 17: 231–261.

ITU (2013). *World Telecommunication / ICT Indicators Database 2013 (17th Edition)*. Geneva, Switzerland: International Telecommunication Union.

Nissan, E., Galindo Martín, M. Á. & Méndez Picazo, M. T. (2011). Relationship between organizations, institutions, entrepreneurship and economic growth process. *International Entrepreneurship and Management Journal*. No. 7: 311–324.

OECD (2001). *The New Economy: Beyond the Hype. The OECD Growth Project*. Paris, France: OECD Publications.

Perotti, R. (1993). Political equilibrium, income distribution and growth. *Review of Economic Studies*. No. 60: 755–776.

Persson, T. & Tabellini, G. (1994). Is inequality harmful for growth? *American Economic Review*. No. 84: 600–621.

Piketty, T. (1997). The dynamics of the wealth distribution and interest rates with credit rationing? *Review of Economic Studies*. No. 64(2): 173–189.

Saint-Paul, G. & Verdier, T. (1993). Education, democracy and growth. *Journal of Development Economics*. No. 42(2): 399–407.

UNESCO (2014). *The Official Source of Literacy Data*. Canada: UNESCO Institute for Statistics.

UNESCO (2008). *Global Education Digest 2008: Comparing Education Statistics Across the World*. Montreal, Canada: UNESCO Institute for Statistics.

UNESCO (2006). *Report of the Ministerial Round Table on Education for All: 33rd Session of the General Conference*. Paris, France: UNESCO Education Sector.

In: Economic Growth in the 21st Century
Editor: Cody Accosi
ISBN: 978-1-63321-589-4

Chapter 5

REGIONAL DEVELOPMENT STRATEGY, MARKET SEGMENTATION AND ECONOMIC GROWTH

Song Donglin, Fan Xin and Zhao Xinyu*
School of Economics, Jilin University, Jilin Changchun, China
Jilin University of Finance and Economics, China

ABSTRACT

In this paper, we adopt glacier model to measure the market segmentation index, and use the inter-provincial panel data from 1985 to 2011 to make an empirical analysis of the relationship between market segmentation and regional economic growth in the context of national regional development strategy. The results show that there will be a trend of consolidation in the domestic regional market, but the regional economic division is stronger than the geographic segmentation. At the same time, the relationship between market segmentation and regional economic growth does not follow a certain rule, and polices bring different gains in four areas with regional development strategy. Therefore, it is of great importance to correctly handle the relationship between government and market, break market segmentation, promote

* Author introduction: Song Donglin, Male, Doctor of Economics. Research Area: Regional Economics. Email: sdl3699@sohu.com; Fan Xin, Male, Doctor of Economics. Research Area: Regional Economics. Email:jlufx@126.com;Zhao Xinyu, Male, Doctor of Economics. Research Area: Development Economics. Email: xinyuchiu@163.com;

regional cooperation, and thoroughly implement national regional development strategy so as to speed up the regional market integration process in China.

Keywords: National regional development strategy; market segmentation; economic growth

1. INTRODUCTION

To uniform a domestic market is an important realistic issue for national comprehensive and deep reform. In the continuous process of marketization, central government has made several measures in hopes of realizing the flow of resources cross different regions, but the market control means of local government is diversified and invisible. As a result, gaming between central and local benefit, leads to complex influence on market consolidation. Currently, national economy is in a key stage of transformation development. To weaken local interventions and advance regional market integration are important means of releasing system dividend. Due to the different levels of regional economic development, different measures are adopted by local governments, which result in various effects of regional segmentation. In particular, since China has carried out the regional developing strategy[1] focusing on "the development of the western region, the invigoration of northeastern, the rise of central China and the eastern take the lead", are there new changes in different regions in China? Does the multi-pronged regional development policy take obvious effects? We pay close attention to these problems.

Market segmentation is one area to which scholars pay close attention. In the early stage, the early work is mainly centered on the measurement of domestic market segmentation and the analysis of tendency. Based on empirical analysis (Yong, 2000), adopting boundary effect (Poncet, 2002) and applying data envelopment analysis (Zheng Yusheng, 2003), some scholars pointed out that market segmentation in China is increasingly severe. However, the majority of scholars have amended the domestic market

[1] The Communist Party of China clearly stated our overall strategy for regional development for the first time in the fifth plenary session of the sixteenth CPC central committee: continue to promote the development of the western region, revitalizing the northeast old industrial bases, promote the rise of the central region and encourage the development of the eastern region. The division method of east, central, west and northeast is according to the Standards of National Bureau.

segmentation measurement. The empirical study concludes, despite of the segmentation phenomenon of regional market in China, the level of market segmentation is continuously decreasing. The methods they adopt mainly involve: Law of Trade (Naughton, 1999; Poncet, 2005), Business Cycle Mode (Xu, 2002), Research Questionnaires (Li Shantong, etc., 2004), Regional Professionalization Index (Bai Enzhong, 2004), Price Index (Gui Qihan, etc., 2006; Zhao Qiwei, etc., 2009). Besides, some analysis aiming at specific industries, such as rice market (Yu Wen, 1998), agriculture market (Huang Jikun, 2002), beer market (Li Ji, etc., 2004) and so on, also got the conclusion that market has demonstrate an integration trend.

Generally speaking, regional protection and degree of opening to the outside are major influential factors of market segmentation. Lin Yifeng, etc., (2004) pointed out that the reason that caused the market segmentation is the result of 'catching-up' strategy in some degrees. The strategic behavior of less developed areas is favorable to themselves in some certain conditions, but it results in the decrease of social output and loss of efficiency of resource allocation (Lu Ming, etc., 2004). The governmental region protection and market segmentation are motivated by material-interests of such act (Ping Xinqiao, 2004). Relevant financial decentralization policy intensified the degree of market segmentation. on the contrary, economic separation of power reduced the degree of market segmentation (Liu Xiaoyong, etc., 2008). In terms of the level of opening to the outside world, the degree of opening to the outside world and market segmentation appears non-linear relationship. When the economic opening level is lower, economic opening intensifies domestic market segmentation. But, if the economic opening is enlarging, the integration of domestic market will be promoted (Chen Min, etc., 2007), behind the robust growth of export trade, the distorted phenomenon of forcing enterprise to export is actually caused by severe domestic market segmentation (Zhu Xiwei, etc., 2005). On the non-government factors, channels for circulation and circulation organization have impact on the establishment of united market. the enlargement of circulation enterprises scale will probably intensify the market segmentation, especially the wholesale process.

In addition, in the aspect of the relationship between market segmentation and economic growth, scholars thought there are two types: "Inverted U" (Lu Ming, etc., 2009) and negative correlation (Liu Xiaoyong, 2009). In the research of transmission mechanism, taking China's entry to WTO as a time point, before entering WTO, market segmentation has increased economic growth by promoting the investment of fixed assets and slowing down government consumption proportion; while after entry to WTO, market segmentation hindered economic growth by slowing down economic opening to the outside and capital investment (Li Wenhao, 2013). At present, there is no final conclusion on the relationship between market segmentation and economic growth and no analysis of the relationship between market segmentation and regional economic growth in the context of regional development strategy.

Compared with previous research, the main contributions of this paper lie in the following three aspects: firstly, verify and amend the hypothesis premise of the market segmentation index and put forward predictable conclusions; secondly, investigate the relationship between market segmentation and economic growth in the regional level and find the variance of the relationship, even the existence of "Inverted U" ; thirdly, based on the regional development strategy background, investigating the changing conditions of market segmentation with regional economic growth in the adjacent periods of regional development strategy in different phrases and try to find out the inner mechanism.

The rest of the paper is as follows: in the second section, we examine the market segmentation index measurement hypothesis and amend the premise of the hypothesis and make use of calculated value to analyze the domestic regional market integration tendency; thirdly, we set the regression model of market segmentation and regional economic growth and make empirical analysis of the relationship on the whole; fourthly, from the perspective of quality and quantity, we investigate the relationship between market segmentation and economic growth in phrases and give further explanation of the relationship; fifthly, we make conclusion and relevant policy suggestions.

2. The Re-examination and Tendency Analysis of Market Segmentation Measurement Hypothesis

(I)The Re-examination of Market Segmentation Measurement Hypothesis

With respect to market segmentation measurement, there is difference on methods in domestic and abroad existing documents.[2] This paper makes use of

[2] The measuring methods of market segmentation mainly include production method, trade method, specialization index method, questionnaire method, the economic cycle method and price index method. Among them, the production method use the industrial structure data to analyze , whose data is easier to obtain , but lack representativeness ; the trade

price index method to calculate the degree of market segmentation and uses the research method of Paresley and Wei (1996, 2001a,2001b) and reflect the changes of market segmentation degree by the variation of comparable price. This method originated from glacier cost model (Samuelson, 1964), that is, due to the exist of path lose and other forms of exchange cost, the commodity value will thaw a part during the trade process, so even with entire arbitrage, there is no absolute equivalence of the commodity price of two places, relative commodity price will fluctuated in a certain section. Supposing in a certain time section, the comparable fluctuation of commodity become convergent day by day, which illustrated that the transaction cost is decreasing, that is, decreased market segmentation degree and vice versa. Scholars like Lu Ming, Chen Zhao (2006) and Fan Aijun (2007) and others also make use of price index method to measure regional market segmentation degree, its formulas are as follows:

$$\Delta Q_{ijt}^{k} = In(PI_{it}^{k}) - In(PI_{jt}^{k}) \quad (1)$$

$$\mathrm{Var}\,(q_{ijt}^{k}) = \mathrm{Var}\,(|\Delta Q_{ijt}^{k}| - |\overline{\Delta Q_{t}^{k}}|) \quad (2)$$

PI denotes commodity price index, i, j denotes different regions, k denotes k good, $\overline{\Delta Q_{t}^{k}}$ denotes t phase, Q denotes average value[3] of relative commodity price. It is to point out that this method contains two hypothesis premises:

Hypothesis 1: The chosen commodity is representative and reflects the whole price change tendency of the whole retail goods market.

method uses inter-provincial trade flows to measure it , although it can eliminate the problem of under-representation , it tends to be easily affected by other factors ; the specialization index method using output data from different industries in different regions to design the regional specialization index, although representative , is essentially different with the degree of market integration (Chen , 2007) ; the questionnaire method mainly come from self- investigation , is first-hand information , can be analyzed from different dimensions, but need a longer investigation period , higher expenses , and with inevitable subjectivity ;the economic cycle method has strong persuasiveness for the degree of market integration between countries , but it is related to many macroeconomic factors (including market segmentation , etc.) , so there is a certain degree of deviation ;the price index method has a data source which is easy and contains relatively rich information , but the provincial statistical data are not consistent and need to be effectively screened.

3 There are two ways to excluding the no- additive effects caused by the heterogeneity of goods: one is to eliminate the systematic bias brought by fixed effects associated with specific goods; another one is to do OLS regression on $|\Delta Q_{ijt}^{k}|$ to obtain its residuals (q_{ijt}^{k}). Wherein, $q_{ijt}^{k} = |\Delta Q_{ijt}^{k}| - |\overline{\Delta Q_{t}^{k}}|$, the effect of the two methods are equivalent.

In the current situation, the appearance of the hypothesis premise mainly lies in no published, uniform retail goods price index. Of course, based on the homogeneity of commodity in different regions, diversity and otherness of retail commodity types and so on, it is hard to seek unity of talking. From empirical analysis, difficulty in reality has forced scholars to adopt reasonable merchandised categories to combine categories in hope of achieving the goal of measuring the whole retail goods market price. Scholars basically adopt 7~9 kinds of retail goods(Lu Ming, Chen Zhao etc. adopted 9 kinds of goods to evaluate, Fan Ai jun and other scholars adopted 7 kinds of goods[4]) to calculate, which has unanimous conclusion from integrating domestic market, but there is still big difference of the amplitude. Here, we will continue to adopt 9 kinds of commodities to calculate, and there are three main reasons: firstly, there is some differences in the classification of statistical yearbook, but some sole goods price index still have some inheritance and representativeness and have limited influence on results; secondly, even some goods are seasonal goods and are impressionable to transportation costs, but with scientific and technological progress, the convenience of traffic facility and lower costs, they has continuously broken the restrictions on space and time. Thirdly, considering the coverage of goods type, we use more goods as far as possible and making them more representative.

Hypothesis 2: in provincial trade, suppose one province set barriers to adjacent areas, and it will naturally set barriers to other provinces as well.

Based on the homogeneity of resource endowment, logistics industry shortened the distance and other factors which brought influence to governments. It is inappropriate to only consider the market segmentation of adjacent provinces. Out of the needs of local economy, in less developed regions, local government has stronger protectionism of local economy and protects local industry from outside impacts. With time passing by, government will realize that the directionality of industry is the mainstream of times, develop competitive industries and make efforts to propel industry chain to take shape across regions, which is beneficial for regional economy

[4] Lu Ming, Chen Zhao, etc., chose nine categories of good from the Retail Price Index by Category of every province , specifically including food, fresh vegetables, drink alcohol and tobacco, clothing and footwear, Chinese and Western medicines, books and magazines, cultural and sports goods, daily necessities and fuel . On this basis, Fan Aijun and some other scholars of the excluded cultural and sports goods as well as fresh vegetables. Their reason is that the cultural and sports goods' had split into cultural goods and Sporting Goods from 2003. as a result, the data was no longer consistence. And fresh vegetables are seriously limited by transport conditions and the distance, and can not reflect the price difference caused by market segmentation well.

development in long run. Specialized division and cooperation, as well as breaking regional limits can be considered as a bottleneck of local economy development.

Chart 1 reflects the ranking of relative price variance in different provinces from 1985 to 2011. Limited by the length of paper, we do not list one by one and list the first three and the last three ones. From the cross-section data of sole year, it is observed that ranking is quietly different in years. On the whole, adjacent provinces has smaller relative variance, that is, there is lower market segmentation degree of neighboring provinces, but there still exists huge economic cooperation space. It is clear that the construction of city circle enjoys closer location and city belt is in favor of realizing the rationalization of specialization of work and scale of economy. While, non-neighboring provinces, on one hand, shows high market segmentation degree of some provinces are partially caused by convergence of specialization of work and fierce competition of major elements; on the other hand, represents low market segmentation degree of many provinces, even though the distance is far or near, there is wide corporation space with the boost of transportation convenience. From the relative price variance of the year between 1985 and 2011, market segmentation mainly concentrates on the well-developed non-neighboring provinces, however, high market integration degree mainly concentrates among the coastal--inner land and well-developed--less developed regions. Above all, it is inappropriate to limit market segmentation to neighboring provinces. It is high priority among priorities to break regions definition, seek cross-region cooperation, realize the ordering of specification of work and rationalization of industry chain in future economy development.

On the data sources, this paper select nine kinds of goods in goods retail price categorizing index of different provinces from 1985 to 2011, including grain, fresh vegetable, liquor and tobacco, clothing, Chinese and Western medicines, books, magazines and newspapers, culture and sports goods, daily necessities and fuel.[5] Due to the loss of statistical data and the founding time of some provinces failed to cover the research time sequence, we get rid of Hainan, Chongqing and Tibet.

---

[5] From 1985 to 1993, we use the data of tobacco and tea, clothing, medicine and medical supplies, Cultural goods instead of that of alcoholic drinks and tobacco, clothing and footwear, Chinese and Western medicine, cultural and sports goods. From 2003 to 2011, lacking the data of fresh vegetables, Chinese and Western medicines, books and magazines, cultural and sports goods, we use that of vegetables, Chinese and western medicine and health care supplies, books and magazines and electronic magazines, cultural and office supplies instead.

Table 1. 1985-2011 variance rank of interprovincial relative price

Year/ Rank	First	Second	Third	Last third	Last second	Last
1985	Beijing- Henan	Henan- Xinjiang	Henan- Yunnan	Jiangsu- Ningxia	Zhejiang- Xinjiang	Tianjin-Fujian
1986	Shanghai- Guizhou	Shanghai- Yunnan	Guizhou- Ningxia	Shandong- Guangxi	Fujian- Guizhou	Fujian- Yunnan
1987	Henan- Guangdong	Tianjin- Guangdong	Liaoning- Guangdong	Neimenggu- Jilin	Zhejiang- Guizhou	Neimenggu- Anhui
1988	Shanghai- Guangdong	Tianjin- Guangdong	Guangdong- Qinghai	Neimenggu- Zhejiang	Henan- Yunnan	Henan- Qinghai
1989	Neimenggu- Shanghai	Hebei- Shanghai	Neimenggu- Anhui	Jilin- Guangdong	Guangdong- Yunnan	Yunnan- Gansu
1990	Guangdong- Ningxia	Hunan- Ningxia	Jiangxi- Ningxia	Hubei- Qinghai	Hebei- Shanxi*	Shanxi*- Neimenggu
1991	Fujian- Henan	Shanghai- Henan	Hebei- Shanghai	Jilin- Fujian	Shanxi**- Qinghai	Heilongjiang- Jiangsu
1992	Anhui- Guangdong	Anhui- Fujian	Hunan- Guangdong	Tianjin- Jilin	Liaoning- Guizhou	Hebei- Liaoning
1993	Guangdong- Shanxi**	Zhejiang- Shanxi**	Hebei- Zhejiang	Liaoning- Jiangxi	Shanxi*- Shandong	Shangdong- Shanxi**
1994	Yunnan- Xinjiang	Ningxia- Xinjiang	Beijing- Xinjiang	Anhui- Henan	Liaoning- Anhui	Liaoning- Ningxia
1995	Beijing- Hunan	Neimenggu- Hunan	Beijing- Yunnan	Liaoning- Xinjiang	Heilongjiang- Xinjiang	Anhui- Shandong
1996	Henan- Hunan	Henan- Guangdong	Jiangsu- Hunan	Ningxia- Xinjiang	Jilin- Sichuan	Jilin-Hubei
1997	Beijing- Hunan	Beijing- Zhejiang	Beijing- Guangdong	Fujian- Hunan	Guangdong- Sichuan	Shandong- Sichuan

Year/ Rank	First	Second	Third	Last third	Last second	Last
1998	Shanghai- Guangxi	Jiangxi- Shanxi**	Shanxi*- Jiangxi	Guizhou- Qingghai	Shandong- Xinjiang	Heilongjiang- Sichuan
1999	Beijing- Henan	Beijing- Hubei	Beijing- Xinjiang	Jiangsu- Shandong	Jiangsu- Yunnan	Jiangxi- Jiangsu
2000	Beijing- Guangxi	Beijing- Hubei	Beijing- Ningxia	Hunan- Guangxi	Hebei- Jiangsu	Guangdong- Guangxi
2001	Tianjin- Sichuan	Tianjin- Ningxia	Tianjin- Hunan	Hebei- Jiangsu	Guangxi- Qinghai	Hunan- Yunnan
2002	Zhejiang- Xinjiang	Anhui- Xinjiang	Hubei- Xinjiang	Jiangsu- Shandong	Hebei-Neimenggu	Hunan- Qinghai
2003	Beijing- Fujian	Beijing- Shanghai	Beijing- Xinjiang	FUjiang- Jiangxi	Jianhxi- Ningxia	Jilin- Zhejiang
2004	Anhui- Yunnan	Jiangxi- Yunnan	Shanxi*- Yunnan	Shanxi**- Gansu	Jilin- Guangxi	Hubei- Guangxi
2005	Hunan- Yunnan	Hubei- Yunnan	Jiangxi- Yunnan	Zhejiang- Guizhou	Hebei- Heilongjiang	Liaoning- Henan
2006	Shanghai- Gansu	Shanghai- Xinjiang	Yunnan- Gansu	Guangdong- Sichuan	Shanxi*- Shandong	Zhejiang- Hunan
2007	Heilongjiang- Yunnan	Heilongjiang- Shandong	Shanghai- Gansu	Shanxi**- Ningxia	Jilin- Hubei	Jilin- Zhejiang
2008	Jilin- Guangxi	Liaoning- Guangxi	Shandong- Guangxi	Shanxi*- Hubei	Shanghai- Anhui	Henan- Sichuan
2009	Guangdong- Sichuan	Guangdong- Gansu	Guangdong- Yunnan	Shanxi*- Gansu	Hubei- Xinjiang	Hubei- Shanxi**
2010	Neimenggu- Hunan	Neimenggu- Gansu	Guangxi- Gansu	Hubei- Guangxi	Liaoning- Xinjiang	Jiangsu- Gansu
2011	Tianjin- Guizhou	Liaoning- Guizhou	Tianjin- Hunan	Neimenggu- Jiangxi	Sichuan- Xinjiang	Zhejiang- Gansu
1985-2011	Shanghai- Huangdong	Hebei- Shanghai	Tianjin- Guangdong	Jilin- Jiangsu	Jiangsu- Anhui	Liaoning- Jiangsu

Table 2. regional rank of provincial market segmentation index

Area		Overall average	Regional rank	Phase I average	Regional rank	Phase II average	Regional rank
Western region	Neimenggu	0.001369	1	0.002151	1	0.000526	9
	Guangxi	0.001303	5	0.001819	5	0.000747	2
	Sichuan	0.001092	7	0.001524	9	0.000628	4
	Guizhou	0.001083	9	0.001583	7	0.000544	8
	Yunnan	0.001328	3	0.001730	6	0.000896	1
	Shanxi**	0.001203	6	0.001846	4	0.000511	10
	Gansu	0.001055	10	0.001490	10	0.000586	5
	Qinghai	0.00107	8	0.001548	8	0.000556	6
	Ningxia	0.001361	2	0.002118	2	0.000546	7
	Xinjiang	0.001309	4	0.001898	3	0.000675	3
Northeast	Liaoning	0.001043	3	0.001300	3	0.000529	1
	Jilin	0.001071	2	0.001350	2	0.000514	3
	Heilongjiang	0.001125	1	0.001431	1	0.000515	2
Central region	Shanxi*	0.001103	4	0.001366	4	0.000480	4
	Anhui	0.001183	3	0.001446	3	0.000558	3
	Jiangxi	0.001099	5	0.001271	5	0.000690	1
	Henan	0.001388	1	0.001797	1	0.000419	6
	Hubei	0.001018	6	0.001267	6	0.000428	5
	Hunan	0.001313	2	0.001600	2	0.000632	2
Eastern region	Beijing	0.001886	1	0.002397	1	0.000425	5
	Tianjin	0.001612	4	0.001957	4	0.000626	1
	Hebei	0.001253	6	0.001566	6	0.000358	9
	Shanghai	0.001878	2	0.002333	2	0.000577	2
	Jiangsu	0.001069	8	0.001270	8	0.000495	4
	Zhejiang	0.001235	7	0.001531	7	0.000386	8
	Fujian	0.001484	5	0.001862	5	0.000404	7
	Shandong	0.001009	9	0.001218	9	0.000412	6
	Guangdong	0.001833	3	0.002294	3	0.000516	3

The data of this section originates from *Chinese Statistical Yearbook* from 1986 to 2012 and statistical yearbook of different provinces.

(II) Trend Analysis of Market Integration on Regional Level

Based on the above results, we combine the relative price index of different regions to get the market segmentation index of each province in different years, so that we can describe the market segmentation degree of every province, region and even the whole country better.

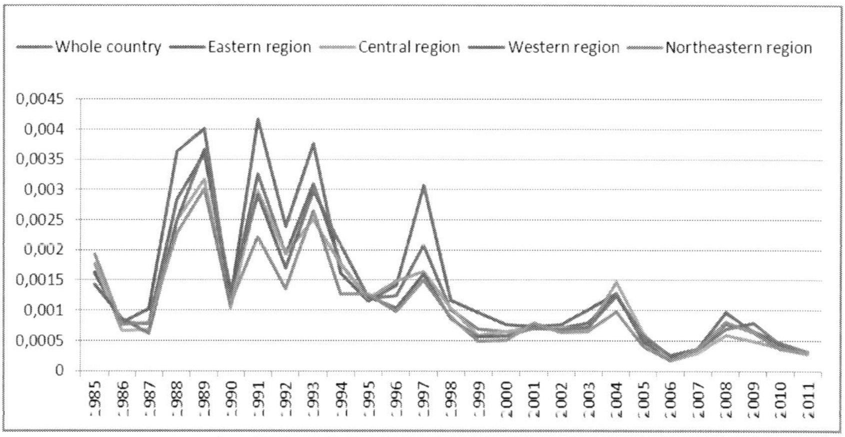

Chart 1. Domestic commodity market segmentation (1985-2011).

From Chart 1, we know that, from the year of 1985 to the year of 2011, even though there are a few big fluctuations in whole market, the integration trend of market on the whole is in line with former research conclusions. For the regional level, the overall trend of four regions on the time sequence is almost the same as that of the whole nation, but amplitude is different. The Northeastern region has the smallest market segmentation degree, for two reasons: first, the northeastern region has intimacy on geography, regional culture is prone to identify with; secondly, the level of economic development is a significant range. There is well-developed region and less-developed region, which are apt to achieve complimentary. Such actions will lower the intervention from government to cross region transactions. However, the Eastern region has the highest market segmentation degree, which is probably because almost all eastern regions are the developed region, the resources are relatively severe and regional overlapping construction is quiet serious. So, government may take administrative measures to intervene for protecting the development of local industry. From 27 years regional average value, the average value of market segmentation in northeastern region is the smallest which is lower than the nationwide average level; the average value of market segmentation in eastern region is the biggest, which is the only region higher than the average level(0.001278) in nationwide.

Chart 2 reflects the regional ranking condition of every province market segmentation index. On the whole, we analyze the figure of every province market segmentation index and find out that there are similarities of market integration degree and obvious difference.[1]From the perspective of regional development strategy, we take phase analysis to find that compared with the former stage of developing strategy of different regions, market segmentation degree in the phase of regional develop strategy decreases by a large margin, eastern region has the largest drop while northeastern region has the smallest drop.[2] From the provinces in different regions, there are different drops.

The reasons of the above phenomenon are surely caused by many aspects. The main reason is: first, the release of policy bonus under regional developing strategy; second, the implementation of reform measures of city circle and city group [3]which break up the administrative barrier within regions and between regions; third, the varied effect of self-policy of different regions.

---

[1] The results show that the provincial markets have a basically same trend of consolidation with the whole domestic market. However, the magnitude of changes in the various provinces is different, and not synchronized in time. Limited by the space of this paper, we will not give a list.

[2] Statistical data shows that before the Western Development , the western region had an average market segmentation index of 0.001771, and during the Western Development period it droped to 0.000621, with decrease of 0.00115; Northeast China had an average segmentation index of 0.00136 before the Northeast China Revitalization, while turned to 0.000519 during the revitalization period, with a decrease of 0.000841;the average index value of the central region reached to 0.001458 before the Rise of Central China, during that period was 0.000534, with a decrease of 0.000924;the eastern region's was 0.001825 before the Eastern New Leap, droped to 0.000467duringthat period ,with a decrease of 0.001358.

[3] In June 2005, the Shanghai Pudong New Area was approved, focusing on the transformation of government functions, exploring and improving the socialist market economic system; In April 2006, the Tianjin Binhai New Area is approved to explore a new model of urban development and improve the lead role on the regional economy; In June 2007, the Chengyu Comprehensive Reform Experimental Zone is approved, exploring ways to change the urban-rural dual economic structure, promoting the coordinated development of urban- rural economy and the society ;In December 2007, the government approved the Wuhan city circle and Changsha, Zhuzhou, Xiangtan (CZT) city group as a national resource-saving and environment-friendly society comprehensive reform pilot areas, promoting economic and social development and the coordinated development of population, resource and environment ;In May 2009, Shenzhen became comprehensive reform spot; In April 2010, the Shenyang Economic Zone National New Industrial Comprehensive Reform Pilot Area was approved; In December 2010, Shanxi province established a national resource-based economy incomprehensive reform pilot area; In March 2011, the State Council approved the implementation of the " Overall Program of

Based on the above analysis, we made the following predictable conclusion: first, with the gradual improvement of market system, market segmentation and regional economy growth show stage characteristics and four regions have different features. Market segmentation isn't always the disadvantage of regional economy growth, market segmentation in rational sections will probably promote the regional economy growth; second, the means of market segmentation have diversification, elusion characteristics. The market segmentation based on regional developing strategy is tending to be reasonable and promote regional economy growth.

3. Market Segmentation and Regional Economic Growth

Based on the economic growth model used by Barro (2000) in his empirical analysis, we add other factors such as market segmentation and the square of market segmentation to build the following regression model:

$$y_t^i = a_0 + a_1 Semg_t^i + a_2 Semg2_t^i + a_3 X_t^i + a_4 LGM_{t-1}^i + \varepsilon_t^i \quad (3)$$

y represents the growth rate of per capita GRP, $Semg$ represents market segmentation, $Semg2$ represents the square of market segmentation, X is a consolidated variable, LGM values the logarithm number of per capita GRP, i represents each corresponding province sectional units, t represents the year, a_0 is a constant vector, a_1、a_2、a_3、a_4 of the coefficient vector, ε is a stochastic disturbance term..

About the selection of the dependent variables indicator. The existing studies have focused on nominal GDP, per capita GDP, per capita real GDP, real per capita GDP growth and other indicators. Considering the great differences in the economic development level of China's various provinces, absolute indicators are not suitable for horizontal comparison between the provinces, so we use a relative indicator- per capita GRP growth rate.

About the selection of the explanatory variables. First, we need to focus on the significance of the coefficients of market segmentation index-Semg, and its square term, in order to determine its effect and shape. X represents the

Yiwu Comprehensive Reform of International Trade" etc.. All of these are conducive to the elimination of administrative barriers and weaken the market segmentation's intervention on the local economy.

consolidated variable, which includes physical capital, human capital, technological innovation, the opening degree and its squared term, government protection, the proportion of state-owned economy and so on. We select the proportion of total fixed assets investment accounted for GRP to measure physical capita; human capital using the average years of schooling;[4] technological innovation using the average number of granted patents out of per million patent applications; degree of openness using the proportion of total import and export trade accounted for GRP as a measure, this indicator along with its squared term mainly determines its shape and significance to verify its effect; government protection using the proportion of non- public financial expenditure accounted for GRP to describe, and the calculation process excluded science and education spending, which have the nature of public goods; the proportion of state-owned economy using the proportion of employment of state-owned enterprises accounted for that of the total economy to measure.

In this part, the data for empirical analysis excludes Hong Kong, Macau and Taiwan. The data also excludes Tibet, due to its difficulty of obtaining data. Chongqing, Hainan were also excluded because of the missing timing data. Considering the availability, we collect data from 1985. We studied four regions, whose panel data set from 1985 to 2011, including 756 sample observations section. Data is from the "China Statistical Yearbook", "New China 60 Years Statistical Information" and Statistical Yearbooks of China's various provinces.

Here, we take the four regional data from 1985 to 2011 as the research object, using the panel generalized least squares (Pooled EGLS) estimate, to examine the relationship between market segmentation and regional economic growth in different regions (see Table 3). According to the regression results of the four regions, we can find some common law: physical capital, technological innovation and regional economic growth, a significant positive correlation, indicating that increased investment in physical capital, promoted technological innovation are conducive to regional economic growth; the degree of openness and regional economic growth has an "Inverted U-shaped"

[4] In calculating the average years of education, we divided the levels of education into the following categories: under primary, primary, secondary (including middle and high school), college degree and above. Respectively, we select 0, 6, 10.5 (junior high school 9 years, senior middle school 12 years) and 16years of education to represent each level. As the "China Statistical Yearbook" has different degrees of refinement on statistical classification, we used the average years of education of junior and senior middle school,10.5=(9+12)/2, as the result for those situations in which the earlier data did not distinguish between the junior and senior high school.

relationship, which indicates the opening of economy is not always visible to promote regional economic growth. Excessive opening may inhibit the formation of domestic brands, which is not conducive to the growth of the regional economy; local protectionism and regional economic growth has a significant negative correlation, indicating that there are still financial expenditures spending toward irrationality in four regions, in urgent need of further optimization. Besides, various regions have its own development characteristics, as follows:

(1) Analysis of the western region as a whole (Table 3, model I). Judging from the coefficients of the control variables about the western region, at the 1% level, the coefficient of market segmentation index is significantly positive, but its squared term coefficient is significantly negative, indicating that the market segmentation and regional economic growth has an "inverted U type "relationship, which indicates that once it leaped over the threshold, market segmentation will not be conducive to regional economic growth. Human capital is significantly positively correlated with regional economic growth, indicating the talent advantages began to play an important role in the western region, but also to some extent reflecting the western region's advantage in gathering talents under the Western Development Strategy; The proportion of state-owned economy and regional economic growth has an significantly positive correlation at the 1% level, indicating that improving the proportion of employees of state-owned enterprises in the western region will stimulate the regional economic growth. Judging from the value of the coefficients, the opening degree has the strongest effect on the regional economic growth, followed by the proportion of state-owned economy, market segmentation and physical capital. So, in the western region, the government's handling of the economy is still in the traditional mode phase, we should remain opening as a baseline, strengthen the construction of state-owned enterprises, control the degree of market segmentation, and increase physical capital investment such as the construction of infrastructure. This is still the focus of the government's work.

(2) Analysis of the Northeast region as a whole (Table 3, model II). We can see from the empirical results of the northeast region, that market segmentation had not a significant effect on regional economic growth, which is different from other regions. The effect of human capital was not significant too, this may because the northeastern region didn't have a talent advantage as well as the attractiveness to top talent, and the "Southeastern Talent" phenomenon still exists. The relationship between the proportion of state-owned economy and regional economic growth is insignificant, indicating that

in the northeast old industrial base, state-owned enterprises play a very important role in the regional economy, and its uncertainty of reform results caused the non-significant effect. In terms of the value of the coefficients, the degree of opening takes the strongest effect on regional economic growth, followed by physical capital. Evidently, in the northeast region, the source of economic growth power lies in the further promotion of opening, increasing the amount of physical capital investment and the upgrading of state-owned enterprises.

Table 3. The FGLS regression results in four regions

Variables	Model I (Western region)	Model II (Northeast)	Model III (Central region)	Model IV (Eastern region)
Segm	0.3876***	-0.2081	0.6035***	0.2179***
	(5.2112)	(-0.6006)	(2.9847)	(2.7608)
Segm2	-0.3912***	0.4554	-1.3236**	-0.1461*
	(-4.6556)	(0.5034)	(-2.6016)	(-1.8759)
KC	0.3363***	0.2223***	0.2795***	0.3956***
	(5.7356)	(4.0603)	(4.9831)	(6.799)
HR	0.0136**	0.0032	0.0244***	0.0136***
	(2.3702)	(0.402)	(4.1412)	(3.0301)
TI	0.0195*	0.0233*	0.0572***	0.0049***
	(1.8405)	(1.8952)	(6.5659)	(2.8843)
IN	0.6613**	0.7851***	2.6366***	0.0434#
	(2.3299)	(3.0039)	(3.2592)	(1.4864)
IN2	-0.692	-1.3076***	-5.2681	-0.014*
	(-0.7468)	(-2.7727)	(-1.2906)	(-1.7022)
FE	-0.1934*	-0.9804***	-1.9999***	-1.6725***
	(-1.6631)	(-2.8519)	(-5.687)	(-4.6321)
NE	0.5404***	0.1132	-0.2187#	0.3199***
	(3.4982)	(0.441)	(-1.3924)	(3.3912)
LGM	-0.1138***	-0.1076***	-0.1093***	-0.1238***
	(-5.9081)	(-3.5283)	(-5.133)	(-6.3727)
C	0.0154	0.4117***	0.3393***	0.3032***
	(-0.179)	(2.9303)	(4.1934)	(4.0078)
Obs	270	81	162	243
R^2	0.4766	0.2692	0.665	0.4252
Model form	Cross-section fixed effect, No time effect	Cross-section fixed effect, Random time effect	Cross-section fixed effect, No time effect	Cross-section fixed effect, No time effect

Note: The values in parentheses are t values, #, *, **, *** represent the 15%, 10%,5% and 1% significance level.

(3) Analysis of the central region as a whole (Table 3, model III). From the control variable coefficients, we see that the market segmentation index has a significantly positive coefficient at the 1% level, while its squared term has a significantly negative coefficient at the 5% level, indicating that the market segmentation and regional economic growth was "Inverted U ", which indicates the market segmentation has a phased impact on regional economic growth. In the central region, before the threshold value, market segmentation is conducive to the protection of local economic development; while after the threshold value, market segmentation is not conducive to the free movement of production factors, so having an adverse impact on economic growth. The proportion of state-owned economy and regional economic growth has a negative correlation at 1% level, indicating the presence of redundant workers in state-owned enterprises were not to promote regional economic growth. Judging from the value of the coefficients, the opening of economy had the strongest effect on regional economic growth, followed by market segmentation and physical capital, and finally technological innovation. So, in the central region, the focus should still be on opening-up, controlling the degree of market segmentation and promoting physical capital investments are the wings. At the meantime, we should not ignore the effects of technology innovation. Obviously, the government has begun to gradually shift to innovative model for the economic growth. Physical capital investments especially infrastructure investments are of most importance. Besides, technology innovation also can not be ignored.

(4) Analysis of the eastern region as a whole (Table 3, Model IV). From each control variable coefficient about the eastern region, we can see that the market segmentation index has a significantly positive coefficient at the 1% level, its squared term has an significantly negative coefficient at the 10% level, indicating that the market segmentation and regional economic growth were "Inverted U ", almost the same shape with the central region and the western region. Between the proportion of state-owned economy and regional economic growth was a significantly positive relationship at the 1% level, indicating that in the east, the state-owned enterprise with a local government background is still the object of the government's regulation and control, despite of the rising standards of the private economy. Judging from the values of the coefficients, physical capital has the strongest effect on regional economic growth, followed by market segmentation and the proportion of state-owned economy. So in the east, we should attach great importance to physical capital, and market segmentation has remained for a long time. State-owned economy still plays an important role in the economic growth, and the

status of opening began to fall, the quality of foreign investment began to get attention.

4. Market Segmentation and Regional Economic Growth: The Impact of Regional Development Strategies

The relationship between market segmentation and China's regional economic growth is not strictly consistent, in some regions it's an "inverted U-shaped" relationship, in some other regions there was no significant relationship. Therefore, considering the basic characteristics of imbalance of China's regional economic development and the difference extent of economic protection in different regions, this paper will divide the time intervals according to the time when the overall strategy for regional development was introduced, and make an empirical analysis of the relationship between market segmentation and regional development under the adjustments of economic development strategies. According to the national policy introduction time, the western, northeast, central and eastern regions will respectively take 1999, 2003, 2004, 2005 as the dividing line, to make a two-stage analysis (summarized in Table 4).

First, we have a phased analysis of the western region (Table 4 model V and model VI). The conclusion shows that before the Western Development, market segmentation has a negative effect on regional economic growth, but turned positive during the western developing period. So market segmentation is not necessarily negative to regional economy growth, it can be conductive to regional economic growth within a reasonable range. Physical capital had no significant impacts on the western economic growth, either before or after the Western Development. This can be due to the efficiency of capital using and desynchronized capital investment with the economic growth, despite of the large amount of investment in physical capital in the western region. The contribution rate of human capital increases slightly and later becomes significant, as an effect of the Western Development Policy, but the ability of gathering talents still need to be strengthened in the western region. The coefficient of technological innovation is significant at the beginning, and then it becomes insignificant, because of the low level of investment in research during the late period of Western Development and the lack of capacity to transform science and technology into productivity.

Table 4. The results of the phased FGLS regression in the four regions

Variables	Western		North eastern		Central		Eastern	
	Model V	Model VI	Model VII	Model VIII	Model IX	Model X	Model XI	Model XII
segm	-0.0656^{**}	$0.1451^{\#}$	-0.0811	0.4318^{*}	0.0248	0.3094^{***}	0.1063^{***}	-0.2515^{*}
	(-2.3756)	(1.6213)	(-1.1094)	(1.8214)	(0.4276)	(5.3847)	(3.5715)	(-1.794)
KC	-0.0395	-0.0563	0.4617^{***}	0.3324^{***}	0.2962^{***}	0.1143^{**}	0.6592^{***}	$0.1802^{\#}$
	(-0.4358)	(-0.9097)	(3.042)	(3.7373)	(3.205)	(2.2359)	(8.5903)	(1.6173)
HR	0.0176	0.0196^{**}	0.0143^{**}	-0.1192^{***}	0.0273^{***}	-0.0007	0.0134^{**}	-0.0058
	(0.9291)	(2.6138)	(2.3284)	(-3.5499)	(3.6956)	(-0.0942)	(2.5483)	(-0.747)
TI	$0.1202^{\#}$	-0.0045	0.1792^{***}	-0.0334	0.1731^{**}	0.027^{***}	0.0274^{***}	0.0039^{***}
	(1.6236)	(-0.5242)	(5.1955)	(-1.2187)	(2.1266)	(4.0095)	(4.8103)	(2.8564)
IN	-2.5644^{***}	1.043^{***}	0.9531^{***}	1.3936^{*}	2.73^{**}	1.1714	-0.0147	0.061
	(-4.1306)	(3.398)	(2.8245)	(2.0688)	(2.2476)	(1.1174)	(0.3116)	(0.7844)
IN2	9.592^{***}	-2.3394^{**}	-1.9916^{**}	-1.6436	-7.2459	-1.7961	0.007	-0.0299
	(3.3333)	(-2.1857)	(-2.5631)	(-1.4449)	(-1.0294)	(-0.417)	(0.5741)	(-0.5706)
FE	$0.3285^{\#}$	-0.0135	-2.597^{***}	-0.8981	-3.6889^{***}	-0.1915	-2.6243^{***}	3.2909^{***}
	(1.5795)	(-1.0729)	(-6.8669)	(-0.9797)	(-8.1102)	(-0.4974)	(-6.5567)	(2.8733)
NE	-0.2414^{*}	0.29^{*}	0.3185	1.3629^{**}	-0.1552	-0.1054	$0.2911^{\#}$	0.5062^{***}
	(-0.9717)	(1.8422)	(1.0869)	(2.1497)	(-0.7228)	(-1.3464)	(1.5651)	(4.672)
LGM	-0.488^{***}	0.1978^{***}	-0.2801^{***}	-0.1166	-0.2037^{***}	-0.0748	-0.1686^{***}	-0.4731^{***}
	(-4.2439)	(4.9469)	(-8.0981)	(-0.9907)	(-6.449)	(-1.3511)	(-8.7144)	(-4.4635)
C	1.8092^{***}	-0.9415^{***}	0.8672^{***}	0.7863^{*}	0.7556^{***}	$0.3749^{\#}$	0.4661^{***}	1.6003^{***}
	(4.3651)	(-7.3282)	(4.7843)	(1.7568)	(5.482)	(1.6033)	(3.9895)	(4.4604)
Obs	140	130	54	27	114	48	180	63
R^2	0.8814	0.8383	0.6063	0.7446	0.721	0.9803	0.633	0.9622
Model form	Cross-section fixed effect, No time effect	Cross-section fixed effect, No time effect	Cross-section fixed effect, Random time effect	Cross-section fixed effect, Fixed time effect	Cross-section fixed effect, No time effect	Cross-section fixed effect, No time effect	Cross-section fixed effect, No time effect	Cross-section fixed effect, No time effect

Note: The values in parentheses are t values, #, *, **, *** represent 15%, 10%, 5% and 1% significance level.

The degree of openness had different effects before and after the West Development. Local protection was turning from significant to insignificant, probably due to the randomness in the direction of government's financial expenditure. The coefficient of the proportion of state-owned economy turn from negative to positive, indicating that in the western region, state-owned enterprises' quality has been improving, relative to its increasing number. Overall, before the Western Development, regional protection contributed the most to regional economic growth, followed by the scientific and technological innovation. During the Western Development period, the opening degree played a major role, the proportion of state-owned economy and market segmentation followed, and the human capital was last.

Secondly, we start to do some analysis of the Northeast region (Table 4 Models VII and Model VII). Before the 'Northeast China Revitalization 'policy, market segmentation coefficient is not significant, but after that, it becomes significant and positive, indicating the significant effect of northeast China revitalization policy. In the 'Northeast Revitalization' period, market segmentation is conducive to economic growth. Physical capital coefficient was significantly positive at the 1% level, and the coefficient value had a trend of becoming smaller, which may be due to the shift of the physical capital investment from emphasis on quantity to emphasis on quality. Human capital, technological innovation coefficients were all positive to negative. This may result from the existing regional development policy to some extent has not been highlighted, the talent advantage is not prominent, and the combination of learning, research with production, remained to be further enhanced. The opening degree has an "inverted U-shaped" relationship with regional economic growth, both before and after the Northeast Revitalization policy, consistent with the overall analysis. Local protection coefficient turns from negative value to insignificant, indicating that the local government is trying to achieve its own transformation of reducing intervention in the market to upgrade the regional economic level. The coefficient value of the proportion of the state-owned economy begins to become larger and significant, indicating that the revitalization of northeast China old industrial base strengthened the reform on state-owned enterprises and improved its operational efficiency. The overall analysis shows that before the Northeast Revitalization, opening degree contributed the most to regional economic growth, followed by the physical capital. During the revitalization period, the opening degree still played a major role in economic growth, the proportion of state-owned economy closely followed, and finally the market segmentation.

Thirdly, phased analysis of the central region (Table 4 model IX and Model X) .Later before the Central Rise period, the impact of market segmentation on regional economic growth had become increasingly significant and positive. With time going by, market segmentation had an increasingly evident effect of directly promoting the economic growth in the central region. This may be derived from the fact that the market segmentation degree in the central region was within the scope where the regional economy can bear, but may also be a means of diversification of market segmentation. It may also be a fake appearance as a result of the diversification and concealment of market segmentation means. The coefficient of physical capital becomes smaller. The reason may be that although the central region increased its infrastructure construction, the growth rate was significantly less than that in the former period. The coefficient value of human capital turns from positively significant to negatively insignificant. This partly results from the top talents' transportation to developed coastal areas. Although the Central China Rise Strategy has been proposed, the policy needs to be further implemented, and the positive effect remains to be seen. The coefficient of technology innovation is positive and turns smaller, related to the regional advantages of central region, which is conductive to factor mobility, and the factors of study, research and production still need to be further combined effectively. The opening degree had an "Inverted U" relationship with regional economic growth, both before and after the Central China Rise policy, consistent with the overall analysis. The coefficient of local protection is negative and has turned from significant to insignificant since the Central China Rise policy. Obviously, local protection in the central region was constantly weakened. The coefficient of state-owned economy proportion is not significant both before and after the Central China Rise policy, which is partly result from the reducing employment of state-owned enterprises in the transformation process, and job placement problems still exist. Overall, before the Central China Rise policy, the opening of economy made the greatest contribution to western economic growth, followed by physical capital and technological innovation. During the Central China Rise period, market segmentation played a major role in economic growth, followed by physical capital.

Finally, the phased analysis of the eastern region (Table 4 model XI and model XII). Before the New Eastern Leap policy, market segmentation has a positive impact on regional economic growth, then after it, its impact becomes negative, consistent with the overall analysis results. So, as time goes on, the direct impact of market segmentation on the eastern region's economic growth converted from promotion to inhibition. The contribution of physical capital to economic growth is significantly greater before the New Eastern Leap than that after it. Evidently, the economic growth mode relying on physical capital investment in the east began to be weakened. The human capital coefficient turned from positive to insignificant. Evidently, in the New Eastern Leap period, human capital began to gradually return back to other regions or liquidity of human capital was too strong, thus coming up the non-synchronization of human capital investments and economic growth. The coefficient value of technological innovation is positive and becoming smaller, from which we can conclude that even in the economically developed eastern regions, increasing efforts to scientific and technological innovation is of great use to economic growth. Seeing from the coefficients of opening degree and its squared term, the relationships between them and economic growth started to become insignificant, the specific impacts of opening up for the eastern region is uncertain now. The coefficient of local protection turns from negative to significantly positive, from which we conclude that in the New Eastern Leap period, the structure of financial expenditure had been becoming more and more reasonable, to promote eastern economic growth. The coefficient value of the proportion of state-owned economy was significant and became larger. We can conclude that during the economic development of the eastern region, state-owned enterprises still played a very important role. Overall, before the New Eastern Leap, physical capita had the greatest contribution to the eastern economic growth, followed by the proportion of state-owned economy and market segmentation. While during the New Eastern Leap time, local protection contributed most to the eastern economic growth, the proportion of state-owned economy and physical capital followed.

CONCLUSION AND POLICY RECOMMENDATIONS

Based on the 1985 - 2011 provincial panel data, the essay made an empirical analysis of the relationship between segmentation and regional economic growth in China's domestic market and studied the internal mechanism of how the relevant factors worked on the regional economic growth. The main conclusions are as follows:

(1) There is an increasing trend of consolidation in the domestic regional market, but there are still differences among regions. From the regional perspective, the northeast market has the highest consolidation degree, while the eastern market has the most serious segmentation, more serious than the

national average level; from the provincial perspective, the market also presents a consolidation trend and different provinces still vary.

(2)The relationship between market segmentation and regional economic growth is not a regular conclusion, and the effect of policy is different in four areas under the influence of national regional development strategy and difference of regional economic development level. Seeing from the overall of time, segmentation had no significant relationship with regional economic growth in the northeast market, while in the western region, central and eastern regions showed “inverted U-shaped” relationship. The phased analysis shows that the development strategy had made positive effects in the western, central and the northeast region, while the eastern market system needs to be further improved. As seen above, segmentation can be conducive to regional economic growth to some extent, and the key is how to handle the relationship between the government and market.

(3)Throughout all periods, market segmentation is no longer merely a geographical concept, the regional economic division is stronger than the geographic segmentation. Seeing from the ranking of relative price index of all the provinces over the years, the most of the province pairs with high degree of market segmentation are not comprised of neighboring provinces, but that with obvious economic characteristics. So the government should pay more attention to economic segmentation.

As can be seen from the above conclusions, the establishment of a unified domestic market system is a long and tortuous process, which can not be achieved overnight. To reduce the degree of market segmentation is an inevitable choice to meet the market demand, and how to eliminate non-inherent risk, weaken inherent risk and decrease it to a reasonable level is the focus. On promoting the rationalization of market segmentation to accelerate the formation of a unified regional and nationwide market system, we give the following suggestions: Firstly, correctly handle the relationship between the government and market. Currently, the government should clearly position itself and minimize the irrational intervention in market, making sure that both government and market function well; strengthen links between regions, to achieve inter-regional, cross-space cooperation. Things like traffic convenience make inter - regional cooperation possible. We should be concerned more about the rationalization of industrial chain and the specialization of labor division, promote the exchanges and cooperation between non-neighboring provinces; finally, to further optimize the results of implementing policies under the regional development strategies, minimize the negative effects of adverse factors, promote the further release of system advantage different angle and different level.

REFERENCES

[1] Young, A. "The Razor's Edge: Distributions and Incremental Reform in the People's Republic of China." *Quarterly Journal of Economics*, 2000, 115, pp. 1091-1136.

[2] Poncet, Sandra: "Chinese Market is Moving towards 'Non-Integration'? -- Comparative Analysis of Market Integration of China's Domestic Market and International Market" *World Economic Papers*, 2002, 1.

[3] Zheng Yusheng, Li Chonggao: "The Efficiency Loss of China's Regional Segmentation", *China Social Science*, 2003, 1.

[4] Naughton, B."How Much Can Regional Integration Do to Unify China's Markets" Conference for Research on Economic Development and Policy, Stanford University, 1999.

[5] Xu, Xinpeng. "Have the Chinese Province Become Integrated under Reform." *China Economic Review*, 2002, 13, pp.116-133.

[6] Li Shantong, Hou Yongzhi, Liu Yunzhong, and Chen Bo: "Investigation and Analysis of China's Domestic Local Protection", *Economic Research*, 2004, 11.

[7] Bai Chongen, Du YingJuan, Tao Zhigang, Tong YueTing: "Determinants and Trends of Local Protectionism and Industrial Regional Concentration", *Economic Research*, 2004 ,4.

[8] Gui Qihan, Chen Min, Lu Ming, Chen Zhao: "Whether China's Domestic Commodity Markets Tend to Segmentation or Consolidation: Based on the Analysis of the Relative Price Method", *World economy*, 2006,2.

[9] Zhao Qiwei, Xiong Xingmei: "Comparative Analysis of Segmentation of China's Three Major Market: Time Trends and Regional Differences", *World Economy*, 2009,4.

[10] Yu Wen Huang Jikun: "To See China's Grain Market Reform from the Rice Market's Integration", *Economic Research*, 1998,3.

[11] Huang Jikun, Scott Rozelle, Xie Yuping, Zhang Min: "Seeing the Impact of WTO Accession on China's Agriculture from the Agricultural Price Protection and Market Consolidation ", *Management World*, 2002,9.

[12] Li Jie, Sun Qunyan: "To See the Impact of WTO on Eliminating Local Protection from the Integration of Beer Market", *World Economy*, 2004, 2.

[13] Poncet, S., "A Fragmented China: Measure and Determinants of Chinese Domestic Market Disintegration", *Review of International Economics*, 2005, 13(3), 409-430.

[14] Lin Yifu, Liu Peilin: "Local Protection and Market Segmentation: a Survey from the Perspective of the Development Strategy", working paper of China's Economic Research Center in Peking University , No C2004015, 2004.

[15] Lu Ming, Chen Zhao, Yan Ji: "Increasing Returns, Development Strategy and Regional Economic Segmentation", *Economic Research*, 2004 1.

[16] Ping Xinqiao: "the Motivation and the Effect of Government Protection -- an Empirical Analysis", *Finance and Economy*, 2004 5.

[17] Liu Xiaoyong, Li Chen: "Empirical Research of Fiscal Decentralization and Regional Market Segmentation", *Financial Research*, 2008 2.

[18] Chen Min, Gui Qihan, Lu Ming, Chen Zhao: "How do China's Economic Growth Continue the Scale Effect ? -- An Empirical Study of Economic Opening and Domestic Commodity Market Segmentation", *Economics (Quarterly)*, 2007, 7(1) .

[19] Zhu Xiwei, Jin Xiangrong, Luo Deming: "China's Domestic Market Segmentation and Export Trade Expansion", *Economic Research*, 2005 12.

[20] Wang Xiaodong, Zhang Hao: "Non-Governmental Factors Analysis of China's Domestic Market Segmentation - Circulation channels, Organization and the Build a Unified Market System", *Finance and Economics*, 2012 11.

[21] Fan Aijun, Li Zhen, Liu Xiaoyong: "Empirical Analysis of Domestic Market Segmentation and Its Influencing Factors - Our Commodity Market For Instance", *Nankai Economic Studies*, 2007 5.

[22] Lu Ming, Chen Zhao: "Economic Growth of Segmentation Market - Why Economic Opening May Exacerbate Local Protection?", *Economic Research* , 2009 3.

[23] Liu Xiaoyong: "Will Market Segmentation Improve the Performance of the Local Economy?", *Shanxi Finance and Economics University* , 2010 10.

[24] Li Wenjie: "The Influence Path of Domestic Market Segmentation on Economic Growth", *Developmental and Research*, 2013 3.

[25] Parsley, David C. and Shang-Jin Wei, 1996, "Convergence to the Law of One Price without Trade Barriers or Currency Fluctuations", *Quarterly Journal of Economics*, 111, 1211-1236.

[26] Parsley, David C. and Shang-Jin Wei, 2001a, "Explaining the Border Effect: The Role of Exchange Rate Variability, Shipping Cost, and Geography", *Journal of International Economics*, 55, 1, 87-105.

[27] Parsley, David C. and Shang-Jin Wei, 2001b, "Limiting Currency Volatility to Stimulate Goods Market Integration: A Price Based Approach", NBER Working Paper 8468.

[28] Samuelson P., "Theoretical Note on Trade Problem", *Review of Economics and Statistics*, 1964, 46, 145- 164.

In: Economic Growth in the 21st Century
Editor: Cody Accosi
ISBN: 978-1-63321-589-4

Chapter 6

DOES ECONOMIC HISTORY REPEAT ITSELF? RELIGION, WORK ETHIC AND ECONOMIC GROWTH IN MODERN TURKEY

Jochen Hirschle [*]
Department of Sociology, University of Innsbruck, Austria

ABSTRACT

In this study I examine the recent economic boom in Turkey and its relationship with the resurge of Islam. The media have reported the proliferation of "Islamic Calvinism" in Turkey, which stresses pro-business values, the importance of work, and the acquisition of scientific knowledge as component of religious duties. Using Max Weber's study The Protestant Ethic and the Spirit of Capitalism as a theoretical background, I test for the impact of this religious development on work ethic values and economic attitudes. First, I take a closer look at the message of the neo-Sufi movement and its implantation into the economic and political context of modern Turkey. Second, I empirically study trends in economic output, religiosity, and economic values between 1990 and 2007. Analyses are conducted based on survey data from the World Value Survey. Results indicate that the neo-Sufi movement has revalued Turkish Islam in a pro-business direction. Empirically, I find that both religiosity and work ethic values significantly increased between 1990 and 2007. However, there is no

---

[*] Corresponding author: Email: Jochen.Hirschle@uibk.ac.at, Phone: +43 (0)512 507 7312.

empirical evidence of organic development of work ethic due to the values of Turkish Islam.

INTRODUCTION

The Turkish economy has developed at a breathtaking speed within the last decade, and has achieved an over 8% growth rate in 2010 while at the same time most European economies have stagnated or only scarcely developed (OECD, 2012). Although the country is still way below the OECD average in terms of gross domestic product (GDP), its recent economic boom has received attention from the media and researchers. This attention has been amplified since the economic trend was accompanied by the resurgence of Islam, and economic growth was created, in great part, by small and medium-sized family companies based in Anatolia rather than by large enterprises from Istanbul or Ankara (OECD, 2008, p. 24).

In a report entitled "Islamic Calvinism" published on behalf of the European Stability Initiative (ESI, 2005, p. 1), which was echoed in different media (BBC, Hürriyet, Sueddeutsche Zeitung, among others), these religious and economic trends were then interpreted as causally interrelated. Obviously, the intention was to draw a connection to Max Weber's seminal work on *The Protestant Ethic and the Spirit of Capitalism*. Weber interpreted the rise of capitalism in the Occident as a result of the development of rationality within the Judeo-Christian tradition and the emergence of the Protestant sects that defined material success as a sign for a state of grace (Weber, 1971). He argued that this cultural shift was central in motivating individuals to systematically and vigorously engage in secular activities, since "a man does not 'by nature' wish to earn more and more money, but simply to live as he is accustomed to live and to earn as much as is necessary for that purpose" (Weber, 1971, p. 60). This perspective also implied that the economic 'backwardness' of non-Christian countries – among them those in the Muslim world – was a result of a different cultural pathway; that is, it was a result of the fact that a positive cultural connection between material success, rationality, and religious values was never established (Davis & Robinson, 2006. p. 167). Even in Muslim countries, especially in Turkey, traditional Islam was (under the reign of Atatürk) interpreted as hindering the process of modernization. It was seen as not being culturally compatible with the value exigencies of modern economies (Yavuz, 2009, p. 38).

The ESI report, in contrast, argues that traditional Islam in Turkey has been reformed in a capitalist-friendly way and that it now "embraces hard work, entrepreneurship and development" (ESI, 2005, p. 2) as essential qualities. In a similar way, the BBC reported that "[a] new form of Turkish Islam is emerging (...), one which is pro-business and pro-free market" (Lodhi, 2006). Economic success in Turkey is, in this reading, not possible *despite*, but precisely *because* of the resurge of Islam. Islam has been successfully reconciled with economic modernity, and Turkey today is a shining example of how countries can both remain Muslim and act successfully in the global market economy.

The aim of this paper is to take a closer look at economic and religious developments in Turkey and its possible interrelations. In specifically, I aim to examine whether religion has contributed to evolve and spread a work ethic that initiated or fostered economic engagement. To achieve this aim we, in the first part, resume the basic premises of Max Weber's study on The Protestant Ethic and the Spirit of Capitalism. Weber's core ideas on the role of a religiously induced economic ethic for the rise of capitalism in the Occident serve as the theoretical background of this paper, and as a template that I use to decide whether the religious-economic process in Turkey takes a similar course. In the second part, I discuss the relevant literature and describe the basic political and religious trends in Turkey. Specifically, I take a closer look at the Fethullah Gülen community and the new Sufi movement to determine their contribution to reforming Islam from within. Moreover, I delineate the political influence of Turgut Özal (the Turkish prime minister between 1983 and 1989), as well as his relation to the religious movements and the neo-liberal structural reforms he enacted. In the third part, I empirically determine economic and religious trends and the development of work ethic values and economic attitudes. Moreover, I try to examine whether and in what way they are causally related. I thereby draw on official statistics and on representative survey data from the World Value Survey (1990, 1996, 2001, and 2007).

Theoretical Background: Religion and the Rise of Capitalism from the Perspective of Max Weber

In *The Protestant Ethic and the Spirit of Capitalism*, Max Weber determined the development of certain Protestant sects and their specific worldview as a central cause for the rise of capitalism (Weber, 1971 [1905]).

While Weber never wanted to provide an unidirectional cultural model (Collins, 1980, p. 925), he nevertheless emphasized the relevance of culture as an independent factor in the economic process (Trigilia, 2002, p. 56).

The aim of this section is not to discuss whether Weber's perspective was wrong, misunderstood, or oversimplified, but to outline some of his central arguments in order to be able to address them in the subsequent sections of the paper.

Basically, Weber's line of argument entails two separate components.

(1) First, Weber conceived of religion in general as developing along the "continuum of rationality-irrationality" (Berger, 1967, p. 59; Weber, 1966 [1922], p. 10). From this perspective, rational ways of thinking and acting have evolved within the religious sphere itself. The driving force behind this trend is the "problem of theodicy" (Weber, 1966, p. 139). It refers to the fact that religions have to interpret (adjust to) and live their core message in an "imperfect" world that permanently tends to threaten its contents (Weber, 1966, p. 139). While therefore the development of rationality is a universal trait of religion, the Judeo-Christian tradition had, at the end of the medieval ages, achieved a comparable high level of progress (Tenbruck, 1975, p. 690). From Weber's perspective, the reformation itself was a result of the increasing pressure of rationalization and the fact that it became more and more difficult for the religious followers to cognitively harmonize their rational worldview with the mystical and spiritual inventory that the Catholic cosmos entailed (Weber, 1966, p. 138; Berger, 1967, p. 111).

(2) The reformation and the development of the Protestant sects, however, brought a second important consequence. The Calvinists directly related the religious issue of salvation to the acquisition of material wealth within economic activities (Weber, 1971, p. 80). To be sure, from the perspective of the doctrine of predestination, the faith of an individual was predetermined and inevitable and could not be changed through individual deeds. However, economic success was seen as a sign for a state of grace of a person, and could therefore answer the pressing question, "Am I one of the elected?" (Weber, 1971, p. 110). As a consequence, individuals affiliated to Calvinism were highly motivated to engage in occupational life in order to receive an answer to this question. In this way the religious culture of the Calvinists created a situation in which it became 'rationale' to

seek profit for profits sake. Spending these profits for hedonistic purposes was not the aim of these efforts. In the contrary, it was inconsistent with religious ideas, since profits could be used to reinvest in further economic activities in order to gain more profit.

The combination of these two elements paved the way for a specific process to evolve: By giving "every-day worldly activity a religious significance" (Weber, 1971, p. 80) the Protestant sects provided a bridge for rationality to flow from the religious sphere – where it was encapsulated in the Catholic tradition – to the economic world (Weber, 1971, p. 181). From now on, individuals were not only highly motivated to make profit. Moreover, they were equipped with the cognitive tools, organizational principles and ascetic practices that enabled them to pursue this goal in the most efficient way.

According to Weber, this cultural model soon revealed to be economically extremely successful and began to force all traditional forms of economy out of the market (Weber, 1971, p. 55). This is true even if the religious ideas were only important as an initial spark for the system to start. With the institutionalization of the economic mode of production within the firm and the market, religion became more and more dispensable.[1] The capitalist economy had at this stage become an "immense cosmos" that was able to socialize its own value patterns and that was, by virtue of its systemic inescapability, able to force the individual "to conform to the capitalistic rules of action" (Weber, 1971, p. 54).

HISTORICAL BACKGROUND: SECULAR TURKEY AND THE RESURGE OF ISLAM

The Kemalist Years: The Failed Project of Secularization

In the 1920s, Turkey was in a stage of transition. Out of the ruins of the Ottoman Empire, Atatürk and the Kemalist elites who had taken over power from the Caliph, tried to form a new Turkish society. Role models were the western European countries that were revealed to be superior both in terms of

[1] I do not discuss, in this paper, the branch of secularization theory that has more or less directly developed out of the idea that capitalism denominates the final victory of rationality over mystical thinking and has therefore incrementally lead to a "secularization of consciousness" (Berger. 1967, p. 108; Hirschle, 2013).

military power and economic performance (Keyman, 2007, p. 220). It was the explicit aim of this project to create modern Turkey as a secular state and society, and therefore to control and downgrade the role of Islam (Yavuz, 2009, p. 25). Islam was then seen as the reason for this backwardness, as well as for the economic and military weaknesses of the Muslim countries in comparison to western industrial societies (Keyman, 2007, p. 220). To reach the goal of secularizing the country, Atatürk installed secular political institutions to exclude Islam from politics. Moreover, and because he knew that it was not possible to simply delete Islam from people's culture, he tried to control religious activities and education by installing an official state version of Islam (Yavuz, 2009, p. 23). Simultaneously, he banned other religious groups, especially the Sufi orders that had played an important political and economic role in the Ottoman Empire (Silverstein, 2008, p. 124). The aim of these measures was to promote a new Turkish national identity, and the Muslim religion was merely utilized in order to pursue this aim (Yavuz, 2009, p. 39).

This project remained, however, unfulfilled. While the Kemalist reforms were never rejected by the Turkish population as such, they were also never completely adopted by them (Silverstein, 2008, p. 120). The "crisis of secularism in Turkey," (Keyman, 2007, p. 223) which became obvious at least since the 1980s is therefore more complicated and involves different aspects.

A central one is related to the country's economy: despite the efforts to turn Turkey into an industrial society, the country was not economically able to close the gap between itself and the western European nations or the United States. Turkey was poor after World War II, and until today it has remained, in comparison to other OECD countries, underdeveloped. The country's GDP is low, over 60% of the working-age population has less than a high school education, and as of 2009 more than 20% of those who are employed are working in the agrarian sector (OECD, 2010, p. 115).

Against the background of these economic parameters, it is comprehensible that the cultural project of modernization has not been too successful: "Turkish secularism has been weak in creating a secular social ethos strong enough to achieve subjective secularization" (Keyman, 2007, p. 223). Life, lifestyle, and social mobility opportunities have, for the larger part of the Turkish population, hardly improved. As a consequence, traditional Islam has remained vital, particularly in the rural areas, but also in urban spaces where many of the new-arrivals live under poor conditions, and social integration and welfare support are organized via religious networks (Kaplan, 1994). Therefore and despite the prohibition of the Sufi orders, a number of them "have continued to function in a somewhat 'public secret' fashion" (Silverstein, 2008, p. 124).

After Turkey had attempted to invent a multi-party system in the 1950s, the claims and interests that had been fostered in these influential and widespread religious networks began to influence the political scene. It took a longer time until these movements were effectively able to shape the political agenda. Different parties, including the Democratic Party (closed in 1960), The Justice Party, and the Milli Nizam Partisi (closed in 1971 after a military coup) tried to articulate the interests of Muslim groups within the secular, Kemalist nation state (Yavuz, 2009, p. 49). They were, however, regularly banned or cut back by the military that protected the secular political institutions against infiltration from religious groups (Jenkins, 2003, p. 48f.). It was not until the military coup in the 1980s, and with the election of Turgut Özal as prime minister, did Islam officially return to the political scene and incrementally began to shape modern Turkey.

The Neo-Sufi Movement

In order to understand the specific economic developments in Turkey after 1980, it is necessary to take a closer look at the religious movement and their influence in shaping politics and the cultural values of the population. I do so by focusing on two actors in this process: *Fethullah Gülen* and *Turgut Özal.*

Fethullah Gülen is an Islamic scholar. Until the 1980s he was serving as a mosque preacher for the state-controlled "Directorate of Religious Affairs". During this time he managed to gain many followers and supporters. In 1999 he had to flee Turkey after being accused of undermining secularism. While he is virtually unknown in the West, he was, in a study of the Royal Islamic Strategic Studies Centre, classified as one of the top ten of the world's most influential Muslims in 2012 (Schleifer, 2012, p. 34). Moreover, his followers voted him the top intellectual in a poll conducted by the US newspaper *Foreign Policy* and the British newspaper *Prospect* in 2008 (Foreign Policy, 2008).

In Turkey he is both influential and controversial, acting between different frontiers. While secular Kemalists accuse him of trying to rebuild the Turkish nation according to the Shariah (Sharon-Krespin, 2009), radical Wahhabi Muslims accuse him of turning Islam away "from its God-given task of building a society in accord with the ideals of Qur'an and Sunnah" (Michel, 2005, p. 343). He sees himself as a moderate Muslim, trying to reconcile traditional Islam with modernity in the sense of Said Nursi (Michel, 2005, p. 345).

Sufism itself is conceived of as the mystical, spiritual-oriented part of Islam; it is "the quest for religious fulfillment and spiritual transcendence" (Lapidus, 1992, p. 15). Its roots go back to the very beginning of Islam and Mohammed is, in principle, regarded as the first Sufi. Despite this long tradition, Sufism is not (as Islam in comparison to Christianity in general) organized via top-down central organizations. A variety of Sufi orders exist that have developed different approaches. A common thread, however, is the "impulse toward asceticism" (Lapidus, 1992, p. 17), which in its extreme forms has led to the denial of all worldly pleasures: "Some ascetics chose the utmost isolation, poverty, and self-renunciation and cringed before the temptations of the world; they curbed the bodily desires and wept in yearning for the paradise to come" (Lapidus, 1992, p. 17). Therefore, from the beginning, Sufism has contained and fostered some of the ingredients that Max Weber determined to be crucial in the development of rationality within Christianity (Tenbruck, 1975, p. 670). In comparison to Christianity where the Protestant sects released the rational principles encapsulated within the religious sphere by adding religious value to secular activities (Weber, 1971, p. 80), the pathway of Islam is different. The straightforward (theologically motivated) development of an Islamic work ethic out of Sufism is not evident; however, recent developments in Turkey point in the direction that a specific (pro-entrepreneurial) interpretation of Islam became virulent in the course of the challenge of Islam by Western culture.

As described above, Islam in the 19th and 20th centuries was under pressure. One basic discussion in virtually all Muslim countries was whether the tradition of Islam itself was to blame for the subordinate role of Muslim countries in the world. A first reaction in many countries was to turn away from Islam. The reforms of Atatürk and the Kemalist elites was a radical, though typical, example for this stage of development. The solution was to get rid of traditional Islam (Jenkins, 2003, p. 45) and to emulate the economically successful model of western countries (Yavuz, 2009, p. 24).

While Islam had never disappeared in Turkey, it was mainly cultivated in the private sphere between 1925 and 1950 (Yavuz, 1999, p. 588). When it became obvious that the strategies of the Kemalists in building a Western industrial society were not successful (Gulay, 2007, p. 38), and Turkey moved to a multi-party political system, religious forces began to reappear on the political scene. This Islamic resurgence was, however, not simply a return to traditional Islam; it was also a reformation process.

One central argument throughout the Muslim world was that the weakness of Muslim countries did not result from Islam itself, but from the fact that Muslims had not followed and lived 'true' Islam. I argue that the neo-Sufi movement inspired by Said Nursi, and later by his follower Fethullah Gülen (Gülen, 2001), was both a typical but also a specific reaction to this challenge. The solution was radical in the sense that it was aiming at "live fully the message contained in the Qur'an and Sunnah" (Michel, 2005, p. 345). However, instead of breaking with Western modern principles and orientations, Nursi and Gülen tried to smoothly integrate them to establish Islam as "the middle way" (Gülen, 2001). This reimagined concept of Islam integrates three basic components:

(1) The development of (inner) *spiritual disciplines* and *asceticism* as one central aspect of traditional Sufism: "As a religion, Islam naturally emphasizes the spiritual realm. It takes the training of the ego as a basic principle. Asceticism, piety, kindness and sincerity are essential to it" (Gülen cited after Michel, 2005, p. 348).
(2) Emphasis on the individual person, on *individual freedom* (Gülen, 2007), and therefore on an individual's responsibility to interpret and live in accordance with Shariah from one's own values. Gülen explicitly turns against blindly following rules because "[t]hrough Sufism, the Muslim learns to move beyond obeying commands and regulations that he or she does not understand to an appreciation of Islamic teaching" (Michel, 2005,p. 348).
(3) And most important, a *practical sense of dealing with the secular world*. Sufism in the sense of Said Nursi and Fethullah Gülen does not aim at divorcing the individual from worldly life in order to engage in "useless metaphysical speculation" (Michel, 2005, p. 348; Yavuz, 2000, p. 7; Gulay, 2007, p. 49). However, in comparison to Said Nursi, who mainly engaged in sophistically interpreting Islam and trying to "raise religious consciousness" (Yavuz, 1999, p. 592), his follower Fethullah Gülen explicitly stressed the importance of secular activities as religious duties. First of all, he drew a connection between Islam and scientific education. He argued that "scientific activity is religious activity" (Yavuz, 1999, p. 591) because "[t]he main duty and purpose of human life is to seek understanding. The effort of doing so, known as education, is a perfecting process through which I earn, in the spiritual, intellectual, and physical dimensions of our beings, the rank appointed for us as the perfect pattern of

> creation" (Gülen, 1981). Second, Gülen explicitly tried to connect religious values with engagement in secular activities. He thereby mixes ingredients that scholars have associated with Max Weber's defining characteristics of the Protestant sects (Özdalga, 2000, p. 95). In fact, the concept of *responsibility*, which plays a central role in Gülen's interpretation, entails a version of the doctrine of predestination. Gülen not only argues that "there can be no promise of salvation" (Robinson, 2000, Gulay, 2007, p. 49), he also defines engagement in worldly activities as a religious duty: "In the face of uncertainty, the Muslim must be tireless in performing as many good deeds as possible" (Gulay, 2007, p. 49). This in effect means that he "is engaged without ceasing in particular activity, always asking 'Oh my Lord, what else can I do?'" (Robinson, 2000). To complete the analogy to the Protestant ethic – or more precisely, to Weber's interpretation of it – Gülen also stresses "the importance of good time management and well-planned activity" (Robinson, 2000, cf. also Özdalga, 2000, p. 95, Gulay, 2007, p. 50). Özdalga thus concludes that "Gülen's vision is based on an ethic that is inclined to constant work, whereby the individual works especially hard because any other way to salvation seems too uncertain and ambiguous" (Özdalga, 2000, p. 95).

There is good reason to doubt that Gülen's interpretation is a genuine theologically motivated cultural development. His concept of responsibility reads partly like an economically-driven reinterpretation of Islam in which the Weberian concepts of Calvinism have been deliberately utilized in order to model a business-adapted version of Islam. Gülen may on the one hand follow the course of Said Nursi by opening religion for education and scientific knowledge; on the other hand, it is uncertain whether his reading of Islam in a liberal capitalist manner is driven mainly by religious or secular (economic) motives.

Neo-Liberal Politics

In order to understand the cultural value trends within the religious sphere, it is necessary at this point to take a closer look at structural economic and political developments in Turkey and their interrelation with religion. These developments provided the concrete context necessary for religious ideas to flourish. Further, they also provided the setting for religion to become tuned in accordance with liberal economic principles and the developing profit motives (Gulay, 2007, p. 46).

In the 1980s the Turkish political agenda was shaped by *Turgut Özal*. He was born in Anatolia and was raised in a conservative religious family closely associated with the Nakşibendi Sufi order (Yavuz, 2003, p. 75). He studied at the Istanbul Technical University, held managerial positions in the private sector, and spent two years at the World Bank (Öniş, 2004, p. 115) before he became Deputy Prime Minister for Economic Affairs after the military coup in 1980. He was then involved in the formation of the Motherland Party (ANAP), and in 1983 was elected prime minister of Turkey. His time of ruling was characterized by two main topics: (i) he changed the role of Islam within the former Kemalist secular state (Yavuz, 2003, p. 75), and (ii) he initiated a political-economic transformation in a neo-liberal, antibureaucratic direction (Öniş, 2004, p. 113).

Özal was both religious but was also explicitly using his involvement in Sufi-related religious networks in order to establish his career. His display of a religious lifestyle – his pilgrimage to Mecca during his term of presidency, and the introduction of official "break the fast" dinners during Ramadan (Yavuz, 2003, p. 75) – increased his popularity among the middle and lower classes.[2] Beyond reincorporating religious symbols into politics, Özal contributed to the revival of Islam by adopting measures to renew religious education. While he was breaking with the secular tradition of Atatürk, he strengthened the national identity by flavoring it with religious values, thereby shaping "a modern Islamic political identity" (Yavuz, 2003, p. 81).

The Turkish economy was in poor shape when Özal became prime minister. The military coup in the 1980s was partly a reaction to the social unrest that arose due to the economic conditions within the country. The state-oriented and state-supported economy as arranged by Atatürk had not achieved its intended objectives. By 1977, the government needed to implement an International Monetary Fund (IMF) adjustment program. While Özal was religiously conservative, he had been pursuing a neo-liberal strategy since the beginning. He closely cooperated with the IMF in order to implement the structural reforms needed to liberalize the market. In his term of office, he "reduced state intervention, alleviated payment difficulties, liberalized domestic pricing, and rationalized the public sector;" moreover, he freed

[2] These classes had hardly improved from the secular reform process of Kemalism. The Turkish society was therefore divided into two groups: a small secular elite and a larger proportion of traditional Islam-oriented groups that Özal was able to attract.

prices, removed agricultural and other state subsidies, and banned trade unions (Yavuz, 2003, p. 87).

This mixture of conservative religious values and neo-liberal economic ideas, which is rather untypical for Muslim countries (Davis & Robinson, 2006), was, among others, a result of the strong entanglement of the religious and economic sphere. The religious movement of Fethullah Gülen was largely economically supported by small or medium-sized companies based in Anatolia. These companies had been virtually excluded from the Kemalist's efforts to create a modern economy because the large industrial companies were developed with the intention of playing a key role in the modernization process. In comparison, smaller rural companies were perceived as representing the cultural backwardness of the country in terms of both production technologies and the religious orientation of their management and workers. By radically implementing the adjustment program of the IMF, Özal therefore supported his own supporters: the petite bourgeoisie consisting of "peddlers, dealers, small constructors, restaurant owners, small industrialists, textile factory owners, and food processors" (Yavuz, 2003, p. 89). Individuals working in this sector had never previously benefited from state interventions, and now they saw an opportunity to gain influence, achieve status, and earn profits (Gulay, 2007, p.39).

This outline reveals that the connection between economic growth and the specific interpretation of Islamic religion by the neo-Sufi movement is more difficult, especially given that the 'material' side of the development and the religious 'values' are hardly separable. The Fethullah Gülen movement was theologically active, and it was generally aimed at constructing "its own modernity with its own available means" (Yavuz, 1999, p. 592). Therefore, it very practically instituted the infrastructures that were necessary to do so. The Gülen community established a broad network of educational facilities, business corporations, and even an Islamic bank (Baskan, 2004); and they used modern media (daily newspapers, magazines, TV channels, and radio stations) to spread their message (Gulay, 2007, p. 45). This structural context of "co-optation" made it difficult for the religious movement to remain ethically independent from the economic sphere (Peifer, 2012, p. 24). The development of pro-entrepreneurial religious values was therefore a possible measure to reduce the tensions between both spheres.

Against this background, the all too obvious similarities between Gülen's "theology of action" (Gulay, 2007, p. 51) and the Protestant ethic – the idea of salvation through worldly activity, and the rational ascetic principles that should be applied in these activities (Özdalga, 2000, p. 95) – can be readily interpreted as attempts to shape Islam in accordance with the economic interests of a certain social class. Since Weber's thesis was well known among scholars in Turkey (ESI, 2005, p. 24), the Calvinist metaphor has, it seems, been utilized in order to enact a specific economic philosophy – or to speak with Marx, in order to provide the cultural superstructure for the material interests of the Anatolian bourgeoisie. The idea that the neo-Sufi movement has shaped a new entrepreneurial mentality by reforming Islam from within, thereby creating economic success, is hardly realistic. Instead, one must assume that the economic success of Anatolian companies, their growing influence within the political and religious movement, and the liberal reforms of Özal have contributed to the incremental readjustment of Islam in the direction of a pro-entrepreneurial religion.

The last part of the story highlights the usage and explicit rearrangement of Islam for economic purposes. This becomes obvious when a member of the Islam-affiliated *Independent Industrialists and Businessmen's Association* (MÜSİAD) explains that, "[t]he rise of Anatolian capitalists is due to their Protestant work ethic. No personal waste, no speculation, reinvest your profits." (ESI, 2005, p. 24).

EMPIRICAL ANALYSES: DEVELOPMENT OF ECONOMY, RELIGION, AND WORK ETHIC

In the previous section, I briefly outlined the resurgence of Islam, liberal political reforms and economic trends, and their interrelations based on information obtained from other studies and the literature. The aim of this section is to empirically trace these changes and developments. Moreover, I examine the question of whether there are any empirical hints indicating that religiosity was causally involved in creating a work ethic in the sense of Weber.

Using indicators and representative survey data, in this part I *first* take a closer look at the development of GDP and its causes, the development of religiosity among the Turkish population, and changes in work-related cultural values and attitudes. *Second*, I examine whether a substantial positive relationship between individual religiosity and work ethic values can be determined.

Operationalization and Data

In order to pursue the above delineated research goals, I have to operationalize four distinct theoretical concepts: economic prosperity, individual religiosity, work ethic values, and economic attitudes.

(1) I operationalize *economic prosperity* using the standard indicator of GDP per capita (in purchasing power standards) from the Organization for Economic Co-operation and Development (OECD, 2012).
To empirically treat the concepts of religiosity, work ethic and economic attitudes, I draw on World Value Survey (WVS) data from 1990, 1996, 2001, and 2007:
(2) The concept of *religiosity* is measured using three variables: self-assessment as a religious person,[3] importance of religion in life,[4] and importance of God in life[5]. Since these variables were measured on different scales in the WVS, I first standardize the individual items and then aggregate the items using a religiosity index.[6]
(3) To study *work ethic*, I use a selection from the WVS's inventory aimed at investigating "important child qualities." This selection is comprised of two child quality items that are closely associated with economic behavior (cf. Miller et al., 2002): "hard work," and "determination, perseverance."[7] Moreover, I use a variable to measure the importance of work in life.[8] Again, and due to the fact that these

---

[3] Respondents were asked whether they conceived of themselves as "a religious person," "not a religious person," or "a convinced atheist." In the analyses, I created a dichotomous variable in which "a religious person" receives the value of "1" and all other answers were given a value of "0."

[4] Importance of religion in life was surveyed on a 4-point-scale with categories including "very important," "rather important," "not very important," and "not at all important."

[5] This question was surveyed on a 10-point-scale with 1="not at all important" and 10="very important."

[6] I do not study the impact of religious practice (Mosque attendance) on work ethics. This is because from a Weberian perspective, religious attendance, as the community part of religion, should not promote an individually-oriented work ethic. In accordance with this hypothesis Barro and McCleary (2003) have shown that religious practice is negatively rather than positively associated with economic growth.

[7] Respondents were asked to choose a maximum of five important items from a list of eleven items. The other items included "good manners," "thrift, saving money," "independence," "feeling of responsibility," "imagination," "tolerance and respect for other people," "religious faith," "unselfishness," and "obedience."

[8] Importance of work in life was surveyed on a 4-point-scale with categories including "very important," "rather important," "not very important," and "not at all important."

variables were measured on different scales, values are standardized before aggregating them to a work ethic index.

(4) The index of *economic attitudes* aims at measuring whether respondents prefer an individual-entrepreneurial idea of economic performance, or whether they prefer a state or community-oriented economy model (Davis & Robinson, 2006, p. 168, p. 177). I use two questions available from the WVS to assess individual orientation: "Private ownership of business should be increased vs. government ownership of business should be increased," and "People should take more responsibility to provide for themselves vs. the government should take more responsibility to ensure that everyone is provided for." Respondents were requested to vote for one of the models described in each statement on a ten-point-scale. I recode these variables such that high values indicate an individualistic economic attitude; next, I aggregate the single items and standardize the resulting index.

Economic Development

Figure 1 provides an overview of the development of GDP (per capita in purchasing power standards) in Turkey between 1980 and 2010. The left graph indicates that GDP has increased in a stepwise manner since 1980, but this pattern was regularly interrupted by short periods of stagnation or even downtrends. A more significant upward trend is apparent between 2001 and 2007, in which the Turkish economy substantially grew from 9,053 US$ to 12,441 US$. The decrease in 2008 was due to the international financial crisis and not to endogenous factors, as was the case in many European countries. This is supported by the fact that the pre-crisis growth slope reappeared after 2009, with yearly growth rates of more than 8% between 2009 and 2011.

The right graph compares the Turkish GDP and average GDP development for all 34 OECD countries. The Turkish economy still falls significantly below the OECD average in all years depicted, and has only recently (between 2000 and 2010) began to catch up. Even in 2010, with a GDP of around 12,500 US$ per capita, Turkey was the poorest OECD country, followed by Mexico (13,000 US$) and Poland (17,300 US$).

Nevertheless, economic growth in the 2000s was impressive. The 2006 OECD economic outlook reported that "[o]ver the 2002-05 period, output increased by a third, representing the strongest pace of growth among OECD countries" (OECD, 2006, p. 11). What were the causes for this economic boost? The main accelerators of the Turkish economy were medium-sized companies, most of them being "highly entrepreneurial family businesses of first generation" located in both urban and rural areas (OECD, 2008, p. 24). These businesses contributed to nearly 50% of the country's export share by producing textiles, clothing, and medium-technology goods. Up to 800,000 new jobs were created in the manufacturing industry between 2000 and 2008; however, most of these jobs were created in the informal sector, while during the same time period, the number of formal sector jobs was declining (OECD, 2008, p. 24).[9]

Development of Religiosity, Work Ethic and Economic Attitudes

Before examining the developments of religious and economic values in Turkey, it should be noted that virtually all Turks are Muslims. In 1996 and 2001 (for which information from the WVS is available) more than 97% of respondents stated that they belong to a religious denomination, of which another 99% (for both years) categorize themselves as Muslims. Moreover, all investigated religiosity items receive high approval rates, while non-religious individuals are rare. For all surveyed years, more than 75% assessed themselves to be "a religious person," an average of 74% stated that they are "very religious", with a mean value on the "importance of God" indicator of 9.1 (surveyed on a 10-point scale for which 10 indicates "very important").

Figure 2 provides an overview of the development of individual religiosity, work ethic, and economic attitudes between 1990 and 2007. It is clearly visible that religiosity and work ethic values are increasing during the depicted timespan. Particularly, between 1990 and 1996 and between 2001 and 2007, during which GDP developed most dynamically, both religious and work ethic values were becoming markedly more important among the Turkish population. In contrast, economic individualism increased only between 1990 and 1996. In 2001, it decreased to the level of 1990 and then only marginally developed between 2001 and 2007.

[9] Turkey also has a relatively high and increasing number of self-employed persons (OECD, 2008, p. 142). Nearly 45% of the Turkish workforce is self-employed, indicating that Özal's attempt to encourage people "to set up their own business and to create an enterprise culture" (Uygur, 2009, p. 213) was successful.

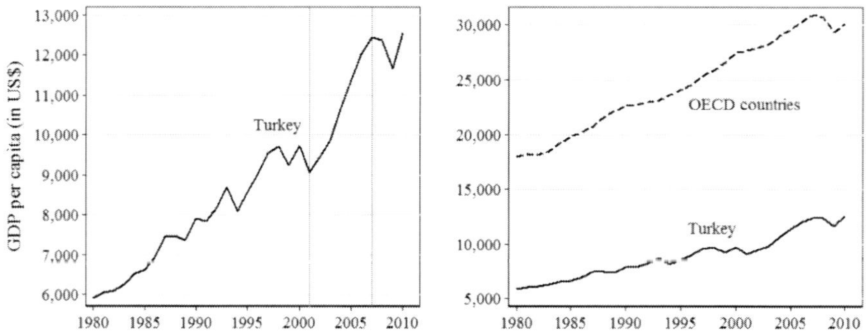

Figure 1. Economic development in Turkey and OECD countries 1980-2010.

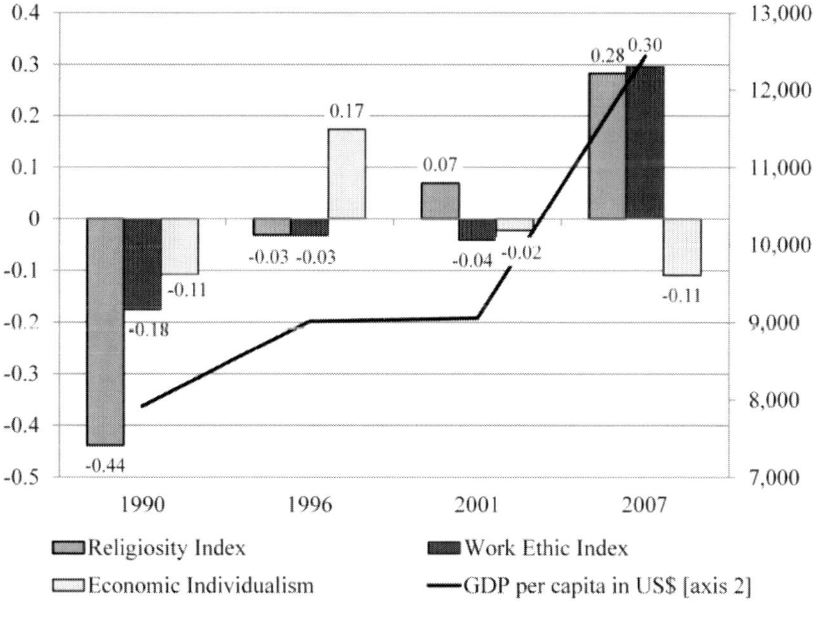

Figure 2. Development of religiosity, work ethic values, economic attitudes, and GDP.

To determine whether these developments over time are significant, I conduct three linear regressions with the religious value index (Model 1), work ethic index (Model 2), and economic attitudes (Model 3) as dependent variables. I control for sex, age, marital status, occupational status, and education.

Model 1 in Table 1 presents the results of the first regression using the religiosity index as a dependent variable. Coefficients of the sociodemographic variables reveal that younger individuals are less religious than older individuals, students are less religious than employed persons, and the higher-educated are less religious than the lower educated. Further, married persons and persons working in the household are significantly more religious. The unusual negative effect of women vs. men is an artifact of inserting an occupation indicator. Individuals working in the household virtually include only women.[10]

The coefficients of the dummy-variable set (years) that operationalize the development over time confirm the bivariate findings. Compared to 1990, individuals in Turkey are more religious in all other years. The sharpest increase is visible for the period between 1990 and 1996. I conducted further regression analysis and changed the reference categories of the year variables to determine whether changes between other years are also significant. The results reveal that the gap between 1996 and 2001 is insignificant; however, the margin between 2007 compared to both 2001 and 1996 is positive and highly significant ($p < 0.001$; results not depicted in the Table).

Next, I test the impact of the same independent variables on work ethic index. The results are presented in Model 2 in Table 1. They reveal an inversely U-shaped age effect: middle-aged individuals are most likely to indicate that work-ethic related values are important. This is clear given that persons between age 30 and 60 are the most strongly involved in economic life. Moreover, I find three significant and obvious effects of occupational status: Self-employed are likely to have higher average values on the work ethic indicator compared to employed persons; individuals working in the household and persons who are retired are, on average, significantly less likely to develop work ethic values. It should also be noted that education is not systematically correlated with the dependent variable, indicating that the development of a work ethic is neither dependent on human capital (and the related factual opportunities on the labor market) nor on the socializing effects of the educational system.

[10] Most studies show that women are more religious than men (Collett & Lizardo, 2009). When conducting the same regression without the occupational variable, the coefficient of women against men is significantly positive.

Table 1. Regression analyses with religiosity, work ethic values and economic attitudes as dependent variables

	DV: Religiosity		DV: Work Ethic Index		DV: Economic individualism	
	Model 1		Model 2		Model 3	
	b	beta	b	beta	b	beta
Sex (female=1)	-0.076	-0.040 *	-0.104	-0.031 +	-0.067	-0.034 +
Age	-0.027	-0.386 ***	0.060	0.486 ***	0.003	0.036
Age squared	0.000	0.381 ***	-0.001	-0.455 ***	0.000	-0.025
Maritial status (married=1)	0.129	0.060 ***	0.014	0.004	0.032	0.014
Occupational status (Ref.: employed):						
| Self-employed	0.043	0.016	0.151	0.031 *	0.121	0.042 ***
| Retired	0.035	0.010	-0.318	-0.052 ***	0.101	0.028
| In household	0.247	0.123 ***	-0.387	-0.109 ***	-0.035	-0.016
| Student	-0.249	-0.050 ***	-0.138	-0.016	0.051	0.010
| Unemployed/other	0.017	0.005	0.024	0.004	-0.076	-0.023 +
Education (Ref.: no formal education):						
| Elementary education	-0.076	-0.040 *	0.014	0.004	0.107	0.053 **
| Secondary education	-0.359	-0.132 ***	-0.046	-0.010	0.261	0.094 ***
| University preparation	-0.526	-0.207 ***	0.198	0.044 *	0.320	0.120 ***
| University degree	-0.922	-0.282 ***	0.046	0.008	0.415	0.124 ***
Year (ref. 1990)						
| 1996	0.336	0.143 ***	0.195	0.050 **	0.229	0.099 ***
| 2001	0.384	0.200 ***	0.113	0.033 +	0.036	0.018
| 2007	0.415	0.172 ***	0.476	0.110 ***	-0.076	-0.029 +
Intercept	2.641	***	-1.241	***	-0.309	**
R-square	0.142		0.039		0.037	
N	6,707		7,150		7,090	

+ $p < 0.1$, * $p < 0.05$, ** $p < 0.01$, *** $p < 0.001$.

Coefficients of the year dummies indicate that a significant increase in work ethic values is in evidence both between 1990 and 1997 and between 1990 and 2007. The gap between 2001 and 1990 is only significant on the 10% level. Separate regressions for which I defined the year 2001 instead of 1990 as a reference category demonstrate that a further significant increase occurred between 2001 and 2007 (not depicted in the Table).

The last model in Table 1 (Model 3) exchanges the work ethic index for the economic attitude indicator (economic individualism) as a dependent variable.

Among the socio-demographics, only self-employed vs. employed and education (basic and higher education as against no formal education) are significantly (positively) associated. The first effect appears to be obvious given that the bourgeoisie is, as a rule, hardly supportive of a strong state economy.

Part of the effect of education may be interpreted in a similar manner. With increasing human capital, individuals have better opportunities to earn a high income on the free market. Another reason is probably that state intervention, for educated individuals in Turkey in general, evoke negative connotations of censorship and paternalism (Yavuz, 2003).

Among the variables describing the passage of time, only the coefficient determining the year 1996 vs. 1990 is positive and significant.

In summary, the regression analyses confirm the general impression determined from the bivariate results (cf. Figure 2). The trends in religiosity and work ethic values clearly resemble the development of GDP. Waxing rates become visible between 1990 and 1997, followed by a short plateau phase between 1997 and 2001, and again a steep increase in 2007 as compared to 2001.

Attitudes towards economic individualism, in contrast, follow the trend of these variables only between 1990 and 1996. In 2001 and 2007, they fall back to the level of 1990.

A New Islamic Work Ethic?

In a second analytical step, I aim to answer one of the main questions of this study: has religion causally contributed to the emphasis of work ethic values and was thereby directly involved in creating economic growth? Admittedly, I cannot directly measure the impact of the Fetullah Gülen movement on the character of religion and on work ethics by means of available data. However, if the reinterpretation of the religious message was linked to economic growth, its impact cannot be restricted to a small religious group.

Rather, it must have influenced the ethics of the religious majority. Second, I hypothesize that if the religious core message has been pursued in a capitalist-friendly direction, individuals who are more religious should also associate more strongly with work ethic values. If this hypothesis applies, I should be able to identify a positive association between individual religiosity and the work ethic indicator.

To empirically test this assumption, I have conducted the regressions depicted in Table 2 (Model 1 to 3). The basic set-up of the variables is the same as in the second model shown in Table 1 above. The *work ethic index* is the dependent variable, the socio-demographics have been inserted as controls, and the year indicators determine the development over time. Additionally, I included the religiosity index as an explanatory variable.

The results (Model 1) do not appear to support the causality-hypothesis. The coefficient of the religiosity index is only marginally positively associated with work ethics and the value is not significant.

An explanation for this result is that religiosity may only account for work ethic differences on the timeline, but not on the cross sectional level (between individuals for one and the same point in time). Associations over time between religiosity and work ethic values can however not be determined by Model 1. This is because the year dummy-variables completely absorb variances on the dependent variable between different points in time. In Models 2 and 3 the year dummys have therefore been removed.

As expected, Model 2 shows that the religiosity index gains strength and becomes significant at the 5% level, indicating a positive relationship between religiosity and work ethics between different time points.

Based on this result, I conduct Model 3, in which I use an additional religiosity measure to separately treat the impact of religiosity on the longitudinal and on the cross-sectional (micro) level. The variable entitled 'religiosity aggregate' is a macro indicator that contains information on the average value on the religiosity index for each point in time (over the entire sample).

By adding this variable to the model, I directly and separately measure the effect of religious change on work ethic transitions on the timeline on the one hand (religiosity aggregate indicator) and on the cross-sectional level on the other hand (religiosity indicator).

Table 2. Impact of religiosity on work ethic values and economic attitudes

	DV: Work ethic indicator						DV: Economic individualism	
	Model 1		Model 2		Model 3		Model 4	
	b	beta	B	beta	b	beta	b	beta
Sex (female=1)	-0.077	-0.023	-0.092	-0.027	-0.082	-0.024	-0.087	-0.043 *
Age	0.059	0.473 ***	0.060	0.485 ***	0.058	0.470 ***	0.004	0.057
Age squared	-0.001	-0.446 ***	-0.001	-0.457 ***	-0.001	-0.445 ***	0.000	-0.042
Maritial status (married=1)	0.010	0.003	-0.006	-0.002	0.005	0.001	0.025	0.011
Occupational status (Ref.: employed):								
| Self-employed	0.185	0.038 **	0.197	0.040 **	0.194	0.040 **	0.122	0.042 **
| Retired	-0.350	-0.057 ***	-0.315	-0.051 ***	-0.335	-0.055 ***	0.076	0.021
| In household	-0.424	-0.118 ***	-0.386	-0.108 ***	-0.415	-0.116 ***	-0.042	-0.020
| Student	-0.065	-0.007	0.041	0.005	-0.010	-0.001	0.067	0.013
| Unemployed/other	0.010	0.002	0.011	0.002	0.005	0.001	-0.079	-0.024 +
Education (Ref.: no formal education):								
| Elementary education	0.009	0.003	0.021	0.006	0.010	0.003	0.117	0.058 **
| Secondary education	-0.019	-0.004	-0.002	-0.001	-0.024	-0.005	0.281	0.099 ***
| University preparation	0.209	0.047 *	0.268	0.060 **	0.204	0.046 *	0.366	0.138 ***
| University degree	0.091	0.016	0.159	0.028	0.081	0.014	0.496	0.146 ***
Year (ref. 1990)								
| 1996	0.132	0.032 +					0.187	0.076 ***
| 2001	0.086	0.025					-0.005	-0.002
| Y2007	0.434	0.102 ***					-0.132	-0.051 **
Religiosity	0.018	0.024 +	0.024	0.033 *	0.017	0.024 +	0.027	0.064 ***
Religiosity / aggregate					0.528	0.064 ***		
Intercept	-1.189	***	-1.095	***	-1.036	***	-0.311	**
R-square	0.040		0.033		0.037		0.041	
N	6,585		6,585		6,585		6,530	

*+ $p < 0.1$, * $p < 0.05$, ** $p < 0.01$, *** $p < 0.001$.*

The results of this analysis, including both the aggregate religious measure and the original micro level indicator, are presented in Model 3; they support the expected patterns of correlations between religiosity and work ethics. A substantial positive association exists only on the timeline (cf. significant coefficient of religiosity aggregate index), but not on the cross-sectional (micro) level (cf. insignificant coefficient of original religiosity index).[11]

In Model 4 (Table 2), I test whether and in what way religiosity is associated with an economic individualistic attitude. Results indicate that religiosity is significantly positively associated with the economic attitude indicator, even when controlling for socio-demographics and year of survey. A further regression model (not depicted in the Table), in which I included the religiosity indicator on the aggregate level and excluded the year variables (resembling the set-up of Model 3), demonstrates that religiosity is only correlated on the cross-sectional (micro) level, but not on the timeline.

It should be mentioned that Model 4 with economic attitudes as a dependent variable was not a strict test of the causality-proposition. This is because, compared to work ethic values, economic individualism has not developed dynamically in correspondence with religiosity and economic growth (cf. Figure 2). Moreover, a positive correlation between religiosity and economic individualism on the micro level, can be better explained from a materialistic perspective than from a cultural perspective. As outlined in the review section of this chapter, the Kemalist elites that have shaped the state economy over a long period of time have been anti-religiously-oriented; thus, religious individuals should (for political reasons) be skeptical of the state (economy) in general.

CONCLUSION

The aim of this paper was to empirically determine the role of religion in the economic process in Turkey between 1990 and 2010. Specifically, I examined the question of whether endogenous religious reforms have shaped the cultural values of individuals in a manner that positively affected the economic process.

[11] This interpretation is also supported by the fact that when separately analyzing the impact of religiosity on work ethics by years, I do not observe any substantial correlation between the two indicators (analyses of these regressions are not reported in the Table).

The theoretical background was Max Weber's seminal study on *The Protestant Ethic and the Spirit of Capitalism.* Weber argued that Protestant sects created an economic ethic that became a central (independent) factor contributing to the rise of capitalism in the Occident. I tested how recent religious and economic developments in Turkey resembled these processes and how they differed.

The results revealed that the development of the religious and economic spheres was indeed strongly intertwined. Economic growth was mainly created by smaller firms owned by families with a religious background. Further, religion in Turkey was, in recent decades, coined by the new Sufi movement and Fethullah Gülen who preached a capitalist-friendly version of Islam. This version conceives of hard work and the acquisition of education as religious duties, as well as stresses the importance of time management and well-planned activity. These contents, it seems, comprise a set of cultural values that Max Weber argued were essential attributes of the 'spirit of capitalism'.

The aim of the quantitative-analytical section was to empirically determine how religion impacted the economic process in Turkey. Using data from the WVS (1990–2007), I first examined the development of religiosity and economic values before and during economic boom years. Second, I evaluated whether religion causally contributed to the spread of a new work ethic, thus serving as the motivational base to create economic prosperity. The results can be summarized as follows:

(1) I found no evidence that Turkish Islam has directly contributed to increase work ethics by virtue of its religious message. To be sure, I could not empirically determine how or whether the neo-Sufi movement has changed the core religious message. Rather, I argued that if the movement has significantly influenced religious contents in a work ethic-friendly manner, individuals that are more religious should also be more affine towards work ethic values. In this case, our data should have revealed a positive association between individual religiosity and the work ethic index. However, regression analyses results did not support this hypothesis.

(2) In contrast, the analyses confirmed a positive correlation between individual religiosity and economic individualism. I do not, however, interpret this finding as an indication that the message of Turkish Islam today is capitalistic rather than communitarian oriented. Rather, the fact that religious individuals prefer economic freedom over state interventionism could be a reaction to the secular, anti-religious

attitude that the Kemalist elites have exerted over a long period of time after the decline of the Ottoman Empire (Yavuz, 2009).

(3) Further, I found clear evidence that religious values and work ethic values have been developing with the same trend over time. Between 1990 and 2007, individuals in Turkey increasingly emphasized the importance of religiosity and the relevance of work ethic values; a development that goes hand in hand with waxing GDP.

In summary, I interpret the empirical results in the direction that Turkish Islam has not organically contributed to create work ethic values. The materialistic "justifications" perspective seems much more appropriate for explaining the interrelation between the economic and cultural process than the Weberian "motivational power of cultural values" approach (Vaisey, 2009, p. 1677). From this perspective, the Gülen movement has mainly provided the "superstructure" requested by the Anatolian bourgeoisie. Religion has, in other words, been secularly upvalued rather than religion having upvalued secular activities. This hypothesis both explains the zero-correlation between individual religiosity and work ethic values, and the increasing attractiveness of Islam which is documented in a resurge of religiosity among the Turkish population over time.

REFERENCES

Barro, R. J. & McCleary, R. M. (2003). Religion and economic growth across countries. *American Sociological Review*, *68*, 760-781.

Baskan, F. (2004). The Politics of Islamic Finance in Turkey. In C. Henry & R. Wilson (Ed.), *The politics of Islamic finance* (216-239). Edinburgh, UK: Edinburgh University Press

Berger, P. L. (1967). *The sacred canopy: Elements of a sociological theory of religion*. New York, NY: Anchor.

Cam, S. (2002). Neo-liberalism and labour within the context of an 'emerging market' economy – Turkey. *Capital & Class*, *26*, 89-114.

Collett, J. L. & Lizardo, O. (2009). A power-control theory of gender and religiosity. *Journal for the Scientific Study of Religion*, *48*, 213-31.

Collins, R. (1980). Weber's last theory of capitalism: A systematization. *American Sociological Review*, *45*, 925-942.

Davis, N. J. & Robinson, R. V. (2006). The egalitarian face of Islamic orthodoxy: Support for Islamic law and economic justice in seven Muslim-majority nations. *American Sociological Review*, *71*, 167-190.

ESI. (2005). Islamic Calvinists. change and conservatism in central Anatolia. *European Stability Initiative (ESI) Reports*. Retrieved 10 August 2012 from http://www.esiweb.org/index.php?lang=en&id=156&document_ID =71.

Foreign Policy. (2008). *The world's top 20 public intellectuals*. Retrieved 10 August 2012 from http://www.foreignpolicy.com/articles/2008/06/16/the_world_s_top_20_public_intellectuals.

Gulay, E. N. (2007). The Gülen phenomenon: A neo-Sufi challenge to Turkey's rival elite? *Critique: Critical middle Eastern Studies*, *16*, 37-61.

Gülen, F. (2007). *Free will*. Retrieved on 10 August 2012 from http://en.mfethullahgulen.net/recent-articles/2427-free-will.html.

———. (2001). *The eelationship of Islam and science and the concept of science*. Retrieved on 10 August 2012 from http://en.mfethullahgulen.net/recent-articles/905-the-relationship-of-islam-and-science-and-the-concept-of-science.html.

———. (1981). *Education from cradle to grave*. Retrieved on 10 August 2012 from http://en.mfethullahgulen.net/love-and-tolerance/274-education/1855-education-from-cradle-to-grave.html.

Hirschle, J. (2013). Secularization of consciousness or alternative opportunities? The impact of economic growth on religious belief and practice in 13 European countries. *Journal for the Scientific Study of Religion*, *52*, 410-424.

Howe, M. (2000). *Turkey. A nation divided over Islam's revival*. Boulder, CO: Westview Press.

Huntington, S. P. (2002). *The clash of civilizations and the remaking of world order*. London, UK: The Free Press.

Jenkins, G. (2003). Muslim democrats inTurkey? *Survival*, *45*, 45-66.

Kaplan, R. D. (1994). The coming anarchy. How scarcity, crime, overpopulation, tribalism, and disease are rapidly destroying the social fabric of our planet. *The Atlantic*. Retrieved 8 August 2012 from http://www.theatlantic.com/magazine/archive/1994/02/the-coming-anarchy/304670/.

Keyman, E. F. (2007). Modernity, secularism and Islam: The case of Turkey. *Theory, Culture & Society*, *24*, 215-234.

Lapidus, I. M. (1992). Sufism and Ottoman Islamic society. In R. Lifchez *(Ed.), The Dervish lodge. Architecture, art, and Sufism in Ottoman Turkey* (15-32). Berkley, CA: University of California Press.

Lodhi, A. (2006). Turkish toil brings new form of faith. *BBC report*. Retrieved 30 August 2012 from http://news.bbc.co.uk/2/hi/business/4788712.stm.

Michel, T. (2005). Sufism and modernity in the thought of Fethullah Gülen. *The Muslim World, 95*, 341-357.

Miller, M. J, Woehr, D. J. & Hudspeth, N. (2002). The meaning and measurement of work ethic: Construction and initial validation of a multidimensional inventory. *Journal of Vocational Behavior, 60*, 451-489.

OECD. (2012). *OECD stat extracts*. Retrieved 8 August 2012 from http://stats.oecd.org/Index.aspx.

———. (2008). *OECD economic surveys: Turkey*, Volume *14*. Paris, France: OECD Publishing.

———. (2006). *OECD Economic surveys: Turkey*, Volume *15*. Paris, France: OECD Publishing.

Öniş, Z. (2009). Beyond the 2001 financial crisis: The political economy of the new phase of neo-liberal restructuring in Turkey. *Review of International Political Economy, 16*, 409-432.

———. (2004). Turgut Özal and his economic legacy: Turkish neo-liberalism in critical perspective. *Middle Eastern Studies, 40*, 113-134.

Özdalga, E. (2003). Secularizing trends in Fethullah Gülen's movement: Impasse or opportunity for further renewal? *Critical Middle Eastern Studies, 12*, 61-73.

Peifer, J. L. (2012). Religious moral authority and the financial market in 20th century America: Privatization, deprivatization or co-optation? *Rice University, Working Paper*. Retrieved 10 July 2012 from http://sociology.rice.edu/uploadedFiles/Peifer%202012%20Religion%20and%20Financial%20Market_working%20draft.pdf?n=2911.

Robinson, S. (2000). *Fethullah Gülen and the concept of responsibility*. Retrieved 8 August 2012 from http://en.fgulen.com/conference-papers/gulen-conference-in-washington-dc/3093-fethullah-gelen-and-the-concept-of-responsibility.

Schleifer, A. (2012). *The Muslim 500. The world's most influential Muslims*. Retrieved on 2 May 2013 from http://themuslim500.com/downloads/2012lo.php.

Sharon-Krespin, R. (2009). Fethullah Gülen's grand ambition. Turkey's Islamist danger. *Middle East Quarterly, XVI*, 55-66.

Silverstein, B. (2008). Disciplines of presence in modern Turkey: Discourse, companionship, and the mass mediation of Islamic practice. *Cultural Anthropology*, *23*, 118-153.

Tenbruck, F. H. (1975). Das Werk Max Webers. *Kölner Zeitschrift für Soziologie und Sozialpsychologie*, *27*, 663-702.

Trigilia, C. (2002). *Economic sociology. State, market, and society in modern capitalism*. Oxford, UK: Blackwell.

Uygur, S. (2009). The Islamic work ethic and the emergence of Turkish SME owner-managers. *Journal of Business Ethics*, *88*, 211–225.

Vaisey, S. (2009). Motivation and justification: A dual-process model of culture in action. *American Journal of Sociology*, *114*, 1675-1715.

Weber, M. (1966 [1922]). *The sociology of religion*. London, UK: Social Science Paperbacks.

Weber, M. (1971 [1905]). *The Protestant ethic and the spirit of capitalism*. London, UK: Unwin.

Yavuz, M. H. (2009). *Secularism and Muslim democracy in Turkey*. Cambridge, UK: Cambridge University Press.

———. (2003). *Islamic political identity in Turkey*. Oxford, UK: Oxford University Press.

———. (2000). Being modern in the Nurcu way. *ISIM Newsletter*, *6*, 7/14.

———. (1999). Towards an Islamic liberalism? The Nurcu movement and Fethullah Gülen. *Middle East Journal*, *53*, 584-605.

In: Economic Growth in the 21st Century
Editor: Cody Accosi
ISBN: 978-1-63321-589-4

Chapter 7

ON BEING HAPPY IN UNCERTAIN ECONOMIC TIMES

Sally Fiona Kelty*
School of Social Sciences, University of Tasmania,
Hobart, Tasmania, Australia

ABSTRACT

Given the uncertain economic times over the past few years, the aim of this research was to investigate whether economic instability affected subjective well-being and if so how. The sample was 135 men and women from a stratified sample of adults living in metropolitan Western Australia. Using scores from the Satisfaction with Life Scale and the Short Happiness-Depression Inventory two happiness groups were formed: adults with high subjective well-being; and adults with lower subjective well-being. Group differences on homeownership, financial liquidity and stress, attitudes towards credit, pursuit of extrinsic goals were assessed. The results showed that income level per se did not make people happier, although not being able to make ends meet was associated with more unhappiness. Happier people were more likely to own their home, to pay off credit balances each month, pay rent/mortgage on time and could save even a small amount of money on a regular basis. Attitudes to credit, number of credit cards owned, and extrinsic life aspirations were not associated with levels of happiness. The results and

* Corresponding author: Phone +061 450230115. Email Sally.kelty@utas.edu.au, or sally.fiona.kelty@gmail.com.

applied implications of the study are discussed with an emphasis on promoting happiness and avoiding financial stress during times of economic uncertainty.

Keywords: Subjective well-being, financial stress, credit attitudes

Introduction

Mental health is not just the absence of mental illness and promoting high subjective well-being has been a major Federal Government initiative (Australian Health Ministers, 2003). Ahuvia (2007) theorised that subjective well-being comprised of cognitive judgments of life satisfaction and the balance of happiness over feelings of depression. Ahuvia suggested that real happiness was not just an affective or cognitive state in isolation but was the combination of both. For example, people who experience deep sadness and depression will rarely judge their life to be worthwhile. Finding a range of holistic ways to promote higher subjective well-being and good mental health for Australian citizens has for the past 6 years been a major Federal Government initiative (Australian Health Ministers, 2003). This goal is not limited to Australia but can be seen in the US and Europe.

What is Subjective Well-being: An Overview

According to Ahuvia (2007) the term happiness in everyday use has many different meanings. Some people consider happiness as a short term affective state (laughing after a joke), or as a long term affective state (feelings of love felt over a long term relationship), while other people consider happiness as cognitive perceptions or judgments (living a good life/having life satisfaction).

Ahuvia devised a dual component model of subjective wellbeing, which he considered was synonymous with happiness. He hypothesised that real happiness was not just an affective state nor a cognitive state in isolation but was the combination of both. For example, people who experience ongoing feelings of sadness will not generally judge their life to be satisfying or worthwhile. The dual component model of subjective wellbeing comprises of perceptions of life satisfaction (the cognitive component) combined with feelings of cheerfulness and sadness (the balance of positive and negative affect). Ahuvia's subjective well-being model was itself grounded in the work of influential subjective well-being researchers like Larsen (1973) and positive psychologist Csikszentmihalyi (1990).

Recent research has suggested that one way people experience lower levels of subjective well-being is by pursuing fiscally oriented (extrinsic) life goals where success and achieving happiness is measured in terms of wealth and power. Kasser (1999) suggested that seeking happiness by pursuing external goals led people to strive to do well in school, get good jobs, enter the "right" profession, accumulate money and possessions, and seek social status among like-minded peers. Kasser argued that one disadvantage for people who place emphasis on their share holdings, how they look, what they do for a living and their social status is that their subjective well-being in the long run tends to diminish because they rely on the approval and opinions of others as a measure of their personal worth.

In 1976, Klagsbrun hypothesised that many cases of adolescent suicide in the US were partly due to the high degree of pressure faced by young people in trying to live up to the standards set by the American dream of wealth, social status and career success. Thirty years later, the same issues appear to be prevalent in contemporary society with similar themes appearing in the mental health literature. For example, in (2007) LIFE presented a number of protective factors promoting good mental health and reduced risk of suicide for Australian adults; these factors were all intrinsic in nature, such as a positive sense of self, a belief that one's life is meaningful and has purpose, and that people have close and supportive relationships with family and/or friends, have affordable housing, and do not experience high levels of financial stress.

Aspirations for the Good Life

In 1972 the King of Bhutan argued that the optimal way to measure the wealth and happiness of a nation was not by Gross Domestic Product (GDP) but rather by Gross National Happiness (GNH). Unlike GDP, GNH is an abstract concept than defies quantification as it is an indicator of happiness, preservation of cultural values and environment, quality of life and the spiritual growth of citizens (Bruni & Porta, 2005).

In contrast to Bhutan, many developed nations like Australia and the US appear to have pursued neo-liberal politics where national prosperity and wealth is measured by GDP, not GNH, and where GDP is generated through free-market trade where all citizens are provided with individual choice in employment and consumer markets (Bruni & Porta, 2005).

Specifically in Australia in recent decades national prosperity was considered by Australian governments to be achieved through annual percentage rises in economic growth (Hamilton, 1999). According to Western et al., (2007) this rise in neo-liberal thinking has created societies where the demand for increased supply and demand of consumer goods has been the main goal of fiscal policy in order to achieve continual increases in economic growth. For corporations to increase growth they must streamline performance, often pursued by offering monetary bonuses to staff and executives. To increase sales a common strategy is to saturate the market with images that encourage people to purchase goods (Hamilton & Denniss, 2005).

In Australia, as well as the UK and US, social analysts have noted from their research (combining media content analyses, with qualitative research and national health surveys) that for many people perceptions of the good life and happiness now equates to the image of corporate employees (the high-flyers) wearing designer label clothes, driving luxury cars, living in large homes furnished in the latest trends, whose children attend private school, and with the annual overseas holiday (Hamilton & Denniss, 2005; James, 2007). As Hamilton (1999) argued, a common belief of individualism found today in many western nations is that contentment and happiness can be achieved via consumerism and extrinsic rewards, such as ownership of luxury commodities and this is one reason why Hamilton (1999) argued that many Australians appear to aspire to wealth, beauty, status and celebrity as evidence of their achievement and success.

Extrinsic and Intrinsic Life Aspirations

Pursuing external rewards has been conceptualised by Kasser and Ryan (1993, 1996) as extrinsic goals which were found to represent three interrelated constructs: money (obtaining financial success and wealth); personal appearance (external image creation); and social recognition (fame and popularity).

Researchers have found that on average people who endorse these three types of extrinsic goals report a lower quality of life, work longer hours, report more depression, more anxiety, are more likely to abuse alcohol and have poorer health outcomes than their peers who do not pursue these goals (Kasser, 1999). Extrinsically oriented people are also significantly more likely to be more narcissistic, score higher on conduct disorders and personality disorders and report more experiences of unpleasant emotions on a daily basis than their peers (Kasser, 1999).

Furthermore, people who pursue extrinsic goals are more likely to have relationships that are of shorter duration, are more conflictual, and based more on competition than reciprocity. As Hamilton noted, this research demonstrated that having the goals of wealth, attractiveness and fame was more likely to be associated with unhappiness and disillusionment than with the good life as assumed.

In contrast, pursuing intrinsic life goals is considered by Kasser (1999) and Grouzet et al., (2005) to be more satisfying and congruent with the self because these goals represent the search for understanding in life. Intrinsic goals promote the search for self-acceptance (growth), investing in and nurturing close relationships (relatedness), and pursuing a career or hobbies that promote stronger communities and help other people (helpfulness) (Grouzet et al., 2005).

Cross cultural research with university student samples from the UK, USA, Korea, Australia, Bulgaria, India, Egypt found that adults who pursue more intrinsic goals tend to report higher levels of happiness (less depressive and anxiety symptomatology) and report higher life satisfaction in that they see their life as meaningful and rich (Chan & Joseph, 2000; Grouzet et al., 2005). Furthermore, people who pursue intrinsic goals are also more likely to score higher on psychometric scales measuring self-actualisation based on Maslow's (1971) hierarchy of needs.

Pursuing the intrinsic goals of affiliation, self-acceptance and bettering the community as a way to experience higher levels of subjective well-being is not a new idea. In the 4th century BC, the philosopher Epicurus theorised that an uncomplicated and simple life was the only way to obtain true happiness. He wrote that life satisfaction could be achieved by meeting three needs: first, the need for close friendship; second, the need for basic necessities (serviceable clothes, food and adequate not elaborate shelter). Third, the need to be free, with freedom referring to the self as master of your time (shorter working hours) and removal of pressure/interference from superiors at work and by engaging in the politics routinely experienced by those who aspire to climb the corporate ladder.

Financial Stress and Health

In addition to the apparent pursuit of neo-liberal principals in Australia which has been associated with the promotion of extrinsic aspirations to increase consumerism (Hamilton & Denniss, 2005), there has also been a large and rapid rise in consumer credit and personal debt levels.

The rise in Australian household debt was of enough concern in 2005 to result in an Australian Federal Senate standing inquiry. The inquiry found that the rapid rise in debt was in part due to deregulation of the credit sector flooding the market with a range of consumer credit options. The report recommended that the government intervene in the credit market through legislation to ensure that credit providers undertake appropriate checks of borrowers‘ capacity to pay before issuing new credit cards or raising credit limits (Senate Economics References Committee, 2006).

Despite the Senate recommendations to regulate the credit sector, recent statistics from the Reserve Bank of Australia (RBA) have shown that household debt has continued to rise. For example, a common measure of household liquidity calculated by the RBA is the ratio of debt (housing and personal credit) to disposable/after tax income. In 1990 debt repayments amounted to 28.2% of disposable income. By March 2008 (18 years later) the ratio was 93.5% (RBA, 2008).

In 2006 with petrol prices rising to an all time high, with interest rates rising rapidly between 2002 to 2006 and with high debt levels an Australian report found that one in three households in metropolitan Sydney were experiencing ongoing financial stress (Wesley Mission, 2006). The Wesley researchers found the two most common predictors of chronic financial stress was related to the amount of different credit options taken up by a household and their inability to service debt repayments as living costs rose (Wesley Mission, 2006).

Researchers exploring the psychological impact of financial stress have found positive relationships whereby increases in financial stress have been related to higher levels of reported depression, higher relationship distress, increases in domestic violence, marital breakdown, self-esteem and obesity (Krause, 1995; Manktelow & Hegarty, 2004; Wesley Mission, 2006). Of concern were the findings of Dossey (2007) in his extensive review which suggested that both men and women with a high level of debt and who experience financial stress are more likely to commit suicide because ongoing financial pressure, especially when current income cannot service debt repayments, often leads to feelings of personal failure, such as beliefs they have been disgracing their family and that the future looks bleak and unbearable.

Financial stress is not just linked to poorer mental health outcomes. It has also been found to predict poorer physical health which leads to behaviours that could have implications for the development of debilitating chronic diseases. One influential study by Drentea and Lavrakas (2000), in a sample of 970 male and female adults from Ohio State in the US, found that higher levels of credit card debt were positively related to higher levels of financial stress which significantly predicted poorer health outcomes. Poorer physical health was partly accounted for by the unhealthy/risky behaviours (drinking, smoking and physical inactivity) that people with high debt levels said they engaged in more often relative to their peers with lower levels of debt (Drentea & Lavrakas, 2000). Of concern is that engaging in high levels of drinking and smoking combined with a sedentary lifestyle as a means of coping with stress, may not just lead to obesity and associated psychological impacts such as poor body image, depression and low self-efficacy and self-worth (Krause, 1995) there is also now wide evidence at the population health level that such behaviours significantly reduce life expectancy. For example, compared with healthy weight peers, adolescents and adults classified as obese (body mass index: BMI >30) on average live 3 to 7 years less and are also at significantly elevated risk of mortality thorough lifestyle related cardiovascular disease, fatty liver disease, stroke and diabetes complications (Kelty, Giles-Corti & Zubrick, 2008).

Is There a Cost to Purchasing the Good Life?

The RBA household debt ratio discussed above indicated that over the last 18 years Australian households on average have trebled their amount of debt. The rise in household debt appears to be due to both housing loans and personal credit debt. The Wesley Mission research (2006) found that the high level of debt when living costs rose appeared to result in over 30% of households experiencing chronic financial stress and many other households reporting negative impacts on their family relationships and physical health.

Given the increase in household debt some researchers have started to explore the relationship between attitudes towards credit and consumer behaviour as measured by actual credit card debt. For example, Boddington (1999) found a predictive relationship in that the more positive the attitude toward credit the higher the level of debt in a sample of New Zealand university students. Boddington also found that for students with high levels of credit (not just education fees), debt was not related to financial mismanagement or impulsive consumer behaviour. A similar finding was found in a US community sample (Watson, 2003). Watson compared adults with high or low scores on a materialism scale with their attitudes towards using credit to fund acquisitions of luxury goods and non-luxury goods. Watson found that both groups of adults supported credit for essential goods, investment and self-education; however for luxury goods the group with high materialism scores were significantly more likely than adults with low materialism scores to use credit to acquire luxury goods like holiday homes, jewellery, luxury cars or boats (Watson, 2003). Finally, Chien and Devaney (2001) found that positive attitudes towards buying five different types of luxury goods predicted higher credit card balances and that positive attitudes towards credit in general predicted higher level of installment debt (such as bank loans).

Of interest, the findings of Boddington, Watson, and Chien and Devaney appear to support the theoretical framework of Ajzen and Madden (1986) who predicted that behaviour was a consequence of an intention to act and where intentions were in part considered a function of positive attitudes towards a specific behaviour. Of note, the research work presented directly above suggested that positive attitudes towards credit predicted higher levels of credit, however what these researchers did not explore was whether there was elevated financial stress associated with servicing high debt used to buy luxury items. Further, the attitude measure used by both Watson (2003) and Chien and Devaney (2001) appeared not to have been fully psychometrically assessed, hence the reliability and generalisability of these findings cannot be assumed (DeVellis, 2001). Exploring both these issues will form part of this project.

Summary of the Literature

It appears that people who aspire to and/or pursue extrinsic life goals in the form of money, image and fame on average experience poorer psychological and physical health outcomes compared with their peers who aspire to more intrinsic life goals. Furthermore, in a separate body of literature it has been found that people exposed to financial stress are suggested to have poorer psychological and interpersonal outcomes. However, no research to date has investigated the relationships between extrinsic life goals, attitudes to buying luxury goods on credit, levels of financial stress and subjective well-being.

Based on previous research findings (Chien & Devaney, 2001; Watson, 2003; Wesley Mission, 2006)) it could be hypothesised that one reason for the financial stress experienced by many households may be due to the pursuit of extrinsic goals through credit, especially luxury image driven commodities, and that the cost of living rises in recent times have increased the financial stress experienced. The aim of this project is to explore this hypothesised relationship.

Aims and Rationale of the Study

This Study Had Two Aims

Aim 1 was to carry out a psychometric assessment of the credit attitude measure used by Watson (2003) and Chien and Devaney (2001). As this attitude measure appears not to have been adequately assessed the validity of this measure for clinical use or as a financial management measure cannot be assured, hence any current findings suggesting that positive attitudes towards using credit may not be generalisable.

Aim 2 The second aim was to explore whether certain demographic and/or financial variables are associated with higher levels of happiness during uncertain economic times. The rapid changes in Australian society caused by the global financial crisis of 2008/9 created a unique opportunity to explore in an adult sample whether types of homeownership, income levels, positive attitudes to credit, number of credit cards held, ability to service household debt and either pursuit of extrinsic or intrinsic life goals were associated with higher levels of subjective well-being and happiness during a global economic crisis. As this was an exploratory study no hypotheses were set.

The rationale for this research was that after an extensive search of the literature this was the first Australian study to explore the differences in a community sample of adults using people high or low on extrinsic values and their attitudes towards buying various goods on credit, range of credit options taken up, financial stress and subjective wellbeing. The information obtained from this study could be used to enhance outcomes for clients seeking assistance for financial stress, couple stress, or life dissatisfaction. For example, if people with high extrinsic goals place themselves in debt to buy goods, therapists maybe able to assist them with exploring their core beliefs of why consumerism may equate to life success for them. It was also possible that the findings could have enhanced medical intervention for older adults if therapists explored the life goals their clients have pursued. For example, older clients may present with symptoms of depression which could be related to difficulties they are experiencing while facing Erickson's mid-life or older-age transitional stages. It is possible that the feelings they are experiencing relate to the dissatisfaction that researchers predict many people who spend years pursing external rewards will experience (Grouzet et al., 2005; Kasser, 1999).

METHOD

Participants

The respondents were adult men and women residing in metropolitan Perth, Western Australia. Six hundred random residences were invited to participate in the study, 146 respondents consented by completing the questionnaire pack and returning it by post (response rate of 24%). Of the 146 packs received, 11 packs were unusable, five were blank and 6 were substantially incomplete. The final sample has 135 adults, 94 women (70%) and 40 men (30%). Five people said they were not Australian citizens, 130 said they were citizens (96%). The age range of the sample was: under 25, n=5; age 25-35, n=20; 35-44, n=40; 45-60, n=43; 61-75, n=22; over 75 years, n=5. Forty-six respondents owned their home, 67 were paying a mortgage and 20 rented their home.

Measures

The Aspiration Index (AI: Kasser & Ryan, 1996) is a 29-item self-report measure assessing two constructs: extrinsic life aspirations (money, image, fame; e.g., "you will be financially successful"); and intrinsic aspirations (affiliation, self-acceptance, community feeling; e.g., "you will know and accept who you really are"). Participants are asked the importance of each goal in their life using a 5-point Likert scale, ranging from "very important", to "not important at all". Evaluation of the AI in a sample of 100 New York residents reported Cronbach's alpha of a = 0.76, and with 192 US university students an alpha of a = 0.79 (Kasser & Ryan, 1996). The construct validity of the index showed positive relationships between high extrinsic goals and higher depression, anxiety, narcissism and positive relationships between high intrinsic goals and self-actualisation and physical health outcomes (Chan & Joseph, 2000; Grouzet et al., 2005).

The Satisfaction with Life Scale (SWLS: Pavot & Diener, 1993) is a widely used unifactorial 5 item scale measuring the cognitive aspect of subjective well-being. Respondents are asked to consider 5 statements (e.g., "If I could live my life over, I would change almost nothing") and agree or disagree using a 7-point Likert scale, range "strongly agree" to "strongly disagree". High scores indicate higher life satisfaction. Evaluation of the SWLS reported Cronbach's alphas of a =0.79 (university students) and a =0.87 (older adults) (Pavot & Diener, 1993). Construct validity of the measure showed negative relationships with depression and anxiety scores and positive relationships with extroversion, physical health and martial harmony (Pavot & Diener, 1993).

The Short Depression-Happiness Scale (SDHS: Joseph et al., 2004) is a short-form 6 item unifactorial scale measuring happiness (3 items positively scored) and depression (3 items, negatively scored). Respondents are asked to consider each question and tick their response using a 4-point Likert scale, ranging from "never" to "often". After reversal of negatively worded items, higher scores reflect greater well-being. Evaluation of the SDHS reported a Cronbach's alpha of a = 0.80 in a sample of 241 British university students. Convergent validity was reported as a negative relationship with scores on the Beck Depression inventory and positive relationships with scores on the Oxford Happiness Inventory. Construct validity was reported through positive relationships with agreeableness and negative relationships with neuroticism as measured by the NEO (Joseph et al., 2004).

Experience of Financial Stress (EFS: Wesley Mission, 2006) was specifically developed for the Wesley Sydney study to assess whether financial stress had impacted across several life domains (partners/health/family/work/leisure time). Respondents are asked to consider whether money stress has impacted across seven life domains. Respondents can agree or disagree with each question using a 5-point Likert scale, ranging from "strongly agree" to "strongly disagree". The EFS can be seen in Section 2, question 4 of the questionnaire pack (refer Appendix B). Validity data for the measure was not available at the time the current study was carried out.

Reasons for Borrowing Money Scale (RBMS). The RBMS is a draft 31 self-report paper and pencil measure developed for this study to measure attitudes towards using credit to buy luxury or investment goods, such as "It's ok to borrow money to buy a swimming pool or spa." The first 24 items were based on items used in a National US financial survey by Godwin (1997) and by Chien and Devaney (2001) and Watson (2003) in their US community surveys. An additional 7 items were sourced from interview data by Hamilton and Denniss (2005) and represent common luxury goods purchased by Australian households over the past decade. Participants rate each item using a 5-point scale ranging from "strongly agree" to "strongly disagree". The psychometric properties for any of these items had not previously been assessed and formed one of the additional aims of this study.

Demographic questions included age, homeownership, education level and gender. Financial liquidity, credit behaviour and ability to service debt were similar to the range of questions by the Australian Bureau of Statistics (ABS) in their national household financial surveys and similar to research questions used in the Wesley Mission (2006) survey.

Procedure: Community Sampling and Data Collection

A questionnaire pack was developed comprising of demographic information (i.e., sex, age range, occupation, household income range) followed by the psychometric measures. On page 2 of the pack respondents were provided with completion instructions for return of the packs, consent to participate and details of how they were selected. No incentives or rewards were provided. All packs were completed anonymously with no identifying data requested or provided by respondents. To provide confidentiality, consent to participate was by completion and return of the pack by post.

A stratified cluster sampling was used to collect a random sample of adults across Perth suburbs. A sampling frame was constructed to locate three socio-economic status (SES) clusters using data from the Census of Population and Housing (ABS, 2002a, 2002b). The ABS reports list suburbs from highest to lowest on a number of socio-economic and demographic variables, primarily median individual weekly income, rent and mortgage repayments per household. The three SES bands used were: High SES (weekly income >$588); Medium SES (income A$314-$587) low SES (individual income <A$314). Six suburbs were then selected from the Census report using random numbers, two suburbs from each of the three SES clusters were selected. Finally the streets to sample within each suburb were selected using a letter and number sequence randomly generated through Microsoft Excel; these numbers corresponded to street directory map references for each of the six suburbs.

Six hundred questionnaire packs were distributed, 100 to each suburb. The packs were labeled "to the resident" and hand delivered to letterboxes. Half of the packs were intended for women, the other for men. On page 2 was a request that the pack should be completed by either an adult female or male. A reply paid envelope was provided to return the pack once complete. Two weeks later a reminder letter was hand delivered to the 600 homes which had received the pack. The questionnaire design and survey distribution method used was based on the recommendations of Dillman, Smyth and Christian (2008)

RESULTS

Data entry was checked for accuracy, missing values, and response sets. Several respondents did not complete all sections of the pack: 2 respondents did not complete the EFS questions, 3 did not complete RBMS, 5 did not complete SDHS; and one did not complete the AI. Missing values within the dataset were replaced using the midpoint value as follows: 9 missing values were replaced on the RBMS, 32 items replaced on the RBMS and 16 values replaced on the AI. No response sets were identified. Data was checked for univariate outliers (with z-scores > 3.29, the cut-off recommended by Tabachnick and Fidell (2013)). Outliers were identified on 3 measures: RMBS, 3 cases; SDHS, 7 cases; SWLS, 4 cases; and AI, 25 cases were identified. As outliers are to be expected in large datasets all cases were retained. Due to the number of tests performed on the data, a conservative alpha level of .01 was set to reduce risk of Type I errors (Norusis, 2011).

Aim 1: Assessing the Psychometric Properties of the RBMS

Aim 1 was to assess the psychometric properties of the draft RBMS developed to measure attitudes towards using credit. DeVellis' (1991) two stage assessment method was utilized where a reliability/item analysis is undertaken to identify weak items and then a Principle Components Analysis (PCA) to access component structure. The reliability of the 31 pool items was assessed. DeVellis (1991) recommended that items with corrected item-total correlations < .30 be removed as they represent poorly performing items. Further, that items which deflate overall alpha should be removed even if their CITC is slightly >.30. Using these guidelines, 5 items were removed. The component structure was then examined to determine whether any remaining items were complex or shared little common variance with other items. This examination showed 9 items required removal as they loaded on 3+ components, making their interpretation complex.

A PCA was performed to explore the component structure of RBMS. Tzeng (1992) noted that when using PCA the eigenvalue of less than 1 for component extraction is sensitive and can overestimate the number of true components. Tzeng recommended using Cattell's (1966) guidelines for locating the turn in the "elbow" on the scree plot. The elbow was located at the point of component 2; suggesting there are two different reasons for borrowing money. However as the eigenvalue for both component 3 and 4 were > 1, all four components were retained in the solution.

After Varimax rotation the 4 Components explained 60.5% of total variance. Component 1, eigenvalue = 5.706, represented attitudes to buying luxury goods on credit (LGS), 27.2% of variance. Component 2, wealth creation using credit (WC), eigenvalue = 2.867, 13.7% of the variance. Component 3, altering current situation using credit (ACS), eigenvalue = 2.258, 10.75% of variance. Component 4, investing in family's future using credit (IFF), eigenvalue = 1.877, which explained 8.93% of the variance. Table 1 below presents the component matrix.

The final RBMS was a 21 item self-report measure with a total scale Cronbach's alpha of .91. This is within DeVellis' (1991) scale range of "very good reliability".

Aim 2: Exploring Happiness in Uncertain Economic Times

In order to explore which variables are associated with happiness two groups were formed: a high SWB group and a lower SWB group. A K-means clustering analysis was used to form the groups using the two measures of SWB: life satisfaction (cognition; as measured by the SWLS) and felt happiness over depression (affective; measured by SDHS). The results from the cluster analysis found two distinct groups: 109 adults with higher SWB; and 20 adults with lower SWB. As the F-tests performed on the group means during K-Means clustering analysis can in some instances be overly liberal (Norusis, 2011) a Multiple Discriminant Analysis (MDA) was carried out to access differences between the two cluster groups as recommended by Drew and Bishop (1999). The MDA results showed that 94.4% of the cases were correctly classified (107 cases to high SWB, and 20 cases to lower SWB) and that the two cluster groups were significantly different from each other at the $p < .0001$ level. The results suggest that adults classified into group 1 (HSWB) report higher life satisfaction and feel happier than group 2 (LSWB). The means and standard deviations for each group can be seen in Table 2.

Table 1. Component Matrix (after Varimax Rotation) for the RBMS

Item		Component 1 Luxury goods services (LGS)	Component 2 Wealth Creation (WC)	Component 3 Alter current situation(ACS)	Component 4 Invest family future (IFF)
28	Quality electrical goods (Flat screen TV/ home theatre / top-end Hi-Fi)	.862			
19	Stay at a resort (interstate/overseas)	.821			
15	Go on a vacation / holiday	.791			
25	Current model mobile telephone, laptops, home computers.	.727			
17	Go on a honeymoon	.725			
20	Expensive sporting goods/home gyms	.724			
22	Quality appliances (e.g., ranges, side by side refrigerator)	.692			
16	Buy a swimming pool / spa	.660			
26	A back-yard make-over/outdoor BBQ	.608	.478		
27	Regular upgrade of main family car to a newer model	.530			
31	Major extension/refit of family home		.737		
18	Buy stocks and shares		.725		
24	Invest in precious metals		.610		
13	Buy second property / holiday home (not strictly investment)		.601		
2	Buy land/property for investment purposes		.550		.524
12	Help a relative who needs money			.690	
14	To cover expenses when income has been reduced			.619	
10	Pay accumulated outstanding bills			.575	
30	Convert to solar/electric panels			.500	
23	Put children through university/TAFE				.745
29	Child's private school education				.691

Table 2. Means and SD by SWB group for the Community Sample. SD in Parentheses

Group	(n)	SWLS [a]	SDHS [b]
Australian sample			
Higher subjective-wellbeing (HSWB)	109	29.07 (3.37)*	20.72 (2.18)*
Lower subjective-wellbeing (LSWB)	20	15.45 (4.89)*	15.40 (3.02)*

Notes: [a] Satisfaction with Life Scale.
[b] Short Depression-Happiness Scale.
*All between cluster differences p <.001

The means obtained for each group were then compared with normative groups.

The HSWB group reported a significantly higher level of life satisfaction than French-Canadian adults (t (107) = 6.163, p <.001), ($M_{\text{French-Canadian}}$ = 27.05) and also reported a higher level of affective happiness than adult English university students (t (107) = 40.693, p <.001), ($M_{\text{UK Students}}$ = 12.13). Overall the HSWB group reported experiencing a highly satisfying life and report feeling very happy.

The LSWB group reported a similar level of life satisfaction compared with a US sample of clients attending a private psychological practice (t (19) = .960, p =.349), ($M_{\text{US clinical}}$ = 14.4), however they reported a significantly higher life satisfaction than psychiatric inpatients (t (19)= 3.336, p = <.01), ($M_{\text{US inpatient}}$ = 11.80). The LSWB did report a higher level of affective happiness than adult English university students (t (107) = 40.693, p <.001), ($M_{\text{UK Students}}$ = 12.13). For affective happiness the LSWB group were above Joseph et al.'s (2000) cut-off score of 10 as an indication of mild clinical depression. It must be noted therefore that although the LSWB group report experiencing a relatively low level of life satisfaction their level of affective happiness is not at a clinically relevant level.

A K-means clustering analysis was then performed to form two independent groups based upon aspirations (adults with higher extrinsic aspirations and adults with higher intrinsic aspirations). The variables used in the analysis were the mean score for extrinsic and intrinsic sub-scale scores (as measured by the AI). The results from the cluster analysis found two distinct groups in the data set, these were: Group 1 (95 adults with high intrinsic and low extrinsic scores); and Group 2 (39 adults with high intrinsic and medium extrinsic scores). However, although the groups endorsed a different level of extrinsic goals (F (132)=264.737, p <.001) they endorsed the same level of endorsement of intrinsic goals ($F(132)=2.790$, $p = .09$). This suggested this Australian sample could not be clustered into two meaningful truly independent groups who endorsed a completely different worldview in terms of what they see as important aspirations in life. Furthermore, when comparing the mean score of Group 2 ($m = 3.37$) with the North American mean ($m = 4.30$; Kasser & Ryan, 1996) the t-test results ($t(38)= 10.305$, $p <.001$) suggested that Australian adults are not as high in extrinsic aspirations as their US peers.

Exploring Differences in Socio-Demographics, Liquidity, Life Aspirations, Financial Stress, and Attitudes to Using Credit between the HSWB and LSWB Groups

The next analyses explored which of the demographic, financial and attitudinal variables measured were associated with high SWB compared with lower SWB.

To explore whether HSWB adults differed on demographic and financial indicators from LSWB adults, a series of group (HSWB/LSWB) x variable two-way contingency tables were constructed. Table 3 shows the results from the Chi-squares with phi-coefficients as estimates of effect size. As some respondents did not complete all questions the number of cases per analysis is reduced.

As can be seen, residential status was not significant which suggests that HSWB is not influenced by whether you live alone or with a partner or family. In contrast the association for home ownership was significant with a medium phi-coefficient as an estimate of effect size. An inspection of the residuals showed that fewer adults in the HSWB rented than would be expected by chance, and that fewer adults in the LSWB group owned outright or were paying a mortgage than would be expected by chance.

All financial indicators were significant with medium phi-coefficient estimates of effect size. The results showed that fewer HSWB adults reported they had to go without household necessities, whereas more LSWB adults could not afford to buy necessities than would be expected by chance. Secondly, fewer adults with HSWB had balances left on their credit cards each month with more LSWB adults having balances rolling over on their credit cards each month. Third, fewer adults with HSWB had to borrow money to cover household costs, whereas more adults with LSWB had to borrow money. Last, more HSWB adults were able to pay their rent/mortgage on time, whereas more LSWB adults said they could not always pay on time than would be expected by chance.

Table 3. Demographic and financial indicator differences between the HSWB and LSWB groups

Variable type	Selected socio-demographics	[a]	HSWB[b]	LSWB[b]	Pearson χ^2 [d]	Sig.	ϕ[e]
1. Family status	Live alone	Count Expected	13 13.5	3 2.5	**.135**	***P*= .713**	**.03**
	Live with partner/family	Count Expected	95 94.5	17 17.5			
2. Home ownership status	House fully owned	Count Expected	37 36.0	5 6.0	**13.431**	***p*<.01***	**.32**
	Paying mortgage	Count Expected	57 55.7	8 9.3			
	renting	Count Expected	14 16.3	5 2.7			
Variable type	**financial indicators**						
1. Ability to buy necessaries	Could afford necessaries	Count Expected	88 81.6	9 15.4	**16.38**	***p*<.01***	**.37**
	Had to go without	Count Expected	13 19.4	10 3.6			
2.Paid credit card balances	Pay card balance to zero each month	Count Expected	73 67.1	6 11.9	**11.40**	***p*<.01***	**.32**
	Have balances on cards	Count Expected	23 28.9	11 5.1			
3. Borrowed money for bills	Yes borrowed money	Count Expected	5 9.3	6 1.7	**13.62**	***p*<.01***	**.34**
	Did not borrow money	Count Expected	96 91.7	13 17.3			
4. Ability to pay mortgage/ rent	Yes paid on time	Count Expected	68 65.3	12 14.7	**7.62**	***p*<.01***	**.30**
	Sometimes could not pay on time	Count Expected	3 5.7	4 1.3			

Notes: *$p < .01$ (significant, 2-tail test, alpha set at .01 for significance).

[a] Counts.

[b] High subjective well-being group.

[c] Low subjective well-being group.

[d] Pearson Chi-square, using 1 d.f.

[e] Phi coefficient.

A series of t-tests were then used to assess between group differences (HSWB and LSWB) on the continuous variables of: age; education; hours worked; household income; concerns about increases in interest rates and petrol prices; ability to save each week; financial stress (EFS); extrinsic and intrinsic aspirations (EA, IA); attitudes towards luxury goods on credit (LGS); wealth creation using credit (WC); altering situation using credit (ACS); and investing in family's future using credit (IFF).

Of the 14 analyses performed the results found only three significant or near significant results. The HSWB group were more likely to be able to save disposable income each week, with more LSWB adults just breaking even or spending more than their household earned ($t(124) = 3.740$, $p = <.001$). The LSWB groups were more likely to experience financial stress ($t(19)= -3.232$, $p = <.01$); and were more concerned with fluctuations in petrol prices ($t(19)= 2.499$, $p = .014$), than the HSWB group.

DISCUSSION

Two primary aims had been set for this study. The first aim was to assess the reliability and component structure of a scale developed to measure attitudes towards borrowing money. The second aim was to explore whether the reported financial stress in Australian households could be due in part to chasing extrinsic goals, especially the purchase of luxury and non-essential goods on credit. A number of areas for future research were identified and possible areas and questions will be presented throughout the discussion.

Aim1: The Psychometric Properties of the Reasons to Borrow Money Scale

The first aim was to assess the psychometric qualities of a 31 item measure devised to measure attitudes towards borrowing money (Reasons to Borrow Money Scale: RBMS). The results found the RBMS had four components, each of which described a qualitatively different reason or aspect for borrowing money. The final 21 item scale had an internal reliability > .90. which is in DeVellis' (1991) scale range of "very good reliability". The RBMS appears to be a valid and reliable scale that could have utility for researchers. For example in market research this scale could be used to discover attitudes towards using credit on four different types of goods and services across different consumer groups. Alternatively this scale could be utilised by clinicians, for example, as a pre and post financial management intervention to discover the attitudes of their clients towards credit and debt. An avenue for future research would be to access the effectiveness of this scale in its ability to predict the success or failure of financial management counselling. For example, research may be able to ascertain at what score level the likelihood of future financial problems are reduced.

Aim 2: Exploring Life Aspirations, Subjective Well-being and Credit Behaviour

The second aim was to explore what types of demographic, attitudes to credit, financial stress and financial liquidity variables are associated with higher levels of life satisfaction and happiness in uncertain economic times. A number of variables were found to differentiate adults with high SWB (combined high life satisfaction and higher happiness) from adults with low SWB in this sample.

First, home ownership was a significant issue with HSWB adults being more likely to own their homes outright (without a mortgage) and were less likely to rent than LSWB adults. The importance of home ownership has long been an important part of Australian culture and both Davison (1994) and Kemeny (1986) argue the importance lies in a sense of belonging and identity with the home providing the stable place for raising children. These results support Maslow's (1971) humanist work in that personal growth, both cognitively and creatively, cannot occur until an adult has a secure base from which they can grow. In Maslow's hierarchy of needs, this second need of a home and security, was considered especially important in times of social disorganisation and crisis and it is noteworthy that in the current erratic and unpredictable economic times that home ownership in contrast to renting clearly discriminated the SWB groups.

Second, the results showed that adults in the HSWB group were more likely than expected by chance to be able to afford household necessities, to pay their credit card balances in full each month, and not to have to borrow money for monthly household bills. For those in the HSWB group who did not own their homes they were more likely to have paid their mortgage/rent instalments on time. Finally, the HSWB group were more likely to have disposable income left each week and were able to save, many of them reported they were not financially stressed and were that concerned by fluctuations in the price of petrol.

Furthermore, in this sample, regardless of household income level, it was the adults in the low SWB group who reported significant levels of financial stress. This could have occurred due to the rapid changes in household income caused by the reduction in interest rates. In June 2008 when this study was initially conceptualised the RBA had set the base lending rate at a 12 year high (Money Au, 2008). By September 2008 mortgage rates averaged 9.16 per cent, petrol was at $1.60 a litre and household food bills were rising rapidly (Australian Property Investor, 2009). Media reports, based on various on-line polls in September 2008, reported that close to 33% of households said if mortgage rates rose again they would have to refinance their homes, with 82% of Australians saying that rising costs were starting to hurt financially. However, between January to April 2009 (the data collection period for this study) the economic climate in Australia changed dramatically. Within a six month period the RBA had dropped the base rate from a 12 year high to a 49 year low (to 3 per cent). Despite cuts to the base lending rate there was still a gloomy outlook for Australian households with threats of job losses and a more severe and sustained recession than forecasted (AAP, 2009a, Denning, 2009). Of note, the reduction in interest rates for the average Australian household with a $250,000 home loan was an increase in disposable income of approximately $546 per month. This may have eased financial stress in many of the households who participated in the study, especially in the HSWB group and this increase in disposable income allowed them to save money each week and experience lower levels of financial stress. In contrast, as more of the adults in the LSWB group rented their homes this group would not have experienced the increase in their disposable income due to rate cuts which could account for the group difference in financial stress and the inability to make ends meet.

Aspirations for the Good Life and Extrinsic Aspirations

One interesting finding was that in this community sample of Australian adults the sample could not be clustered into groups with either high extrinsic and low intrinsic aspirations. There are several potential explanations for why this occurred in this sample. First, as Dillman et al. (2008) noted, community samples do not always fully represent the community and are often biased in that respondents are usually over-represented by middle aged highly educated men and women who are often higher on altruism scores. It is therefore possible that the 27% of people who did participate in this study were more intrinsic in their worldview and that people with a more extrinsic worldview chose not to participate.

A second explanation is that Australian adults in general place less emphasis on achieving wealth and image (extrinsic rewards) than their US or UK peers. In essence the American dream of wealth (as noted by Kasser, 1999), of acquisition of valuable and high status possessions, self-made wealth and high social status may not be as powerful a motivator for Australians as it is for adults in the US, or in the UK. This explanation of the current findings is however contrary to the argument of several cultural social analysts and researchers who have suggested the American dream is also the Australian dream. For example, Hamilton (1999), Hamilton and Denniss (2005), James (2007) and Wesley Mission (2006) all argued at length that over the past 20 years Australian adults, especially Generation Y adults (people born after 1981), have placed less emphasis on living within their means and saving for goods and services. This new "want-it-now" generation of adults is far more willing, it is argued, to hold high debt to income ratios. Hamilton and Denniss (2005) also strenuously argued that many Australian adults have also embraced image and luxury and have large credit debts due to buying and furnishing larger homes, having multiple luxury cars and wearing designer/status label clothing. Of note, the argument that the contemporary Australian dream is a mirror of the American dream of wealth, power and image was made several years ago and it is possible that the recent global financial crisis has been the necessary catalyst within society for creating the circumstances under which there is widespread attitude change (Aronson, 2004). The rationale for this hypothesis is presented below.

From February 2009 onwards reports were published which suggested that the root cause of the global financial crisis was deregulated credit markets in combination with corporate/executive greed. Scathing critiques were published which highlighted the level of bonus payments paid to CEOs and banking executives of failed companies. In essence, the crisis occurred because many financial institutions gave too much credit to people/companies with poor credit histories and/or an inability to adequately service debt. High risk lending was bolstered by packaging low risk loans with very high-risk loans in increasingly complex and highly unsustainable debt packages. As the former US Federal Reserve chairman, Alan Greenspan, noted recently the US Reserve made a mistake in thinking that bankers and credit lenders would be able to self-regulate.

To help sustain banks and companies through the crisis many governments provided vast amounts of tax revenue to failing firms. Public outrage at taxes being used to bolster firms whose executives appeared unable to adjust their level of spending was highlighted recently in the US. The CEOs from US car manufacturers General Motors, Ford and Chrysler all flew by private jet (at US $20,000 per trip) to the US Senate to ask for tax relief to bolster their failing businesses during the recession. One senator (Rep. Gary L. Ackerman) noted during the public hearing "there's a delicious irony in seeing private luxury jets flying into Washington, D.C., and people coming off of them with tin cups in their hands. It's almost like seeing a guy show up at the soup kitchen in high-hat and tuxedo. . . . I mean, couldn't you all have downgraded to first class or jet-pooled or something to get here?" (Milbank, 2008). Furthermore executive salaries became a topic for public scrutiny in Australia when the former CEOs of Telstra and Qantas received multi-million leaving bonuses despite their companies making substantial losses (Tennant, 2009).

With many homeowners in the US and UK following the sub-prime mortgage crisis having their homes repossessed, with many thousands of people worldwide unable to retire due to the superannuation/investment market decline, and with many people facing the prospect of job losses it is not unreasonable to hypothesis that in the current economic climate the pursuit of wealth, possession acquisition, power and image is not at present high on people's aspirations for the good life. This socio-cultural explanation is a hypothesis only and its validity would need to be tested in a study specifically designed to measure attitude change under opposing economic climates. It would also be of interest to explore whether Australians become more extrinsic in their aspirations after the current global recession eases and as investment and job markets improve.

Happiness, Financial Stress and the Implications of These Findings

Overall, the results of this study suggested that although income level was not a significant factor, financial liquidity was vitally important. In essence, having more money per se did not appear to make people happier. However what appeared to make people less happy was not being able to make ends meet. Research has shown that ongoing financial stress is associated with depression, relationship distress, increases in domestic violence, marital breakdown, reduction in self-esteem and higher obesity (Krause, 1995; Wesley Mission, 2006) and where the financial stress is related to high debt there is an increased risk of suicide (Dossey, 2007). The findings of this study not only appear to support the work of the financial stress research but also support the dual component theory of Ahuvia (2007) in that people who experience financial stress and worry and who cannot make ends meet on a regular basis are more likely to report ongoing feelings of sadness, hence they are more unlikely to view their lives as satisfying or worthwhile.

One implication of this study for clinical practice and financial management intervention is the result that not being able to make ends meet on a regular basis was associated with low life satisfaction and higher unhappiness. It may be possible that clients who come to counselling describing feelings of exhaustion, frustration and an opinion that life is not worthwhile may be experiencing ongoing financial stress. It may be possible that a thorough financial assessment and a money management intervention may for some clients enhance therapy outcomes.

Ongoing financial strain and poorer psychological outcomes have been found to be associated with high levels of debt (Dossey, 2007) and the more credit options people take the more likely they are to become financially stressed (Wesley Mission, 2006). A surprising result was that the number of credit options/loans taken out and the number of credit cards did not differ for each of the SWB groups. Of note however was that in this study we did not ask for actual monetary debt amounts so it cannot be assumed that just because the adults did not hold a wide range of credit options that the amount of debt was low as well. A further study could explore this question in more detail by asking adults more questions about the nature and total amount of their loans.

Conclusion

This study had two primary aims. The first was to carry out a psychometric evaluation of a new scale to measure attitudes towards credit. The scale was found to have four dimensions which measures reasons for borrowing money to borrow for qualitatively different types of consumer goods, namely: purchasing luxury goods, increasing wealth, altering current financial situation, and investing in the family's future. The results showed the measure had very high internal reliability and with some further assessment may prove to be useful for clinicians pre and post financial management intervention. It is also possible the RBMS has utility for researchers exploring relationships between credit attitudes and credit behaviour.

The second aim of this study was to explore what makes people happy in uncertain economic times. This study found that happiness during uncertain and unpredictable economic times was more about good personal financial management than a household's income level per se. Happiness was also associated with owning your own home, being able to pay household bills on time, being able to pay off credit card balances each month (free of credit card debt) and being able to buy everyday necessities. It also appeared that making sure you have at least some disposable income left to save each week is good for subjective well-being.

Not what we have, but we enjoy, constitutes our abundance (Epicurus)

References

AAP. (2009). Borrowing rises, but consumers wary about extra debt. from the World Wide Web: http://www.lendingcentral.com/.

Ahuvia, A. C. (2007). If money doesn't make us happy, why do we act as if it does? *Journal of Economic Psychology*, *18*, 491-507.

Ajzen, I. & Madden, T. J. (1986). Prediction of goal-directed behavior: Attitudes, intentions and perceived behavioural control. *Journal of Experimental Social Psychology*, *22*, 453-473.

Aronson, E. A. (2004). *The social animal* (9th ed.). New York: Worth Publishers.

Australian Bureau of Statistics. (2002a). 2001 Census: Expanded community profile: Central metropolitan Perth, statistical district 50505. Catalogue number 2005.00, AusStats, From the World Wide Web: http://www.abs.gov.au/.

Australian Bureau of Statistics. (2002b). Census of population and housing: Selected social and housing characteristics for suburbs and postal areas for 2001 census. Catalogue 2029.5, AusStats, from the World Wide Web: http://www.abs.gov.au/.

Australian Health Ministers, (2003). National Mental Health Plan 2003–2008. Publication number 3329/JN7947, The Department of Health and Ageing, 2008. From the World Wide Web: www.mentalhealth.gov.au.

Australian Property Investor (API; 7.4.2009). *RBA cuts rates to 49-year low*. From the World Wide Web: http://www.apimagazine.com.au/

Boddington, L. (1999). Student debt, attitudes towards debt, impulsive buying, and financial management. *New Zealand Journal of Psychology*, *10*, 1-7.

Bruni, L. & Porta, P. L. (2005). *Economics and Happiness: Framing the Analysis*. London: Oxford University Press.

Cattell, R. B. (1966). The scree test for the number of factors. *Multivariate Behavioural Research*, *1*, 245-276.

Chien, Y. W. & Devaney, S. A. (2001). The effects of credit attitude and socioeconomic factors on credit card and installment debt. *The Journal of Consumer Affairs*, *35*, 162-179.

Csikszentmihalyi, M. (1990). *Flow: The psychology of optimal experience*. New York: Harper & Row.

Davison, G. *The past and future of the Australian suburb*. Australian Planner, Dec. 1994, 63-69.

Denning, D. (2009). *We do not live in normal times*, from the World Wide Web: http://www.dailyreckoning.com.au/we-do-not-live-in-normal-times/ 2009/03/02.

Drentea, P. & Lavrakas, P. J. (2000). Over the limit: the association among health, race and debt. *Social Science & Medicine*, *50*, 517-529

DeVellis, R. (1991). Scale development: theory and applications. London: Sage Publications.

Dillman, D. A., Smyth, J. D. & Christian, L. M. (2008). 'Internet, Mail, and Mixed-Mode Surveys: The Tailored Design Method, (3rd Ed.). Hoboken, NJ: Wiley.Dossey, L. (2007) Debt and Health. *Explore: Journal of Science and Healing*, *3*, 83-90.

Drew, N. & Bishop, B. (1999). Cluster Analysis. In S.J. Coakes & L.G. Steed (Eds.), SPSS: Analysis without anguish: Versions 7.0, 7.5, 8.0 (243-257). Brisbane, Australia: John Wiley.

Godwin, D. H. (1997). Dynamics of households' income, debt, and attitudes towards credit, 1983-1989. *The Journal of Consumer Affairs*, *31*, 303-325.

Grouzet, F., Kasser, T., Ahuvia., A., Ferna´ndez, J. M., Kim, Y. et al. (2005). The structure of goal contents across 5 cultures. *Journal of Personality and Social Psychology*, *89*, 800–816.

Hamilton, C. (1999). Economic Growth: The dark side of the Australian dream. Paper presented at the Horizons of Science Forum, University of Technology, Sydney, Australia.

Hamilton, C. & Denniss, R. (2005). *Affluenza: When too much is never enough*. Crows Nest, NSW, Australia: Allen & Unwin.

James, O. (2007). Affluenza. London: Vermilion.

Joseph, S., Linley. P. A., Harwood, J., Lewis, C. A. & McCollam, P. (2004). Rapid assessment of well- being: The Short Depression-Happiness Scale (SDHS). *Psychology and Psychotherapy*, *77*, 463-478.

Kasser, T. (1999). *Personal aspirations, the "good life" & the law*. Deakin Law Review, 2005, 1-14.

Kasser, T., & Ryan, R. M. (1993). A dark side of the American dream: correlates of financial success as a central life aspiration. *Journal of Personality and Social Psychology*, *65*, 410–422.

Kasser, T., & Ryan, R. M. (1996). Further examining the American dream: Differential correlates of intrinsic and extrinsic goals. *Personality and Social Psychology Bulletin*, *22*, 280–287.

Kelty, S. F., Giles-Corti, B., & Zubrick, S. R. (2008). Physical activity and young people: The impact of the built environment in encouraging play, fun and being active. In N. P. Beaulieu (Ed.), *Physical Activity and Children: New Research*, (7-33). New York; Nova Science Publishers.

Kemeny , J. (1986). *The ideology of home ownership*. In J. B. McLoughlin & M. Huxley (Eds.), Urban planning in Australia: Critical readings (256-270). Melbourne: Longman Cheshire.

Klagsbrun, F. (1976). *Too young to die: Youth and suicide*. Boston, MA: Houghton Mifflin.

Krause. N. (1995). Assessing stress-buffering effects: A cautionary note. *Psychology and Aging*, *10*, 518-526.

Larson. R. (1978). Thirsty years of research on the subjective well-being of older Americans. *Journal of Gerontology*, *33*, 109-125.

LIFE (Living Is For Everyone). (2007). A framework for prevention of suicide in Australia. Publication Number 2060, The Australian Government Department of Health and Ageing: Canberra. Australian Captial Terrtiory.

Manktelow, R. & Hegarty, M. (2004). *Debt, consumerism and disadvantage*. Northern Ireland, United Kingdom: Western Health Action Zone and Hazlebank Community Partnership.

Maslow, A. H. (1971). *The farther reaches of human nature*. New York: Penguin Compass.

Milbank, D. (2008). Auto Execs fly corporate jets to D.C., *Tin cups in hand*. The Washington Post, Thursday, November 20, 2008; Page A03.

Money A. U. (2008). RBA increased interest rates to a 12 year high, from the World Wide Web: http://www.money-au.com.au/news/Banking/RBA-increases-interest-rates-to-12-year-high_18456831.php

Norusis, M J. (2011). *SPSS 19.0 Statistical Procedures Companion*. Upper Saddle River, NJ. Prentice Hall.

Pavot, W. & Diener, E. (1993) Review of the satisfaction with life scale. *Psychological Assessment*, 5, 164-172.

Reserve Bank of Australia. (2008). *Debt to disposable income ratio.* Household finances, selected ratios, from the World Wide Web: http://www.rba.gov.au/.

Senate Economics References Committee, Parliament of Australia Senate. (2005). Links between Australia's current account deficit, the demand for imported goods and household debt. from the World Wide Web: http://www.aph.gov.au/senate/committee/economics_ctte/completed_inquiries/2004-07/household debt/report/index.

Tabachnick, B. G. and Fidell, L. S. (2013). 'Using Multivariate Statistics' (6th ed) Boston: Allyn and Bacon.

Tennant, D. (2009). Payday paralysis. *In the Black* (Australian CPA), *79*, 28-31.

Tzeng, O. C. S. (1992). On reliability and number of Principal components: Joinder with Cliffe and Kaiser. *Perceptual and Motor Skills*, *75*, 929-930.

Watson, J. J. (2003). The relationship of materialism to spending tendencies, saving, and debt. *Journal of Economic Psychology*, *24*, 723-739.

Wesley Mission. (2006). *Financial Stress and it's Impact on the Individual, Family and Community*. Sydney, NSW: Author.

Western, M., Baxter, J. Pakulski, J., Tranter, B., Western, J, van Egmond, M., Chesters, J., Hosking, A., O'Flaherty, M. & van Gellecum, Y. (2007) Neoliberalism, Inequality and Politics: The Changing Face of Australia. *Australian Journal of Social Issues*, *42*, 401-418.

In: Economic Growth in the 21st Century
Editor: Cody Accosi
ISBN: 978-1-63321-589-4

Chapter 8

FINANCIAL EDUCATION AND ECONOMIC GROWTH: AN OVERVIEW OF PUBLIC AND PRIVATE POLICIES AROUND THE WORLD

Víctor M. González-Sánchez and Susana de los Ríos Sastre*

[1]UNED – National University of Distance Education
Department of Applied Economy
Paseo Senda del Rey, Madrid, Spain
[2]Comillas Pontifical University
Department of Financial Management
Calle Alberto Aguilera, Madrid, Spain

ABSTRACT

Particularly since the financial crisis, it is widely recognized the importance of consumers' financial decisions around the world. At the same time, several studies have shown that consumers worldwide have an insufficient knowledge of financial issues and a limited confidence in financial institutions and how that factors may complicate making informed financial decisions. That is the main reason why financial education is identified as a key driver to improve the stability of the financial system which would be a positive factor for economic growth.

* E-mail: srios@cee.upcomillas.es

During the last years many public and private institutions have launched initiatives in the field of financial education, but now it´d be necessary to ensure the efficiency and usefulness of those programmes. The first objective of this chapter is to present a review of some relevant initiatives on financial literacy and education, developed by public and private organizations around the world. Secondly, it focuses on the effectiveness and efficacy of those initiatives, analyzing how those programmes could have a positive impact on economic growth.

1. Introduction

The importance of financial education is increasingly acknowledged at an international level. Recently, the relevance of financial education and literacy has been highlighted by the G20 leaders, even more since the Russian G20 Presidency in 2013. In fact, the Russian Government has included measures to promote financial literacy in the long-term strategy to reinforce the financial sector. In their opinion, financial education supported by effective consumer protection would help in promoting economic recovery and growth, pushing up the creation of employment as well as decreasing poverty (OECD, 2013a).

At the same time, financial education stands as the main topic of a large number of debates and work meetings held on the five continents. Year after year, these events present the progress made in the field of financial education, but also highlight areas for improvement. And, without a doubt, they also underscore the role of financial education in the world-wide economy.

In this respect, at the beginning of 2014, Korea held the "High-level Global Symposium on Financial Education[1]: Promoting Long-term Savings and Investments”. This event acknowledged financial education as key common tool, not only to support consumers‘ decision making to balance their budget or identify risk factors and plan for their long term future correctly, but to get trust in financial institutions and markets (OECD/INFE, 2014). Another interesting symposium on financial literacy[2] took place in Paris at the end of

---

[1] This event took place in Seoul (Korea) in February 2014 and it was organized by the Organisation for Economic Co-operation and Development (OECD) and the Financial Services Commission and the Financial Supervisory Service of Korea. Further details are available at http://www.oecd.org/daf/fin/financial-education/globalsymposiumonfinancialeducationforlong-termsavingsandinvestments.htm

[2] The “Global Policy Research Symposium to Advance Financial Literacy” was organized by the OECD, the International Gateway for Financial Education (INFE) and the Global Financial Literacy Excellence Centre (GFLEC).

2013, stating that "financial literacy is like reading and writing", that is, an essential skill for the 21st Century (Lusardi, 2013).

In the scope of Europe, the European Economic Social and Committee (EESC) has acknowledged the role of financial education as a strategic instrument that can help in regulating the international financial system. A higher level of financial knowledge would help reduce financial exclusion and prevent consumers from getting into excessive debt, and this would benefit society as a whole. Nevertheless, we should stress that the goal should not only be to transfer knowledge and financial abilities, but also to give consumers the capacity to make informed, grounded decisions on their personal economy, that is, what is known as financial empowerment (EESC, 2013). However, the interest in adequate financial education among consumers of financial products is not something new, for example, in 1998, the European Commission for the International Organization of Securities Commissions highlighted the relevance of the education of participants in capital markets (IOSCO, 1998).

Furthermore, almost a decade has elapsed since the Organisation for Economic Co-operation and Development carried out the first major study of financial education at an international level, whose results were published in the report entitled *Improving Financial Literacy: Analysis of Issues and Policies* (OECD, 2005a). This report underscored the growing importance of financial education, owing, among other factors, to: the increase in the number of financial products, the greater complexity of such financial products, access to information and financial markets via Internet, an increase in life expectancy, the changes in pension arrangements and the low financial literacy level among consumers. The main conclusions of this study[3] were: There was a low level of financial understanding among consumers and it was correlated with education and income levels. And, on the other hand, consumers felt that financial information is difficult to find and understand, while surveys also showed that consumers often overrate their knowledge about financial matters.

As a consequence of this concern, a wide range of initiatives have been launched by international and national institutions over recent years. Currently, financial education is provided by public and private organizations in a variety of ways (e.g., information through websites, media campaigns, distribution of brochures or publications, training courses) and on a number of issues (e.g., credit, investment, insurance, pensions). There is even a large

[3] Based on the results of this study, the representatives of the OECD 30 member countries developed a *Recommendation on Principles and Good Practices for Financial Education and Awareness* (OECD, 2005b).

number of countries from all over the world that are developing and implementing national strategies regarding financial education, following the recommendations of the OECD. However, this does not seem to have achieved the goal of: obtaining a high level of financial literacy and a responsible use of financial products around the world. Therefore, the efforts to improve people's financial knowledge and develop their financial capability must continue. And, at the same time, it would be recommendable to know more about the impact and effectiveness of the different financial education initiatives and programmes.

In this context, the first section of this chapter briefly reviews the evolution that the concept of financial education has undergone. Secondly, it examines the current state of financial education initiatives around the world and some specific initiatives are presented. The third section deals with the controversial matter of measuring and evaluating financial education programmes.

2. Financial Education, Financial Literacy and Financial Capability

In the existing literature, we can find different ways of defining the term financial education and, in all cases it is very closely linked to other, also widely-used terms such as: financial literacy and financial capability. One of the main conceptual references is the OECD's definition, according to which:

"Financial education is the process by which financial consumers/ investors improve their understanding of financial products and concepts and, through information, instruction and/or objective advice, develop the skills and confidence to become more aware of financial risks and opportunities, to make informed choices, to know where to go for help, and to take other effective actions to improve their financial wellbeing" (OECD, 2005a).

The challenge is to make any person around the world capable of making financial decisions in line with their needs, bearing in mind their financial situation, their expectations and with proper knowledge of the risks assumed. For this reason, most programmes intended to improve financial education are aimed at the public in general, as it is not a matter that only affects investors. The underlying idea is that any family should be able to properly plan and budget its saving and investment, as it is exclusively responsible for the risk associated with its financial decisions.

Initially, financial knowledge has been identified with financial literacy. However, in recent years the empirical evidence[4] has shown that it is not enough for people to have greater knowledge of financial concepts and of how financial markets operate, but rather it is necessary that they know how to apply this knowledge to their personal circumstances. It is also necessary to bear in mind that the term "financial knowledge" is broad and may refer to at least three different aspects (Kempson et al., 2013): mathematical abilities, knowledge about the existence of financial issues and institutions, and knowing how to interact with financial services providers. Nevertheless, to transform such "financial knowledge" into "behaviour", something more is required.

In fact, at present, there is a tendency to use a broader definition of financial literacy. In this respect, it is interesting to note the definition of financial literacy used in the recent works of the OECD: "Financial literacy is a combination of awareness, knowledge, skill, attitude and behaviour necessary to make sound financial decisions and ultimately achieve individual financial wellbeing" (Atkinson and Messy, 2012). There have even been efforts to have the definition include the possible impact that the environment may have on individuals' capacity to achieve positive results as a consequence of their financial behaviour.

In this respect, use of the term "financial capability" is increasingly widespread, instead of "financial literacy", to show these new aspects relating to financial education (Kempson et al., 2013). Nevertheless, we have to be aware that the broader the concept is, the more difficult it will be to establish a single definition. Although there does not yet exist a definition of financial capability[5] accepted all over the world, the first steps have been taken to describe this term. In the recent works of the OECD on financial education for young people, several descriptions of this term appear. For example, the Australian authorities describe financial capability as "the ability to apply knowledge, understanding, skills and values in consumer and financial contexts to make informed and effective decisions that have a positive impact on themselves, their families, the broader community and the environment". Therefore, on one hand, the need has arisen to apply financial knowledge in

---

[4] Among others, see OECD/INFE (2013), Atkinson and Messy (2012) and Lusardi and Mitchell (2011).

[5] A conceptual model of financial capability has been proposed in World Bank (2013). And it's also interesting to see the results of the "Money Lives" research study conducted in the United Kingdom about the determinants of an individual's financial capability (Ipsos MORI, 2014).

decision-making and, on the other hand, the search for positive results. Additionally, in the United States, they have acknowledged that "...Becoming financially capable involves acquiring understanding, developing skills and fostering values ... it means being able both to think critically about financial issues and to draw together and apply knowledge and skills in particular situations whilst having due regard to the impact of financial decisions on people's lives and on the environment" (OECD, 2014).

In parallel, as progress is made in the study and development of financial education programmes, new, more specific definitions are appearing. Recently, the OECD has proposed the following working definition for financial education for long-term savings and investments[6] (OECD/INFE, 2014): "A specific and focused strand of financial education which complements existing financial regulation and consumer protection, to provide current and future consumers/investors with the knowledge, skills and capability to manage and accumulate savings (in order to cover the risks that they face and their long-term needs and to make confident and informed decisions about saving and investment), with the intention of increasing their future financial wellbeing whilst also supporting economic and financial development."

As the aim of this chapter is to provide an overview of the current state of financial education around the world, the terms financial education, financial literacy and financial capability are used without distinction.

3. Review of Relevant Initiatives on Financial Education Around the World

One of the most significant public initiatives in this field has been the establishment of national strategies for financial education[7] in a large number

[6] In 2012, an expert group on financial education for long-term savings and investments was created by the OECD International Network on Financial Education (INFE) and this is the working definition they have adopted.

[7] A national strategy for financial education is "a nationally co-ordinated approach to financial education that consists of an adapted framework or programme, which: recognises the importance of financial education (including possibly through legislation) and defines its meaning and scope at the national level in relation to identified national needs and gaps; involves the cooperation of different stakeholders as well as the identification of a national leader or co-ordinating body/council; establishes a roadmap to achieve specific and predetermined objectives within a set period of time; and, provides guidance to be applied

of countries around the world. According to reports by the OECD/INFE, in 2013, 45 countries around the world had designed or implemented a national strategy for financial education (OECD, 2013a). This trend began in the early 2000s in developed countries (e.g., Japan, the Netherlands, New Zealand, Singapore, the United Kingdom or the United States) and, little by little, also spread to emerging countries. Table 1 shows the different levels of development of the national strategies in those 45 countries, according to their situation at the end of 2013. In several countries, the national strategies for financial education are fully established (*implemented*), while in others they are in the process of development (*advanced design*) or their implementation is at a planning stage (*being considered*).

Table 1. Status of National Strategies for Financial Education

NATIONAL STRATEGY	Implemented	Advanced design	Being considered
G20 members	Australia, Brazil, Japan, Netherlands, Singapore, South Africa, Spain, United Kingdom and United States	Canada, India, Indonesia, Korea, Mexico, Russian Federation and Turkey	Argentina, China, France, Italy and Saudi Arabia
Other countries	Czech Republic, El Salvador, Estonia, Ghana, Ireland, Malaysia, New Zealand, Nigeria, Portugal, Slovenia and Zambia	Armenia, Chile, Colombia, Israel, Kenya, Latvia, Lebanon, Malawi, Morocco, Peru, Poland, Romania, Serbia, Sweden, Tanzania, Thailand, Uganda and Uruguay	

Source: Compiled by authors from information of OECD (2013a).

The establishment of national strategies for financial education varies greatly from one country to another, according to government priorities, the target groups or the funding available. They all worked with the same goal, to

by individual programmes in order to efficiently and appropriately contribute to the national strategy" (OECD/INFE, 2012).

improve the financial literacy and capability of their populations, but they show different levels of economic development and also greatly varying financial systems, so it is necessary to adapt the financial literacy programmes to each country's needs. For example, the United Kingdom and the United States launched their first national strategy for improving financial capability in 2006, whilst there are countries just starting to develop some initiatives on financial education. However, one of the aspects where there exists greater coincidence is in introducing financial education in schools.

Additionally, although there are countries in the five continents that have still not had the opportunity to design and establish a national strategy for financial education that does not mean they have not developed programmes to foster their population's financial literacy. At present, a large number of initiatives exist in the field of the financial education in countries in all five continents. Below we present, by way of example and in summary, some of these initiatives.

Latin America and the Caribbean

Up to now, few countries in Latin America have established a national strategy for financial education, but almost all have developed some kind of programme or initiative to encourage financial literacy. Recently, the *Banco de la República* (Colombia), the *Fondo de Garantías de Instituciones Financieras* (Fogafin) and the *Corporación Andina de Fomento (CAF-Banco de Desarrollo de América Latina)* have analysed the main existing financial education[8] initiatives in 16 countries of the area: Argentina, Bolivia, Brazil, Chile, Colombia, Costa Rica, Ecuador, El Salvador, Guatemala, Mexico, Nicaragua, Paraguay, Peru, the Dominican Republic, Uruguay and Venezuela (García et al., 2013). Of the countries analysed, only six have implemented or are at the design stage to establish a national strategy for financial education: Brazil (national strategy established in 2010), Chile, Colombia, El Salvador, Mexico and Peru. One of the most innovative initiatives in this region is the use of financial education in Conditional Cash Transfer programmes[9] (CCT).

---

[8] A summary of financial education initiatives launched in Argentina, Brazil and Mexico is available in OECD (2013a).

[9] CCT programmes consist "of monetary grants that some governments deliver directly to households in conditions of poverty or vulnerability, depending on compliance with a series of requirements such as children's attendance in school (primary and secondary), as well as nutritional and health controls of small children and pregnant women" (García et al., 2013).

According to García et al. (2013), at present, only nine of the countries offer financial education programmes associated with CCT and these are: Argentina, Brazil, Chile, Colombia, Costa Rica, Ecuador, Mexico, Paraguay and Peru. Some of these programs are focused on the use and management of financial services to facilitate the use of prepaid and debit cards (e.g., "Asignación Universal por hijo", in Argentina and "Tekoporâ", in Paraguay), while others are dedicated to promoting access to bank credit and savings products (e.g., "Crediamigo", in Brazil; "Programa de Ahorro", in Chile and "Mujeres Ahorradoras en Acción", in Colombia) and there are also programmes focusing on the management of personal finances and entrepreneurship (e.g., "Crédito de Desarrollo Humano", in Ecuador and "Juntos", in Peru). All these programmes offer the opportunity to promote financial inclusion through improvement in the financial literacy of the target population.

European Union

In the European Union, the community institutions themselves have frequently expressed the need to improve the level of information for investors and consumers of financial services, as well as the quality of their financial education With this in mind, the European Commission[10] has promoted a series of initiatives and has carried out a number of activities, including:

- *Consumer Classroom*[11]: This is a digital community designed with the aim of promoting consumer education in secondary schools. The website allows teachers in the European Union, mainly with students between 12 and

---

[10] For years, the European Commission has been expressing its interest in promoting and improving high-quality financial education for European consumers, both through communications, and in organising meetings or creating panels of experts in this field. In this respect, it is worth noting: the Communication from the Commission on Financial Education adopted on December 2007 (European Commission, 2007), the organisation of the conference "Increasing Financial Capability" to encourage the provision of high-quality financial education to consumers on March 2007 (detailed information about that event is available at http://ec.europa.eu/internal_market/finservices-retail/capability/index_en.htm) and the Expert Group on Financial Education (EGFE) created in 2008 to advise the Commission on its policy-making in the area of financial education.

In 2009 the European Commission launched a European Database for Financial Education (EDFE) to reference numerous financial education programmes offered by public or private institutions in the European Union. It was a useful online database, but since 17 June 2011 the EDFE was discontinued and taken offline.

[11] The information is available in all official European Union languages at www.consumerclassroom.eu.

18 years old, to compile resources there on consumer education. It also provides interactive and collaboration tools to help prepare and share lessons among students and other teachers. It replaces a previous online tool for consumer education, called Dolceta (Development of On-line Consumer Education Tools for Adults), which was operating from 2003.

- *Information campaign on consumer credit rights*[12]: In 2013, the European Commission launched a campaign to inform consumers on their rights when signing for credit. This information campaign has been launched in four EU Member States: Cyprus, Ireland, Malta and Spain, using the language of each country. The campaign slogan is "Need credit? Don't just sign. You have rights". It is accompanied with a traffic light system to help consumers: "stop" (the red light), "think" (the orange light) and "act" (the green light). The campaign focuses on five consumer rights: The right to transparent advertising, the right to pre-contractual information, the right to clear information in the contract, the right to withdraw from the contract and the right to repay early.

- *Sponsorship of financial education initiatives in EU member states*: The European Commission also provides support in the form of patronage to increase the credibility and visibility of financial education programmes and initiatives. Typically, this is a sponsorship without any kind of financial aid and is devoted to programmes with no commercial goal. Sometimes, European Commission officials participate directly in the event in question.

Significant efforts are also being made in the European Union by other kinds of organisations or associations, such as the work carried out in recent years by the European Federation on Finance House Associations (Eurofinas), for example. In 2012, it published the second edition of its report on Financial Education (Eurofinas, 2012), describing financial literacy initiatives implemented in several European countries. Table 2 shows a summary of some initiatives undertaken by national consumer credit associations.

---

[12] Completed information about the campaign is available at http://ec.europa.eu/consumers/citizen/my_rights/consumer-credit.

Table 2. Consumer Credit: National associations' initiatives in EU (I)

	Objectives	Target group	Results
UPC-BVK (*Belgium*) Union Professionnelle du crédit/Beroepsvereniging van het Kredie	To inform about the consumer's rights and duties, as well as the main characteristics of consumer credit products	All consumers	Concrete results have not been yet measured. Website is frequently visited
	www.upc-bvk.be/FR/creditguide www.upc-bvk.be/NL/creditguide		
CLFA (*Czech Republic*) Czech Leasing and Finance Association	Information and knowledge on particularities of non-banking consumer credit	General public Media Schools Vulnerable consumer	Positive reactions by media, State authorities and a number of consumer
	www.clfa.cz		
FFI (*Finland*) Federation of Finnish Financial Service	To increase financial literacy (management of personal finances) To raise awareness on the importance of financial literacy	Young people Students Teachers	Increased interest in economic and financial issues Measure the number of schools that take part in the competitions and campaigns and collect feedback
	www.fkl.fi Projects: www.zaldo.fi and www.keepitrolling.fi		
ASF (*France*) Association Française des Sociétés Financière	To inform about consumer credit To advise on how: - To elaborate a monthly budget - To finance a project - To evaluate the credit cost	Consumers: - who wish to sign a consumer credit agreement -who have difficulties paying off their debts	Number of published copies of the guides
	www.asf-france.com		
BANKENFACHVERBAND (*Germany*)	To inform about consumer credit and about responsible lending and borrowing	Consumer	Website is available to all consumers
	www.kredit-mit-verantwortung.de		

Table 2. (Continued))

ASSOFIN (*Italy*) Italian Association for Consumer Credit and Mortgages	To inform about consumer credit To give some explanations about financial terminology To guide on how to elaborate a family budget	Adults who are considering taking out a loan	Positive reactions of government officials, consumer organisations or media
	www.monitorata.it		
FNO / FINFO (*Norway*) The Norwegian Financial Services Association / The Association of Norwegian Finance House	To increase the understanding of economic and financial issues (mainly personal finances)	Young people	Employees from different banks and insurance companies have been teaching in schools (10,000 pupils in 2011)
	www.fno.no		
KPF (*Poland*) Konferencja Przedsiębiorstw Finansowych w Polsce	To bring financial knowledge (how to borrow responsibly and how to avoid over-indebtedness)	Active consumers in the consumer credit market and who seek advise	Number of distributed copies of the guides
	www.kpf.pl/index.php/program-etyczny/wydawnictwa-edukacyjne		
ASFAC (*Portugal*) Associação de Instituições de Crédito Especializado	To change the Portuguese mentality towards financial education To create a more financially aware consumer	General public and specific target groups (women, teachers, children, etc.)	ASFAC's credibility and visibility have been increased. The association is recognised by government and media
	www.asfac.pt		
FLA (*United Kingdom*) Finance and Leasing Association	To improve the knowledge of motor dealership staff involved in the sale of motor finance and to increase the confidence in motor finance	Car buyers	The Specialist Automotive Finance SAF) project has been recognised as the standard for industry knowledge on motor finance
	www.FinancingYourCar.org.uk www.specialistautomotivefinance.org.uk		

Source: Compiled by authors from Eurofinas (2012).

Africa

In accordance with the available information, there is considerable heterogeneity in Africa in the initiatives to promote financial education and also in the number of programmes implemented, maybe as a reflection of the socio-economic differences that exist among countries and within each one. Ghana adopted a National Strategy for Financial Literacy and Consumer Protection in the Microfinance Sector in 2009, while there is a small group of countries trying to develop their national strategies for financial education (Kenya, Malawi, South Africa, Tanzania, Uganda and Zambia). In other countries, such as Namibia, Lesotho or Zimbabwe, no national strategies according to the guidelines marked by the OECD as yet exists, but the public authorities have launched several financial literacy initiatives. There are also countries where it seems only private initiatives exist to promote financial education, including: Botswana, Burkina Faso, Mali or Senegal. Nevertheless, according to the study carried out by Messy and Monticone (2012) there is a group of countries where financial education programmes have not yet been identified, mainly in Central Africa.

At present, the main goals of the financial education programmes in Africa are: improving financial knowledge and skills, increasing awareness of consumers' rights or financial issues and the improvement of financial inclusion. They generally target vulnerable groups (women, youth or low-income persons).

Most of the initiatives are supported by national public bodies (governments, central banks or financial sector regulators), but as mentioned above, there also exist programmes promoted by Non-Governmental Organisations (NGOs) and by the private sector.

Those public sector initiatives take shape in national strategies, while there are other initiatives (financed by the private sector or supported by NGOs) shared by several countries, such as, for example:

- The project "An opportunity for all, Financial Education in Africa" was implemented by local microfinance institutions in Ghana, Malawi, Mozambique and Uganda and coordinated by Opportunity International[13]. The objectives are to raise awareness of financial

[13] Detailed information on this project is available on the website of the Financial Education Fund (www.financialeducationfund.com).

education and to promote the use of some financial services as well as a better management of credit and debt.

- The Financial Education Programme for training of microfinance institutions staff that was launched in 2010 in Burkina Faso, Mali, Senegal and Madagascar. It is financed by Monaco's development agency and coordinated by Participatory Microfinance Group for Africa (PAMIGA). The goal of this project is not only raising awareness of financial knowledge, but also helping microfinance institutions to improve financial education of their customers.
- The "Aflatoun Social and Financial Education Curriculum[14]" is taught in some schools in Ghana and Uganda. The objective is targeted at children or young people to improve their financial knowledge and attitudes.
- The programmes support by "Junior Achievement" to encourage young people to be economically active, improving their business skills and their financial education. These programmes are operating in Nigeria, Uganda and Zambia.

Australia

It has been implementing a national strategy[15] since 2011. The first pillar of Australia's National Financial Literacy Strategy was "Using educational pathways to build financial literacy for all Australians" and it focused on three sectors: Schools (they will integrate financial literacy into the Australian Curriculum), tertiary education and adult and community education. Two of the most visited portals are: "The MoneySmart Teaching" website (www.teaching.moneysmart.gov.au) that provides resources and materials about financial terminology and how to manage your finances, and it's a good support for parents and educators; and "ASIC's MoneySmart" website (www.moneysmart.gov.au) that offers information available in 26 languages.

---

[14] All the details of this project can be consulted on the website of Innovations for Poverty Action (IPA) (www.poverty-action.org).

[15] The National Strategy is available at www.financialliteracy.gov.au.

4. COST-BENEFIT RELATIONSHIP OF FINANCIAL EDUCATION INITIATIVES

As mentioned in the previous section, there are numerous initiatives and programmes that have started in recent years, with the sole purpose of bringing about an improvement in people's financial capability. Of course, all these programmes and initiatives involve certain costs for the institutions that support them and, therefore, it is very important to know their real impact; that is, their effectiveness and efficiency.

As stated by the OECD (2013b) "evaluation is crucial" for any type of financial education initiative, irrespective of the size of the programme, because increasingly more funds are being devoted to this kind of initiatives and national governments and private institutions should allocate funds efficiently. Information and telecommunication technologies (ICT) have helped in the diffusion of financial education programmes around the world and they have multiplied the number of people receiving information, but it would be recommendable to optimise resources and not to duplicate efforts. Nowadays, all high-income countries and many low - and middle-income countries have Internet portals devoted to financial education.

We may say that, at present, the analysis and evaluation of the financial education programmes and initiatives are aspects that require urgent improvement. Some recent reports even cast doubt on the suitability of current financial education programmes and draw attention to their limited impact (EESC, 2013). The fact is that there is no consensus regarding the effectiveness of the financial education programmes. Instead, there are a lot of unanswered questions that we could summarise in just one: what is it the cost-benefit relationship of the currently-existing initiatives and programmes on financial education? In other words, does financial education work?, and if so, what types of financial education are most cost effective"? (Hastings et al., 2012). Unfortunately, there is no consensus about the effectiveness of financial education programmes, so cannot we provide an answer yet.

In the existing literature, we can find studies[16] addressing the evaluation of different financial education programmes, but each one uses a different method of analysis and, in general, they are investigations limited to one country or to a specific programme, and do not offer a global view. The OECD and the World Bank are working on the development of a common framework which may be used as a guide for anyone responsible for evaluating this kind

[16] Some of them are referenced in Lusardi and Mitchell (2011, 2013).

of programmes and to measure the population's levels of financial literacy, but we still have some way to go. At the same time, both international bodies are conducting pilot studies to find out the state of financial literacy around the world.

In 2012, the OECD published a report with the results of an interesting pilot study on levels of financial knowledge, financial behaviour and some financial attitudes, carried out in 14 countries[17] on 4 continents (Atkinson and Messy, 2012). Specifically, the core questionnaire included 8 questions about financial knowledge, 9 questions about financial behaviour and three scaled attitudinal questions, which is summarised below (see Table 3).

Table 3. Financial Literacy Core Questionnaire

The financial knowledge questions: • Division • Time-value of money • Interest paid on a loan • Calculation of interest plus principle • Compound interest • Risk and return • Definition of inflation • Diversification
The financial behaviour questions: • Carefully considered purchases • Timely bill payment • Keeping watch of financial affairs • Long term financial goal setting • Responsible and has a household budget • Active saving or buying investments in the past year • Financial product choice after gathering some information • Financial product choice after shopping around and using independent information • Borrowing to make ends meet
The attitude questions: • I find it more satisfying to spend money than to save it for the long term • I tend to live for today and let tomorrow take care of itself • Money is there to be spent

Source: Atkinson and Messy (2012).

[17] In particular, 12 countries have voluntarily participated in the study (Armenia, Czech Republic, Estonia, Germany, Hungary, Ireland, Malaysia, Norway, Peru, Poland, South Africa and the United Kingdom), while Albania and the British Virgin Islands (BVI) joined the pilot at a later stage.

This first study demonstrated that it is possible to apply the same kind of questionnaire to evaluate different programmes and populations around the world and thus create a series of basic indicators on financial literacy. As may be seen, the questionnaire on financial knowledge consists of eight questions, but it is very similar to the form used in the 2004 U.S. Health and Retirement Study (HRS) and the 2009 U.S. National Financial Capability Study (NFCS).

Now the goal will be to continue collecting data in coming years and develop an extensive database of indicators across countries and over time.

The results of the study are interesting, insofar as they offer greater knowledge on the state of financial education in the countries analysed. Table 4 shows, by way of summary, the proportion of population that achieved a high level on each component of financial literacy by country.

Table 4. High Score on Financial Literacy

	High knowledge score	High behaviour score	High attitude score
Albania	45%	39%	69%
Armenia	46%	41%	11%
Czech Republic	57%	48%	62%
Estonia	61%	27%	46%
Germany	58%	67%	63%
Hungary	69%	38%	69%
Ireland	60%	57%	49%
Malaysia	51%	67%	53%
Norway	40%	59%	57%
Peru	41%	60%	71%
Poland	49%	43%	27%
South Africa	33%	43%	54%
United Kingdom	53%	51%	49%
BVI	57%	71%	67%

Source: Atkinson and Messy, 2012.

Each of the columns reports percentage of respondents gaining a high score on each component of financial literacy (6 or more on knowledge and behaviour, more than 3 on attitudes).

The aim is not to rank the countries, but to have a benchmark to observe each country's evolution and, therefore, know the effectiveness and efficiency of the different financial education programmes. At the same time, the study helps to better understand the relationship between financial knowledge, behaviour and attitudes.

The report highlighted areas for improvement in terms of financial knowledge as well as behaviour and attitudes. In fact, in all the countries at least 30% of the population could benefit from additional financial knowledge. By calculating an average of the qualifications by country, including the three aspects mentioned, Malaysia, Hungary, Germany and BVI had the highest scores, whilst Armenia, South Africa and Poland showed considerable room for improvement. Nevertheless, once again it appears that having greater knowledge of financial issues and products does not necessarily imply a better behaviour in the financial market. And, of course, it cannot be claimed that there is a direct relationship between financial literacy and financial outcomes (Hastings et al., 2012).

Furthermore, in accordance with OCDE/INFE (2013) if we take into consideration other variables such as socio-economic conditions or gender, the results are also sometimes contradictory. In general, there does seem to exist a relationship between low educational and low income levels and low levels of financial literacy, but it cannot be claimed that there is a cause-effect relationship. Additionally, differences are identified in the levels of financial literacy and behaviour by gender. Women display lower financial knowledge and confidence than men in many countries, although their financial attitude is better than men's in some aspects and they obtain better scores, for example, in planning a family budget.

CONCLUSION

For decades, international institutions have been highlighting the potential benefits derived from proper financial capability, both for the economy and for society as a whole. Initially, it seems certain that a society with good financial knowledge, able to seek out the most appropriate financial services at every given time, could foster efficiency in the financial sector by promoting greater competition between markets and providers, and stimulating financial innovation by requiring better quality and diversity in financial services and products. This could lead to financial stability, as taking more adequate decisions on savings and investment could decrease overall delinquency rates; that is, preventing a repeat of the situations we have seen in the recent international financial crisis (European Commission, 2007; OECD, 2005).

Little by little, initiatives, programmes and strategies have multiplied in the field of financial education, promoted both by public institutions, and by the private sector or by NGOs. Nevertheless, empirical evidence shows that it would be necessary to improve coordination among the stakeholders of financial education, at least to avoid duplicating resources and efforts.

On the other hand, it is essential to improve and increase the assessment of financial education programmes, and to analyse in depth the population's real needs, in order to offer genuinely efficient programmes. Although the empirical evidence is still limited, financial education programmes aimed at more specific population groups are shown to be more effective (for example, Lusardi and Mitchell, 2011). There is some consensus that it would be necessary to intensify programmes to improve financial literacy aimed at young people, women and the more vulnerable groups of society.

In any event, the population's financial capability is a factor with considerable economic potential, though it is necessary to have proper regulation of the financial markets or consumer protection regulations in accordance with the current circumstances, which could lead to an improvement in economic and social wellbeing.

REFERENCES

Atkinson, A. & Messy F. (2012). Measuring Financial Literacy: Results of the OECD / International Network on Financial Education (INFE) Pilot Study. *OECD Working Papers on Finance, Insurance and Private Pensions*, No. 15, OECD Publishing.

Eurofinas (2012). *Financial Education E-Publication*, second edition. Brussels, Belgium.

European Commission (2007). *Financial Education*. Communication from the Commission 808 final. Brussels, Belgium.

European Economic and Social Committee (2013). *Financial education for all: Financial education strategies and best practices within the European Union*. Brussels, Belgium.

García, N., Grifoni, A., López, J.C. & Mejía, D.M. (2013). Financial Education in Latin America and the Caribbean: Rationale, Overview and Way Forward. *OECD Working Papers on Finance, Insurance and Private Pensions*, No. 33. OECD Publishing.

Hastings, J. S., Madrian, B. C. & Skimmyhorn, W. L. (2012). Financial Literacy, Financial Education and Economic Outcomes. *NBER Working Paper* No. 18412, September.

IOSCO (1998). *Objectives and Principles of Securities Regulation*. Report of the International Organization of Securities Commissions, September.

Ipsos MORI (2014). *Money Lives: the financial behaviour of the UK.* Money Advice Service. London, UK.

Kempson, E., Perotti V. & Scott, K. (2013). *Measuring financial capability: a new instrument and results from low- and middle-income countries*. The Russia Financial Literacy and Education Trust Fund/The World Bank. Washington, DC.

Lusardi, A. (2013). Financial Literacy around the World: Evidence and Policy Implications. *OECD/INFE/GFLEC Global Policy Research Symposium to Advance Financial Literacy*, October. Paris, France.

Lusardi, A. & Mitchell, O. S. (2013). The Economic Importance of Financial Literacy: Theory and Evidence. *NBER Working Paper* No. 18952, April.

Lusardi, A. & Mitchell, O. S. (2011). Financial Literacy around the World: An Overview. *NBER Working Paper* No. 17107, June.

Messy, F. & Monticone, C. (2012). The Status of Financial Education in Africa. *OECD Working Papers on Finance, Insurance and Private Pensions*, No. 25, OECD Publishing.

OECD (2014). *Financial Education for Youth: The Role of Schools*. OECD Publishing.

OECD (2013a). *Advancing National Strategies for Financial Education*. A Joint Publication by Russia's G20 Presidency and the OECD.

OECD (2013b). *Evaluating financial education programmes: survey, evidence, policy instruments and guidance*.

OECD (2005a). *Improving Financial Literacy: Analysis of Issues and Policies*.

OECD (2005b). *Principles and Good Practices for Financial Education and Awareness*. Recommendation of the Council. Directorate for Financial and Enterprise Affairs, July.

OECD/INFE (2014). Concept Note on Financial Education for long-term savings and investments. *High-level Global Symposium on Financial Education: Promoting Long-term Savings and Investments* jointly organised by the Financial Services Commission, the Financial Supervisory Service of Korea and the OECD, 26-27 February. Seoul, Korea.

OECD/INFE (2013). *Financial literacy and inclusion: Results of OECD/INFE survey across countries and by gender*, June.

OECD/INFE (2012). *High-Level Principles on National Strategies for Financial Education*, August.

World Bank (2013). *A toolkit for the evaluation of financial capability programs in low-and middle-income countries*. A Report on the World Bank's Research Program and the Knowledge from the Russia Financial Literacy and Education Trust Fund. Washington, DC: World Bank.

INDEX

C

D

E

F

G

H

I

N

O

P

Q

R

S

T

U

V

W

Y

Z